ENDURING THE MOST

The Life and Death of Terence MacSwiney

Francis J. Costello

BRANDON

First published in 1995 by
Brandon Book Publishers Ltd
Dingle,Co. Kerry, Ireland.

Copyright © Francis J. Costello 1995

The moral rights of the author have been asserted.

British Library Cataloguing in Publication-Data
is available for this book.

ISBN 0 86322 214 5

The publishers wish to acknowledge the kind permission of the
MacSwiney family, George Morrisson, Cork Municipal Museum
and The Kilmainham Jail archive for permission to reproduce the
photographs used in this book.

Jacket photographs: FRONT *right*, Terence MacSwiney;
left, MacSwiney's funeral in Cork, 1920. BACK *top right*, Cork
city centre, after it had been burned by Black and Tans, 1920;
centre, Terence and Muriel MacSwiney's wedding party, 1917;
bottom, MacSwiney in Brixton Prison, 1920.

Jacket designed by Public Communications Centre Ltd, Dublin
Typset by Koinonia, Bury
Printed by Redwood Books, Trowbridge, Wiltshire

ENDURING THE MOST

To Owen and Emmett,
may you always be true to yourselves
and to one another,
and with deepest thanks to Anne

Contents

Acknowledgements		7
Introduction		9
1	The Weaning of a Revolutionary	15
2	The Writer Turns to the Gun	43
3	Imprisonment and Love	75
4	Serving the Republic	109
5	The Last Arrest	139
6	Diary of a Hunger Strike	157
7	The Aftermath	223
Bibliography		249
Index		251

Acknowledgements

There are many who must be heartfully thanked for their generosity and help in making this book a reality. Particular gratitude must be expressed by me to Máire MacSwiney Brugha, Terence MacSwiney's daughter and only child. Her willingness to answer questions and provide information, often of a personal nature, particularly about her late mother, Muriel, was vital. I thank her also for her kind permission to consult and quote from her father's papers, as well as those of her aunt, Mary MacSwiney.

Sincerest thanks must also be extended to Seamus Helferty, of the Archives Department at University College, Dublin, for his guidance and help during virtually every phase of this enterprise. I also gratefully acknowledge the courteousness and kind help of the staffs of the National Library of Ireland; the State Paper's Office, Dublin; the Cork Municipal Archives; the House of Lords Records Office, London; the Public Records Office at Kew; and the Widener Library at Harvard University. My thanks are also due to Peter Malone and Sean Cronin for their excellent advice and assistance.

Special thanks must go to my wife, Anne, and our sons, Owen and Emmett, for having endured the research and writing of this book at a time when I am also involved in a number of other projects.

Introduction

HE WOULD LIVE for the remarkable period of seventy-three full days without food. While his was not the longest hunger strike to be waged during the Anglo-Irish war, it was in the end one of the pivotal events of that conflict. Pitted directly against the might of the British Empire, Terence MacSwiney's solitary protest would be seen, in the context of the Irish struggle, as personifying the triumph of the weak over the strong. Six decades later in Northern Ireland, other young Irishmen engaged in hunger strikes claimed him as an example.

When he began the first day of a two-year sentence at England's Brixton Prison for the possession of a police cipher code, MacSwiney was not simply a political prisoner. He was also the lord mayor of the city of Cork, and commandant of the Cork No. 1 Brigade of the Irish Republican Army. He succeeded to both positions following the murder of his friend Tomás MacCurtain, probably by members of the Royal Irish Constabulary.

Few controversies stirred Britain so deeply as did Terence MacSwiney's ordeal and the British government's reaction to it. One commentator, recalling the Boer War, called it the most provocative event "since the one that centred upon Cecil Rhodes, when the Jamestown raid was balked by Paul Kruger and the raiders imprisoned".[1] Efforts to have MacSwiney released grew to encompass all shades of opinion, including the Quakers (Society of Friends), many southern Irish Unionists, the British Labour movement, along with a range of Irish independence support groups in Ireland, Britain and the US. This protest was made largely on humanitarian grounds, although efforts by the Irish Self-Determination League in Britain and the US to exploit the propaganda value of MacSwiney's hunger strike achieved considerable success.

The liberal press in Britain, especially the London *Times*, advocated MacSwiney's outright release, and, in the aftermath of his death, held the government accountable for it. King George V was himself drawn into the controversy. The British government, for its part, made a number of attempts to persuade MacSwiney to take food voluntarily, and tried to encourage dissension within Republican ranks in a somewhat improbable bid to have Sinn Féin order MacSwiney off his protest.

Given that the offences which Terence MacSwiney had been convicted of were not exceptionally grave, why was greater leniency not afforded by the British government in an effort to end his hunger strike? Or was the lord mayor of Cork in fact an early and deliberate target of the government's coercive legislation, which provided the legal basis for his arrest and subsequent trial by a military tribunal? To the British government Terence MacSwiney, as well as being a Republican lord mayor of Cork and an IRA leader, was a principal participant in the establishment and operation of the Republican courts which had served to undermine the king's writ in much of Ireland. He had also played a prominent role in ensuring the success of the Dáil Loan, both in Cork and the country at large. His own actions and writings, both published and in documents captured by the British, had shown him to be a threat to the crown long before his arrest in August 1920.

The British government's handling of the MacSwiney hunger strike may have been tied, in part, to a misreading of the situation by its agents abroad. A report submitted by the British Foreign Office Information Bureau in the US stated that: "The Irish here will, of course, make every effort to exploit MacSwiney's death, but I do not think that an incident of this kind is likely, under present circumstances, to do us much damage here, even if it is successfully represented as having been attended with circumstances of oppression and hardness." The information officer contended that the government's handling of the MacSwiney hunger strike would not have a negative impact in the US since "in the first place the national conscience of this country is very far from active as regards the humane treatment of persons under sentence of law". The report also emphasised that the Irish question had come to be viewed in the United States as something of an irritant in the body politic: "Those who will attempt to stir up anti-British feeling over the case must reckon with the general irritation towards the Irish, of which I have spoken before, and which has been largely produced by their persistent and menacing interference on racial lines in the operations of domestic politics, which are at present the country's chief interest."[2]

In fact, MacSwiney's hunger strike proved to be a source of consternation and embarrassment to the British government throughout the protest and after his death. Indeed, it has been singled out by some writers as perhaps the event which, more than any other during the Anglo-Irish war, encouraged British public opinion to turn against the government's Irish policy. Charles Mowat has written that MacSwiney's death "was a shocking thing to countless people".[3] Robert Kee noted that MacSwiney's death made a profound impression on all observers of the Irish scene. "Of all the many individual acts," Kee writes, "that had made that year of 1920 so extraordinary in the history of Ireland, none seemed to convey so solemnly the message that whatever resources of civilisation the British might continue to summon to its aid in the form of solace or military reinforcements, there was at last a force in Ireland which could not be deflected from its notion of Irish freedom and which would never give in."[4]

In previous hunger strikes of that period – in Mountjoy Jail in 1919 and in 1920, and in Wormwood Scrubbs in 1920 – the government had given in when the hunger strikers had appeared close to death. The crown was unwilling to create more Irish martyrs. In the case of MacSwiney, however, the government announced, with a certain amount of courage of its own, that it did not intend to surrender to moral blackmail. What they underestimated, though, was both the physical courage of MacSwiney and the amount of time it took a resting man to die of hunger. After a fortnight on hunger strike it was assumed that MacSwiney was on the point of death, and public opinion, not only in Ireland but in Britain and much of the rest of the world, focused on the figure of this defiant Irishman, suffering in a British cell. He became an easily graspable symbol of the entire political situation in the country.[5]

F.M. Carroll has written that the lord mayor's hunger strike "drew appeals to the American Government from diverse sources ... Secretary of State Colby," he noted, "was willing to consider making an unofficial appeal to the British Embassy and to listen patiently to Frank P. Walsh, James K. McGuire and Daniel C. O'Flaherty, but the tired and sick Wilson lashed out at a rather tactless telegram to him by telling Tumulty, 'This is more than futile; it is grossly impertinent'."[6] Boston's Cardinal O'Connell, followed by Roman Catholic Bishop William Turner of Buffalo, wrote to Secretary Colby, requesting that the government intervene with Britain on MacSwiney's behalf on humanitarian grounds.[7] The State Department responded, however, that the US government was without a legal basis for intervening in the MacSwiney case.

An examination of British official records reveals the uncertainty with which the British government grappled with the problem presented by MacSwiney's action. The range of options considered underscore the disagreement which existed within the government, though the cabinet sought to present outwardly a determination to maintain its policy towards MacSwiney, and towards Ireland.

It can be argued that for the British government, in its outright refusal to treat MacSwiney as anything less than a disloyal subject to be confined to prison for the duration of his sentence, and for the lord mayor himself, in rejecting the right of the crown to pass sentence on him, the fundamental issue was one of principle. Both sought with grim determination to stay the course. An insight into MacSwiney's own will-power is given in his own words in his collection of essays, *Principles of Freedom*:

> In a physical contest on the field of battle it is allowable to use tactics and strategy, to retreat as well as to advance, to have recourse to a ruse as well as an open attack; but in matters of principle there can be no false tactics, there is one straightforward course to follow, and that course must be found and followed without swerving to the end.[8]

Like Patrick Pearse, MacSwiney believed that "A man must be prepared to labour for an end that may be reached only in another generation."[9]

Yet the story of Terence MacSwiney's life is more than the story of a heroic and tragic hunger strike which would unsettle the mightiest empire of its time. MacSwiney lived for a total of forty years, married and fathered a child who would never know him. He played a significant role in the Anglo-Irish conflict, in both civil and military capacities, up to the time of his arrest. There were many parts to Terence MacSwiney – teacher, playwright, propagandist, soldier, elected official, husband, father and Catholic mystic – which combined to produce a man of considerable complexity.

Who was Terence MacSwiney beyond the heroic figure? To a large extent his image has been locked in time; he is an icon, not unlike other Irish patriots, whose humanity has been subsumed in the legend of his suffering and death. This image of Terence MacSwiney provides no insight into the husband and father, the literary man who, as an individual with practical experience in the commercial sector, sought to serve his country in practical ways also. He was quiet, reserved, and driven by strong convictions, as well as by a degree of guilt that led him to one of the most painful of protests. He was also ruthless in his pursuit of Irish independence.

Despite the attention and outpouring of sympathy which MacSwiney's lengthy protest and resultant death attracted at the time, his life receives little attention now, over seven decades later. The seventieth anniversary of his death in 1990, for example, drew no mention in the pages of his city's paper, the *Cork Examiner*, nor in other Irish publications. Nor was there a civil ceremony of any note held in Ireland. The omission was noteworthy, especially when just a week earlier considerable attention had been focused on the 100th anniversary of the birth of Michael Collins.

It is hoped that this biography will help to provoke a greater interest in the life of Terence MacSwiney, and offer a broader perspective on his life as a whole. I hope to deal with his life on its own terms. The years spent on this project, which included reading MacSwiney's essays, plays and other written works, as well as examining his political and military activities in Sinn Féin and the Irish Volunteers, produced for this writer the image of a man who sought and gave little quarter in pursuit of his vision of Irish independence. Yet he also left behind a body of creative work, encompassing political philosophy as well as ideas for the Irish nation's economic development. Now more than seventy years since his death, the life of this unique figure merits more than a work of hagiography.

Terence MacSwiney's death by hunger strike, and the phrase uttered by him, "Victory is won not by those who can inflict the most, but by those who can endure the most," has been laid claim to by some in justification of hunger strikes in Ireland in more recent times. I hope that more meaning may be taken from Terence MacSwiney's life as well as his death, a life in which considerable reflection was given to the meaning of individual honour as well as service to the nation.

Notes

1. Associated Press account in the Atlanta *Constitution*, 26 October 1920.
2. Bonar Law Collection, HLRO, l02/9/22.
3. Charles Mowat, *Britain Between the Wars* (Chicago 1963) p. 76.
4. Robert Kee, *The Green Flag* (London 1972) p.697.
5. Ibid.
6. F.M. Carroll, *American Opinion and the Irish Question* (Dublin 1978) p. 161.
7. US State Department Files 84ld, 00/225 and 84ld, 00/227.
8. Terence MacSwiney, *Principles of Freedom* (Buffalo 1975) p. 216.
9. Cited by Moirin Chevasse in *Terence MacSwiney* (Dublin 1961) p. vi.

Chapter I
The Weaning of a Revolutionary

FOR ALMOST TWENTY years, during the 1870s and '80s, Ireland's political ambitions had been championed by parliamentary means. But following the downfall of Parnell, the "uncrowned King of Ireland", those who sought to win Ireland's separation from England by force came once more to the fore. Tom Garvin situates the context in which violence returned to the surface:

> Irish separatist nationalist elites of the immediate pre-independence period had an ideology which was romantic and almost anti-political; this has commonly been ascribed to the fact that most of these leaders came of age politically during the years of bitterness and disillusion with parliamentarianism that followed the collapse of Parnellism in 1890 ... The separatist leaders were children of their time and resembled ideologically other radical movements of the period, whether nationalist, leftist, paleo-fascist or some other indeterminate ideological mixture. A conspicuous feature of the politics of the period was the rise of political movements of an often visionary and romantic character, commonly dominated by relatively well-educated young people from the middle reaches of society.[1]

It was in just such an environment that Terence MacSwiney came of age in Cork, Ireland's third largest city after Dublin and Belfast and the capital of the southern region. MacSwiney is easily identifiable as one of the "visionary", "well educated", and "romantic" young men "from the middle reaches of society" which Garvin describes.

A friend and colleague described Terence MacSwiney as a young man as "tall, very dark, with a lock of jet-black hair falling over his forehead, and his dark grey eyes half hooded by the lids. His spare frame had not the easeful co-ordination of the athlete. His walk, a wee bit ungainly, with its short, nervous stride, was always brisk, and the tails of his ever-open top-coat streaming in the rear, as if he were constantly urged by that inner restlessness that plagued him."[2]

MacSwiney's father John, a man whom little "Terry" (as he was called at home) barely knew, was born in the decade before the Great Famine. Like his English-born wife Mary, MacSwiney appears to have been filled with a deep Catholic fervour. John MacSwiney's faith, in fact, had called him to action. In 1868 he made the journey from East Cork to Rome hoping to offer his services to the pontiff as a papal guard to help repel Garibaldi's attack. It was a belated visit, however, and by the time of his arrival the conflict was over. For most of the next decade, he lived in London, working as a school-teacher, where he married Mary Wilkinson.

A fateful decision came with the uprooting of the family to Cork, with the couple's three children, Mary, Catherine and Peter. John MacSwiney had an ambition to start a tobacco factory there with his brother-in-law. The enterprise ended, however, in failure, and reduced both households to bankruptcy. Terence MacSwiney arrived in the midst of this family destitution in 1879. In all, eight of the nine children born to John and Mary MacSwiney survived to adulthood.

In his early years Terence and his siblings were given the task of learning a poem every week for recitation to their father on a Sunday afternoon. In an early account of MacSwiney's life, his boyhood friend and fellow rebel P.S. O'Hegarty wrote that the poem "had to be an Irish poem, the more rebel the poem selected, the better the father was pleased". O'Hegarty described his friend as "a boy with jet-black hair, clear complexion, bright blue eyes and a disposition which could be both serious and merry".[3]

In 1885, when Terry was only six years old, John MacSwiney again got the urge to travel, this time as an emigrant to Australia. He remained there on his own, poor and in ill-health, until his death in Melbourne at the age of sixty, ten years later. The absence of a father figure undoubtedly accounted for Terence's attachment to his mother. (His brother Peter was only a few years his senior). His personal background gives another example of an Irish patriot of the physical force tradition who was without a father during his formative years. It was also the case with men as varied in background as Eamon de Valera, Michael Collins, Dan Breen, Sean Treacy and Liam Lynch, and like Patrick Pearse, MacSwiney also had an English-born parent.

In Terence MacSwiney's case, the most lasting effect his mother had on him was to inculcate in him strict religious principles. Her Catholic faith was at the centre of her life, and his faith later proved fundamental to MacSwiney. Although financially poor, the family possessed spiritual and intellectual wealth. Much was also made within the household by his parents of a claim that the MacSwineys were direct descendants of an ancient County Donegal warrior clan that was dispossessed of its lands by the Saxon invader and driven to Cork centuries before.

All in all, young Terry's boyhood seems to have been a happy one. Yet as he grew to manhood, a marked change in his disposition was noted. "When he was quite young," one longtime acquaintance recalled, "he always joined the family tea parties." The young MacSwiney, the friend recalled, was "quite bright, most talkative and argumentative, but as he got deeper into the movements of the time, he seemed to withdraw himself more from these functions."[4]

In his diary, as a twenty year old, MacSwiney sought to "review my life up to the present ... I don't know that my childhood was in any way particularly interesting," he wrote. He recounted a number of instances when, as a small child, he had wandered away from home. "Of course, when small boys go astray," he noted, "there is a lot of commotion raising the alarm and dispatching couriers to institute a search." In one adventure, little Terry followed the path of a visiting organ grinder along King Street, where the family home was at the time. Looking back in early adulthood, MacSwiney recalled that he had been "an ardent admirer of the monkey". In another instance his journey led him to the shop of an old woman from whom he purchased an orange with his pennies. The boy was found asleep alongside her.[5]

His early years saw Terry involved in boyhood fights. One instance he recounted involved his turning the tables on a stronger boy by an "outburst" of temper. "It was, I think, conscience rather than fear held me so far," he wrote in his diary, "but for the time being everything was forgotten." In a remark on the incident MacSwiney wrote that "the aggressor was vanquished, as I hope will ever be the case with aggressors, be they small boys or big nations".[6]

A year younger than most of his classmates, MacSwiney completed a preparatory grade before going on to secondary school. "I think if I had to select one out of all my school years as the happiest," he wrote some years later, "it would be this year." As a secondary school-boy he excelled at the famed Christian Brothers school at North Monastery in Cork city. He earned special honours in English, the Irish language and in Irish history, receiving a prize of £20 for three consecutive years for his scholastic performance. The national fervour that was instilled in the boy at home received further nurturing at the hands of the Christian Brothers. So committed were his teachers to imparting what they saw as an accurate account of his country's history that they crossed out in blue pencil those passages in Collier's *History of Ireland* which they had found offensive, adding corrections of their own as they went along. In one lively family discussion around the dinner table in which the topic revolved around what each of them would do with the wealth of John D. Rockefeller, Terry responded: "I would free Ireland."[7]

The young MacSwiney left secondary school in the summer of 1894. Shortly afterwards an entry level clerking position became available at Dwyer and Co, a Cork warehousing and distribution company, and, through the intercession of one of his teachers, MacSwiney was hired for the job. In his diary he remarked that "after a few preliminary visits, I was installed in their office on the first of July, 1894, being then only fifteen years old". However, MacSwiney's employment at Dwyer and Co. was not a source of contentment, even though he would work there for a total of sixteen years. His youthfulness curtailed, MacSwiney noted that he did not know "how long I was at business before I got restless, but certainly before twelve months had expired I was utterly sick in office life. I realised I was wasting my time and wanted to get out of Dwyer's, however I could manage it."[8] Years later, his sister Eithne described him in one account as having been in 1894 "only a schoolboy, just beginning to think and plan his future life, as far as his new work permitted."⁹

He grappled with the idea of emigrating. "How we all manage at some time or other to get the notion into our heads that we will win our fortune at once if we could only go away somewhere," he remarked. Australia, New Zealand, North and South America, all seemed to beckon. Australia was his "favourite, if I had any".¹⁰ That it was to Australia his father had emigrated years before might have been a reason for this attraction.

But over time the young man adapted to his job, with the necessity of providing financial support for his fatherless household apparent to him. His thoughts shifted away from emigration. "I conceived the perhaps more practical idea of studying for some profession; and the profession I thought most of was medicine," he remarked in his diary. MacSwiney began to study at night, but while preparing for the matriculation exam for admission to the Royal University, Cork, he suffered a breakdown. He described the condition himself. "As well as I can calculate, when I first began I was about 19 years of age. I remember the time was shortly before Xmas when we used to be very busy in Dwyer's and I consequently had not much time for study. The result was as might have been anticipated that I over-did it and broke down. I did not get knocked up but my head used to pain me a good deal and I had to suspend studying. This would have been, I think, in the winter of '98."¹¹

His plan for university education temporarily sidetracked, MacSwiney took up shorthand and contemplated a career in journalism, but the following year his ambition of furthering his education returned. He passed the matriculation exam and began a degree course in Mental and Moral Science at the Royal University of Cork, while continuing to work at Dwyer and Co. By now, too, he was also becoming politically conscious and active.

MacSwiney was determined to keep these concerns to himself as much as possible while working at Dwyer and Co. When queried by the firm's manager, R.S. Parker, as to his future plans, MacSwiney recorded that "Of course I did not tell him the profession I have my heart in, merely giving him an idea by saying I had ideas of journalism ... I let him see that I had no notion of going on with medicine," he added, "and I think though I would make £500 or £600 a year at that profession, I would still have the same unsatisfied feeling." At the same time, the young office worker wrote in his diary that he would have preferred that he "had not spoken so freely nevertheless, it must only help to attract attention which above all things I wish to avoid."[12]

What truly animated him was the cause of Irish separatism. "I know it is the Irish spirit blazing in me – as it blazes in my brothers," he wrote. He described that spirit as "like the fire in a charger on the course, that impatient for the start chafes at the reins and would kick the ground from under it. But it must have the rein." The agenda he entertained – of armed insurrection on an unparalleled scale – would also need tempering, he wrote:

> And so be it with us – we must curb our souls – nurse our raging spirits – till 100,000 of us, inspired by righteous wrath, and hearing in our ears the appeal of freedom from the mountain tops, rush well armed and ready, on the garrisons and the barracks – then no more stifled anger and silent wrath, but glorious fruitful action. Oh God, speed the day, God speed the day.[13]

It was a tone high in emotional content and one filled at the same time with romantic optimism in hopes of a mass response to the cause of Irish independence. How much his ready adoption of physical force was motivated, like others his age, by the failure of the Gaelic League to inspire a national revival which would counter British dominance in Ireland, might also be considered.

In these early years, it appears that MacSwiney sensed that the road before those who felt as he did would be a difficult one. Nonetheless, he concluded, their efforts of self sacrifice "might have fruitful results if followed even against opposition and with suffering ... Such would be the case with those who challenge many of the conventions of the time that are threatening Religion and Country."[14] MacSwiney's nationalism, despite his renunciation of sectarianism in his writing, carried with it a view that Irish nationhood and Catholicism were joined. If what he in fact sought was a revolution, it was a conservative one. His sister, Mary, recalled his dislike of James Connolly's socialism.[15]

Mary MacSwiney was one of the single greatest influences on Terence's personal and political development, and she remained one of the persons closest to him throughout his life. After the death of their mother in 1904, Mary MacSwiney figured large in most of the decisions he made. They appear to have influenced one another, and their nationalist ideals developed along parallel lines.

Mary, who was eight years older than her brother, was educated in England and taught school there for some years. Her introduction to politics came through the suffragette movement in Cork, after she had returned to teach in St Angela's convent school in the city. Her own politics, however, evolved to a position of extreme nationalism. At the same time, the one constant in her adult life was her devotion to a mystical and uncompromising version of Roman Catholicism. She never married. Handicapped by poor eyesight and the loss of her left foot due to a childhood accident, her religious faith served as a driving force behind both her private and public actions. In the aftermath of the 1916 Easter Rising, following her arrest for her activities with Cumann na mBan, the women's arm of the Irish Volunteers, she was dismissed from her position as a teacher. Soon after, with her sister Annie, she opened a school at 4 Belgrave Place named St Ita's. The school admitted boys and girls at the elementary level and girls to the adjoining secondary school. It would also, on occasion, serve as a safe house for her brother.

MacSwiney carried with him for most of his life a dislike of crowds. It was an aversion he had held since his schooldays at the North Monastery. "I imagine I shall always remain so," he remarked in November 1905. "I am always much happier when the party is limited to say six to eight of those very warm friends."[16]

His aloofness was captured by his friend Daniel Corkery's statement that "Of his own he had no amusements, no hobbies" – although Irish ballads of a patriotic nature held a particular appeal for him, particularly Thomas Moore's ballad, "She is

Far From the Land". "I do not think he ever carried cigarettes
of his own" Corkery recalled, "but of a social evening he
would accept of one." He also described some of MacSwiney's
less endearing qualities:

> Yes, he was too anxious, would burn himself away and all others
> about him. He was a "Brand". He had only small respect for
> tact, which is the homely word for diplomacy. "He treated us
> like small boys," one who was just as long in the movement as
> himself says of him.[17]

At Dwyer and Co, although a diligent worker, he was
distant from the management and staff. One fellow employee
noted that MacSwiney "had no interest in the life around
him, but his aloofness was not resented as he was quite
incapable of doing anything, even by carelessness, that might
cause annoyance or give trouble". MacSwiney had his own
interpretation of his performance at Dwyer and Co. "I wished
to work loyally with everyone in a spirit of comradeship," he
wrote in his diary. "If I had adopted superior airs," he
remarked defensively, "the fellows would have had the right
to resent it." MacSwiney believed that he enjoyed a good
working relationship with his superiors. But Mr Dwyer had
a different view. In a somewhat heated exchange, the young
MacSwiney told his employer that "Some people when they
get on in life looked down on others beneath them." Dwyer
responded that Terry's problem was he "looked down on
those above him".[18]

As the century drew to a close, Terence MacSwiney turned
to matters far removed from the commercial sector in which
he worked. In 1899, as a nineteen year old, he was joined by
his friend Liam de Roiste, among others, in forming the Cork
Celtic Literary Society, after the failure of the Wolfe Tone
Club in the city. It appears that the latter's demise was due
more to generational differences than to internal dissent over
the imposition of limits on the extent of Irish independence.
The more energetic young men of MacSwiney's generation
saw the old Fenians as complacent, content to pass resolu-
tions and erect monuments.

Established essentially as a vehicle for promoting ideas
rooted in advanced nationalism, the Literary Society's journal

was circulated among similar societies in Dublin, Belfast, London and Glasgow. It was in this context that Terence MacSwiney had his first contact with Bulmer Hobson, the architect of the separatist Dungannon Clubs which proved vital to the rejuvenation of the Irish Republican Brotherhood. Hobson was among the first to provide an outlet for MacSwiney's political essays and creative work.

The Cork Literary Society also involved itself in staging public protests over matters tied to the national question. A female contemporary remarked years later that the young men of the society "took themselves far more seriously than the majority of the citizens were inclined to do". The visit of King Edward to the Cork Exhibition in 1902 was a case in point. MacSwiney threw himself into the thick of the action by writing a letter for the society protesting the royal visit, and emphasising its opposition to the British government's recruitment effort in Ireland for the Boer War. As Edward VII made his way down the main thoroughfare of Great George's Street, MacSwiney and the others unfurled a large black flag from the window of their small office. The protest led to his first arrest for activities against the crown.

Before the royal visit MacSwiney commented to a colleague that he was afraid "your hopes that E. Rex will stay clear of us in Cork will not be gratified and I need not say how much we regret it ... Still," he added, "there is many a slip etc. and the pleasure!!! may be denied us!" Though the young men who protested the monarch's visit were few in number, MacSwiney saw their action as important in showing that there was "no danger of people considering Cork as favourable to welcoming a foreigner as Ireland's King ... The power does not belong to any generation," he argued, "to bind lands for those who will follow, and so please God, we need not fear for Ireland's future."[19]

"Everyone," MacSwiney wrote in his diary on 9 September 1902, "should have as many interests in his life as he finds his circumstances will allow him and his tastes give him an inclination for." Reflecting on his own effort to keep a diary, he noted that "probably if my time were not so well filled – albeit not all pleasantly so – I might have begun this diary before". Nonetheless, he noted, "It is more with a view to the future than anything else; for I am sure nothing can be more interesting than to go back on what you have written for a number of years and see what were your opinions when you were five or six years younger."[20]

A bicycle trip that covered much of the south-west coast of Ireland in 1902 proved one of his most memorable experiences. At the close of one particular day, MacSwiney noted that he was "at my journey's end ... What a blessing in disguise to have lost that train – not for anything would I have missed the thrilling moonlight ride."[21] In another passage MacSwiney writes with appreciation of what he saw as the Creator's role in shaping the natural beauty he had witnessed:

> And truly it was glorious; the road was good with a decline in my favour and so I could sit erect on my bicycle and look around. A half-moon lit up the land with its partial light; occasionally it hid itself behind clouds, a dense mask that hung in the heavens not suggesting of darkness or of storm, but as it were of a robe or veil that cloaked the majesty of the mighty Creator of this beauteous landscape – a God whose wonder so far surpassed His work that the eye might only gaze on His Splendour reflected ... but the landscape; on either side of me there spread waving field and meadow land to meet on the horizons the mountains lifting their heads to the heavens – dim and mysterious.[22]

While his prose in describing the trip might be ponderous and repetitive, it is filled at the same time with insights into the extent which the beauty he saw added to the young Corkman's patriotic fervour.[23] There are clear political overtones, as there are in virtually everything he wrote from 1901 onward. His diary contrasts the basic kindliness of the people he met with the harshness of British rule. The sight of once populated stretches of countryside evoked particular resentment in MacSwiney.

> I think of them flying, flying from their land so beautiful that angels from heaven might not disdain it; and there come other feelings – I know not if it be so with others but so is it always with me – above the feelings of awe and solemnity, there surged raging anger and wrath – that the hellish materialistic Power that had fastened itself on this our country by trickery and treachery;

that had rooted one half of the people from the land and was stifling the soul in the other half; and had now stationed amongst us barracks and garrisons like the fang of some devilish ogre that we might not rush upon and struggle forever.[24]

He concluded his travel account by quoting a remark attributed to both Oliver Cromwell and St Ruth: "This is a land worth fighting for."[25]

This type of patriotic writing was not to be confined to the private entries found in his diary. Within a decade, a wider forum for his views became available in the pages of the Dublin-based separatist weekly, *Irish Freedom*.

The year 1904 brought the death of his beloved mother. For the twenty-five-year-old MacSwiney, it was a painful blow from which recovery would prove long and hard. Years later, when seeking the approval of his future mother-in-law for her daughter's hand, MacSwiney wrote of his mother:

I had a devoted mother whose life was one long act of self-sacrifice. Her presence always made home sacred and her memory keeps it safer for me. No matter what I could have done, I could never have equalled her devotion. But I prayed for the opportunity of making good to another all that I owed her ... The happiness of Muriel's future home will rest largely on me and it will be my happiness to safeguard hers and make it true and lasting ... Because of the reverence in which I hold my mother's memory, I am conscious of the respect due to you ... [26]

It was to his sister, Mary, that the role as anchor of the household now fell. She encouraged his literary pursuits and with that his passions on the national question. She also, in spite of some misgivings, stood by some of his more rash actions.

His biographer, Moirin Chevasse, described an incident at Dwyer and Co. which might be seen as reflective of later instances in which he went to extreme limits to assert his own rectitude, regardless of the outcome.

At his office in order to prevent unpunctuality, the management enforced a humiliating method of penalising those who came late: the door was shut for a few minutes at half past eight so that they had to wait in the street outside. This plan, however, was unjust, for although the door was shut at what seemed the appointed time, the office clock was not accurate ... One morning when MacSwiney arrived he found the door closed before the time, thus shutting him out. He went straight home. After thinking it over he wrote a letter of complaint to the management. Mary, already struggling against financial difficulties and ill health, heard of his action at first with dismay. He, however, had considered that it would be better for them to all go back to extreme poverty then to submit to degrading regulation.[27]

At the Royal University of Cork (now University College), he made enduring friendships among those who were instructors there. Among them was Professor William Stockley, who lectured in English literature. His relationship with Professor Stockley would be a longstanding one. In one instance, after viewing the library at the university, MacSwiney remarked to Professor Stockley: "This is where I should like to spend my life."[28] Later, the professor became involved with MacSwiney in the national movement on a number of fronts.

Following his graduation in 1907, with a degree in Mental and Moral Science, MacSwiney turned his sights to teaching. He was attracted to the role of educator out of a desire for greater fulfilment. In a letter written to a boyhood friend who had gone on to study for the priesthood, he offered a glimpse of his restlessness at this time.

> You may trust me not to forget you. I will be with you in spirit. In return give me a remembrance of the great occasion. It is a happy occasion that the 28th March is my birthday – an appropriate time for a prayer in my behalf. Don't stagger, Vin, at the news. I will be thirty years old tomorrow! It nearly staggers me to think of it, and I have done so little to justify such an awful expenditure of time![29]

While remaining in the accounting department of Dwyer and Co., he was appointed lecturer in business methods at Cork Municipal School of Commerce. He said in his letter of application that he had "always been in touch with educational matters", and noted that since his degree from the Royal University included course work in psychology, it would "prove of great service to me in a teaching capacity."[30]

In April MacSwiney was informed that his application for the post "has been provisionally sanctioned by the Department for the current session. The continuance of this recognition," he was informed by the school's secretary, "will depend on the reports of the inspectors on your work."[31]

The following year he applied for the post of commercial instructor at the Joint Technical Instruction Committee for County Cork. He furnished the school with written recommendations from three individuals. D.J. Coakley, the principal of the Cork Municipal School of Commerce, stated that MacSwiney's performance had been "a decided success". He went on to write that MacSwiney "has shown that he possesses the capacity for organising and efficiently conducting commercial classes". Coakley noted also that the young educator had shown a "clear insight into the practical requirements of the students who attend commercial classes". Further testimony as to Terence MacSwiney's abilities came from J. J. Gallagher of Dwyer and Co., who stated that he was "perfectly conversant with our business methods, and the principles of bookkeeping – single and double entry – and office work in all its details".[32]

Accepted for the post, which was a full-time position, he resigned from Dwyer and Co. A testimonial letter, signed by a large number of MacSwiney's co-workers at the company in June 1912, expressed their regret at his decision to leave.

> We feel confident that your future will be a brilliant one and few will be more glad to see your ambitions realised in the fullest measure than we who have been for so many years acquainted with you in business. May we ask you to accept the accompanying as a memento of the esteem and respect which your many excellent attainments have inspired? It is our pleasure to point out that although this letter ostensibly emanates from the office staff, the managing Director of the firm was one of the first to suggest and to subscribe to this testimonial.[33]

In his new job, MacSwiney spent much of his time "travelling County Cork, travelling for commerce the routes he was later to travel for the Irish Volunteers, forming as commercial organiser the links, and the knowledge which were to be so effectively used later on for the furtherance of the Irish Volunteers".[34]

By this time, MacSwiney's literary efforts had begun to bear fruit, and his first two plays – *The Last Warriors of Coole* and *The Holocaust* – were put on in Cork. Both were generally well received by critics; *The Holocaust* was described by one Dublin writer as "a poignant little etching of the problems of slum life". The plays were presented by the Cork Dramatic Society, which MacSwiney had con-founded with Daniel Corkery; the society's objective lay not so much in the production of plays but "to the actual writ-ing of plays".[35] The play as a work of literature was the group's primary objective.

In his early literary and dramatic work, Terence MacSwiney laid great emphasis on the need to keep faith with the past. In 1903, then twenty-three years old and active in the Gaelic League in Cork, he sought to use the centenary of Robert Emmet's rebellion and death as a poetic vehicle for motivating what he saw as a moribund Ireland, corrupted politically and spiritually by England. In Stanza I of a poem titled "Address for the Emmet Centenary", MacSwiney summons his readers to understand the meaning behind Emmet's efforts 100 years before and to grasp their relevance to the present:

> Hear ye that message, ringing down the years,
> Rise sons of Eire! Rise! Your sloth off shackle;
> No longer lie thus bound in slavish fears –
> Hark to that voice, cry from the tombs awake,
> Spring to that call that pleads for Eire's sake.
> Look back across the century that's sped;
> From Emmet learn the course that ye should take,
> Thus did he point the path for us to tread:
> "Till Eire is unfettered let my name be dead."

Stanza II represents an outright call to arms, combined with a plea that MacSwiney's generation of Irishmen and women not let Emmet's memory and Ireland down by Home Rule:

> This was his dying wish – until our land
> Amongst the nations takes her rightful place
> His grave should be unmarked – to this command
> List ye of faltering heart, who would retrace
> The path he, fearless, trod mid the brief space

Of that young life he to his country gave.
Half measure now, must not our cause disgrace,
His creed – o'er us no foreign flag must wave.
Young hearts of Eire learn 'tis ye this land must save.[36]

Keeping faith with the past was again MacSwiney's theme in "The Insurgents Farewell, AD 1798". His characterisation of Ireland as "our mother" is similar to invocations by Patrick Pearse and also to Yeats's image of Ireland as "Kathleen Ní hUalacháin". In the poem's second stanza, he portrays his view of Ireland as a mother waiting for her children to come to her defence:

Again our Mother rears her drooping head,
Invokes her sons in freedom's course to tread,
And we her cause with freedom soon will be wed
    Or sink to death.[37]

MacSwiney's interest in literature and in art itself was driven by his political outlook. He was no advocate of free expression. "Art for art's sake," he wrote, "has come to have a meaning which must be challenged, but yet it can be used in a sense that is both high and sacred."[38] As to what he saw as the obligations of the dramatist, MacSwiney was equally direct: "A dramatist cannot make a great play out of little people. His chief characters, at least, must be great of heart and soul, the great hearts that fight great causes." His friend Daniel Corkery wrote that MacSwiney "practised literature for the sake of Ireland – never to become famous or to make money".[39]

Terence MacSwiney the playwright also showed himself to be something of a risk taker. For one of his productions he committed the Cork Dramatic Society to a one-week contract for the city's Opera House, even though the agreement included penalties for failure. He noted later that the group entered into the contract despite the fact that "we had no single part understudied".[40] The difficulties the society faced in this and other engagements were described somewhat wistfully:

Well, 'twas good training if the crowd were numerically sufficiently strong and well round enthusiasts for the work it could do no other mischief. But the crowd is small and there are always some dropping out and it is very hard to keep them together even under favourable circumstances. What will it be under favourable circumstances? Most of the fellows have improved so much and I hope it will give them an interest in persevering, but the numbers at present hamper any sort of development.[41]

In *The Last Warriors of Coole*, MacSwiney dealt with the rescue of the defeated warriors of Coole by Fionn, the son of Coole. It was his first play, produced on the stage in Cork city in 1910 by the Cork Dramatic Society. The play's theme dealt with how the will to fight on against adversity might be instilled. Despite the approval of the audience, MacSwiney himself declined to take a curtain call. The *Cork Examiner's* critic wrote that the play's verse "is remarkably good, resonant, full of beautiful cadences, and was well spoken by several players."

A central character in the play is Crimal, a young man possessed of undaunting faith that the group will triumph in the end. He tells his comrades that Fionn will return and victory will be theirs.

"No brother, not failure, but success delays them now. They will return well-laden." Crimal is rebutted by Forger, who tells him that "we are grown old. Our brothers sink from the weight of years. You weary them ... with vain dreams."

"There was one shining dream," Crimal responds.[42]

At the play's end, Fionn returns and summons the faithful, while praising Crimal for his stouteartedness: "While still the fight undaunted you maintained. You kept men thinking of the ways of freedom."[43]

In a final exhortation, MacSwiney's Fionn delivers a call for commitment to purpose that is universal in its scope, but in its message of fealty to a cause, is especially directed towards Ireland at the turn of the century:

And in memory of the after time, our day shall shine with all the glow of dawn light. The dream and hope of the morning. ...where dark deeds triumph for a little day, beware the dreamer: When a wandering soul inspires the dauntless heart, a mind acute, a heart both strong and quick to strike ... Let tyrannies them trouble. There shall flash like quickening fire through the quivering earth a message to all nations: Like a star shattering an ocean's darkness: like a song bearing its burden in a simple line: A few men faithful and a deathless dream – to show the freedom of a race ... No people shall despair to hear it told.[44]

His reference to "a few men faithful" offered a vision of what would occur during Easter Week 1916.

In general, MacSwiney's plays received better notices in the local Cork press than from the Dublin theatre critics. The *Cork Constitution* viewed *The Last Warriors of Coole* as a "really commendable piece of work, indicating promise in the author". The paper commented on what it saw as the author's technique and future prospects:

> He seems to have written slowly and studiously, for the verse beautifully embodies the central idea. Many lines are of much beauty of phrase, and there is more than one striking descriptive passage. What amazes the spectator, who follows the play studiously, is the wonderful atmosphere produced by the stage setting, the players and the words. One becomes interested and then absorbed in thought as the idea is unfolded, until there is fully realised "Crimal's deathless hope and Fionn's saving of his people". If space permitted, a good deal could be written about the play, but it must be sufficient to state that it was a success, as it certainly deserved to be.

In his one act play, graphically titled *The Holocaust*, Mac-Swiney showed a great deal of empathy with people trapped in poverty, and forced in some cases to see their children die of a lack of medical treatment. In *The Holocaust*, produced in 1910, Polly, the poor and broken-hearted mother, tends to her fever-ridden little girl in a slum dwelling. She is comforted by Fr Cahill, but she and her child are treated dismissively by Dr Condon, the local dispensary physician, more concerned with completing his social schedule. The play is the closest the author comes in his dramatic work to an indictment of the Irish social system. Nonetheless, in *The Holocaust*, the antagonist is clearly the selfish physician, and not British rule, while the Catholic clergyman acts as the force for righteousness.

At the play's outset, MacSwiney painted the scene of the unfolding tragedy, though without giving a specific location:

Scene: One room hovel in the slums. Window looking onto land on right back; glass broken, stuffed with old cloth. Door at back left. Fireplace at side right. Child's bed in centre back; an old mattress laid on two boxes lengthways together. The child lying on mattress very thinly covered...[45]

The story is told in a type of stage Irish vernacular not uncommon to more celebrated theatrical words of the period from the pen of Synge and others.

MacSwiney's *Holocaust* is a tale of utter hopelessness from beginning to end. The virtuous Cahill and the distraught Polly can do little more than watch the child, given no name except "The Girleen", die in her fitful sleep. In one scene, the priest is standing by the child's bed "looking after Polly, utterly wretched". He exclaims, "My God! My God! The misery of it all ... where will it all end?" Fr Cahill then makes an emotional plea to God, filled with a desire for a condition of "justice" that is left unexplained: "My poor, poor little sufferer ... Justice for this suffering child! We have no divine patience. We will do wild things and leave the great thing undone. If we arraign them who make these horrors, they can crush us and we are futile. Justice would endure annihilation but to be futile. They cannot challenge you! Give us chastening justice, to purify the earth, to redeem the Christ! Hear the cry of the tortured children."[46]

Later Fr Cahill, in imploring Dr Condon to intercede, notes the disparity between the love of God for the poor in the scriptures and the coarse reality of their earthly condition: "Of course, the poor are God's poor, and the rich man will find it hard to get to Heaven. But for all that, the rich Catholic is courted, while the poor one is patronised."[47]

In the end, the little girl dies, and is followed to the grave by her mother, who succumbs that night to a broken heart. The man of the house has by the end arrived on the scene. He leaves the house in a rage and as MacSwiney writes: "Throwing the priest from him, pauses a moment by the bodies in livid wrath." The child's father then "rushes out wildly" while Fr Cahill "alone, helpless, sinks on one knee in distress by two bodies."[48] But the audience is not told who the father seeks to strike out at, and so the object of MacSwiney's wrath is left unclear.

From a critical standpoint, *The Holocaust* elicited the favourable comment of at least one Dublin writer in *The Leader*, who called it "A poignant little etching of the problem of slum life, of unemployment, underfeeding, joylessness and unregarded misery..." A later play, *Manner's Masketh Man*, met with a less than enthusiastic response from the *Cork Constitution*. While complimenting the play for being "well written" and possessing "characters well drawn", its critic opined nonetheless that "the piece never becomes a real, full-bodied one act comedy ... The defects were a certain stiffness at some points, and emphasis, or want of it, at moments in the dialogue ... Mr MacSwiney should do better, and in all probability will, but perhaps it will take the trend of *The Last Warriors of Coole*".

In MacSwiney's work, the influence of his sister can be seen, particularly as it relates to his view of the role of women in politics. The dialogue in *The Breamers* between the characters Dermott, Tom and Mrs Kennedy, regarding the entry of women into the Wolfe Tone Club, might be read against the backdrop of Mary MacSwiney's experience as an early activist in the suffragette movement and in Cumann na mBan. The Irish women's Republican organisation, like its male counterparts, was also an advocate of physical force.

Foley: I admit women are not fitted for politics.

Nora: Why?

Foley: They jump at conclusions.

Nora: While the man walks around and runs away from it.

Mistress Kennedy: Be frank and tell us what you think.

Tom: We wouldn't criticise the girls. We'll say our say to the men.

Mistress Kennedy: Here we won't have the women treated as hothouse plants by the men.

Dermot: A woman wouldn't be expected to be as dexterous as a man at the game.

Hugh: I think you're mistaken.

Dermott: But a man wouldn't care to press his point.

Mistress Kennedy: What condescension! If it were honest condescension.

Dermot: That is rather candid.

Hugh: That's right, Mistress Kennedy. I'd like to hear Tom on
             the kind of girls that come here.
Mistress Kennedy: To shrink argument for want of a plea under
             cloak of magnaminity is cowardly.
Tom: Too damn smart.
Dermott: But women in politics are wasted and politics is tire-
             some. Keep to the social life. There, woman is queen.
Mistress   Kennedy: Queen. More like a toy lamb in a Noah's ark.
             I wonder we are all not put in an institution placarded
             "girls to be married when of age – pleasing appearance
             – state colour eyes and hair".
Dermot: Don't speak as if all girls were panting for an intellectual
             and national revival. Get near a batch of them talking
             after Mass some day. The humour of the occasion is the
             discourse ... the backbiting and small scandal, and the
             scandal is so very small.
Mistress Kennedy: That's the reason for our coming here. The
             average girl's petty outlook dismays us. We want to
             make her a comrade, not a plaything.[49]

For the *Irish Citizen's* critic, this passage represented "an
oasis in a desert of banality ... Mr. MacSwiney must try it
again ... The best that be said of him," L.C. concluded, "is
that it is worth his while."

MacSwiney's own views on the role of women in Irish life
in general formed the basis for an essay titled
"Womanhood" in *Principles of Freedom*. In it we see a
Terence MacSwiney capable of dealing with women in a
manner beyond the conventions of the time. He criticised the
relegation of women to what he called the "Doll's House".

We have noticed the man who prefers his ease to any troubling
duty: he has his mate in the woman who prefers to be wooed
with trinkets, chocolates, and the theatre to a more beautiful way
of life, that would give her a nobler place but far more strenuous
conditions.[50]

The patronising of women was not the sole thrust of the essay.
He contended, in reference to both sexes, that "we have
allowed a standard to gain recognition that is a danger alike
to the dignity of our womanhood and the virility of our

manhood". To the women of Ireland, he emphasised the need to understand "that greater than the need of the suffrage is the more urgent need of making her fellow woman spirited and self reliant, ready to anticipate a danger then to evade it ... When she is thus trained," MacSwiney argued, "not all the men of all the nations can deny her recognition and equality." Nonetheless, in his prescription MacSwiney was at best vague. Appealing for a rejection of materialism among Irishmen and women alike, while stating the case for a heightened role for women in general, MacSwiney wrote: "Let us, then, in the name of our common nature, ask those who have her training in hand, to teach the woman to despise the man of the menial soul and to loath the luxury that is his price."[51]

Despite his calls for a greater role for women in Ireland, Terence MacSwiney was also a product of his times. Hence he was prone to holding up some women from the pages of Irish history as an example to be followed in a manner that may be seen as patronising. Such was the case with Sarah Tone, the wife of one of his heroes, Theobald Wolfe Tone.

> We can speak her praise without fear, for she was put to the test in every way ... For her devotion to, and encouragement of her husband in his great work, she would have won our high praise, even if, when he was stricken down and she was bereft of his wonderful love and buoyant spirits, she had proved forgetful of his work and the glory of his name ... Her devotion to Tone, while he was living and fighting, might be explained by the woman's passionate attachment to the man she loved.[52]

In *The Breamers*, MacSwiney also focused on the wider debate between the various strands of Irish separatism. At the centre of the play is a debate within the Wolfe Tone Club in the fictitious town of Marshtown over whether the organisation's constitution should withdraw its demand for an Irish Republic in exchange for a more general statement advocating Irish separatism. This topic anticipated an issue MacSwiney himself would not live to contend with: the bitter Dáil Éireann debate on the Anglo-Irish Treaty from December 1921 to January 1922, in which the question was whether the ideal of unfettered independence should be held to at all costs, or whether dominion status should be accepted. In *The*

Breamers, MacSwiney's characters discuss the merits of adhering rigidly to the Republican ideal as a requisite for membership in the Wolfe Tone Club:

Conn: There's no question of changing the constitution tonight.

Hugh: No? Why? ... That would involve no violent change. We're fighting for freedom, not a particular form of government.

Conn: Wolfe Tone was a Republican.

Hugh: In action he would separate from England under any form of government.

Conn: But the fellows who dislike pleading for a Republic say separation ought not to be emphasised.

Hugh: Separation must be emphasised.

Conn: Then you must pin them to a Republic.

Hugh: Frankly, I'm less of a democrat now then when we began to work. Men now defy democracy and majority rule. A thing is not right simply for having majority to back it.

Conn: But the wavering of the others from the Republic is for backsliding.

Hugh: There must be no backsliding ... Pleading for the Republic means debating side issues, kingship, democracy, imperialism, communism. We must not waste energy.

Conn: You can't put your philosophy into the rules, and we must be clear on separation.

Hugh: Yes, and the rule for the Republic makes it clear ... And is Sean wavering?

Conn: He is tired of working with little result.[53]

In another segment of *The Breamers*, the need for those seeking Irish independence to stay the course is seen as central. This exchange between the beleaguered Sean, pressing the need for the Wolfe Tone Club to expand its membership, and the more doctrinaire Dermot, is illustrative of a debate which was central to MacSwiney throughout his twenty years of involvement with the Irish separatist struggle.

Sean: You judge those lacking character as having it. Our strength, such as it is, has grown with us. The strength of others must grow. Burden it now, and it will snap and be done with.

Hugh: We keep the strength of others to grow by adherence to principle. To retreat a stage would waste our strength without nursing theirs.

Sean: (depressed) What will our attitude be with newcomers? Give them our object, to separate from England and found a Republic, and they will either not understand or laugh at us or grasp the idea and shrink away.

Hugh: We must make them understand; better they shrink away beforehand, then desert in a crisis.

Sean: Where does that leave us? It doesn't settle the difficulty.

Hugh: I know the difficulty. It weighs on me. But I see a danger more grim. We have a standard. If we propose another standard to others, we must let go our own.[54]

This dilemma, well presented by MacSwiney in this exchange, was never far from the surface within the Sinn Féin movement. The Sinn Féin Convention of October 1917, which accorded a narrow victory to the advocates of a Republic and replaced Arthur Griffith and his more moderate line with Eamon de Valera as the organisation's president, followed by the Anglo-Irish war itself, deferred that debate.*

Throughout *The Breamers*, Dermot, a central character, is seen to grow from a position of being willing to dilute the organisation's Republican character as a means of attracting more members, to one of appreciating the importance of standing fast by principle. Before the curtain falls, he is shown alone, reflecting on the importance of pursuing the path of virtue over expediency.

More than simply serving as a vehicle for asserting what he saw as the virtues of the Republican cause, MacSwiney's message in *The Breamers* was also consistent with what he saw as a fundamental reality: an alliance between those supporting full Irish independence in the form of a Republic, and those favouring something less, was doomed to failure and bitterness. MacSwiney also made this argument in an essay first published in *Irish Freedom* in 1911. "Let not the hands of the men in the vanguard," he wrote, "be tied by

---

* But it would return in earnest, on the floor of Dáil Éireann during the Anglo-Irish Treaty debates in December 1921. Ironically, the vote taken on the Treaty saw Arthur Griffith succeed Eamon de Valera as head of the Irish nation. But tragically for Ireland and all involved, the discussion was not confined to chambers of the Dáil. Carnage and atrocities committed by Irishman against Irishman on the roadways and fields of Ireland instead rendered internecine horror as the outlet for the resolution of differences over the path Irish nationalism should take.

alien King, Constitution or Parliament".[55] Richard Davis has
observed that MacSwiney's use of the word "Vanguard",
had a "Leninist ring, suggesting a small disciplined cadre
rather than the broadly based national movement of
Griffith's dreams".[56]

A similar undercurrent can be found in his play *The
Revolutionist*, in which he stressed the need for adherence to
principle in defence of the elusive Republic. A certain criticism is also evinced by MacSwiney in this extract from the
play, in which he scorns the wishes of popular democracy.

> Men standing by a premature grave are apt to reconsider their
> hasty judgments and indolent lives. Then who has succeeded?
> That, I think, is the moral we need to point now at a time when
> in a natural desire for majorities and armies it is being obscured
> ... It's not our ideas that are at fault, but ourselves. It may be we
> are given the work of angels and the nature of men, and the man
> cuts a sorry figure at times.[57]

"When things seem just hopeless," one of his characters
remarks, "someone is always found to do a brave thing or a
beautiful thing that renews the fire and we're ready to begin
again as from the first." In a message aimed at those he feared
might be considering compromise, "Tell them nothing
matters if they don't give in – nothing, nothing – the last
moment – that's the important time – the grip then ... What's
the good of being alive, if we give in?"[58]

Given the course that MacSwiney's own life was to take,
these remarks were apocryphal. The message emphasising
the Republican ideal of an independent Ireland in his play,
The Breamers, was given deeper meaning by the playwright's own attempt to personify that ideal. MacSwiney's
intellectual honesty would be established beyond question
by his willingness to put his life on the line for the ideals he
cherished most; this fact would be conceded even by his enemies. Terence MacSwiney did not need to ponder, as Yeats
did, whether his work "brought young men out to die".
Instead, he actively sought to join the pantheon of those
who had died in 1916. Rather than be content to write
about the need for revolution, he would help lead one. But
in his attempt to undertake "a brave thing or a beautiful

thing", we will see that he was motivated also by the shame he felt in not having participated in the Easter Rising.

MacSwiney's view that art should express high principles carried over into his political writings. This passage from *Principles of Freedom* is instructive in revealing the extent to which he had developed a framework of ideas with which he later opposed the force used against him:

> Now, and in every phase of the coming struggle, the strong mind is a greater need than the strong hand ... In the aberrations of the weak mind decrying resistance, let us not lose our balance and defy brute strength ... Let the cultivation of a brave high spirit be our great task; it will make of each man's soul an unassailable fortress. Armies may fall, but it resists forever. The body it informs may be crushed, the spirit in passing breaths on other souls, and other hearts are fired into action, and the fight goes on to victory. To the man whose mind is true and resolute ultimate victory is assured. No sophistry can sap his resistance; no weakness can tempt him to savage reprisals. He will neither abandon his heritage nor poison his nature.[59]

But he was not always so serious. "Revolutions fail," Mac-Swiney observed, "when their leaders have no sense of humour."[60] MacSwiney's own sense of humour came through in his play *Manner Masketh Man,* in which he poked fun at the image of the indecisive male figure surrounded by stronger females. One publication described *Manner Masketh Man* as "a very pretty and appealing *morceau*".[61] The play dealt with the inherent contradictions of unending politeness. O'Hegarty noted that "It should not surprise us that Terence MacSwiney could write such comedy as this," and this despite the fact that his friend's mind "was ever dwelling on the heights."[62]

A somewhat mixed review appeared in the pages of the *Cork Constitution* for his play *The Wooing of Emer*. The play dealt with the mythical Cuchulain's pursuit of the enchantress Emer, and the resultant opposition to their romance by the girl's father, Forgel. The *Constitution*'s reviewer commented that "There are some fine and some impressive scenes in the play, but the end is hardly effective." While praising the "fine rhythm and balance of the play's blank verse," the paper's critic cited what he saw as the defect of "a certain floridity, and an attenuation of an image or idea by an elaborate embroidery of words".

One of the harshest reviews of Terence MacSwiney's creative work was directed at *The Revolutionist* by the critic "L.C." in the *Irish Citizen*. The reviewer wrote that the "scenes of keen political controversy were among the best in the play; though even here, Mr. MacSwiney's vagueness, his reluctance to use definitely the words Home Rule, separatism, and the like, keep the puzzled reader in a mood of dissatisfaction and needless obscurity". The critic noted that "the characters of the committee men, and their varying attitudes towards political principles and methods, are well drawn, and apparently from an inside knowledge of what goes on in many political conventicals of little political coteries in Dublin". He reserved his severest criticism for the play's attempted "love interest", finding this "the weakest part of the play". On MacSwiney's treatment of women "L.C." wrote that he "does not understand the modern woman, as if his women are mere reproductions of types long antiquated – if they ever had any real existence outside the mind of the 'romantic' fictionist".

Such criticism no doubt contributed to the frustration of the young writer. Now aged thirty-four, he began to feel that he had reached a dead end as a creative writer. This feeling was expressed in letters to his sister Margaret, a nun in America. He urged her to pray for him and wondered about his literary prospects if he emigrated to the US.[63] It was now 1913. Soon his attention moved away from creative writing toward a more direct form of prose: that of the separatist propagandist. In a short time these efforts led him from the pen to the gun.

Notes

1. Tom Garvin, "Great Hatred, Little Room: Social Background and Political Sentiment Among Revolutionary Activists in Ireland, 1890-1922," *The Revolution of Ireland 1879-1923* (D.G. Boyce ed. London 1988) pp. 90-91.
2. Sean Nolan, account provided by Máire MacSwiney Brugha.
3. P.S. O'Hegarty, *Terence MacSwiney* (Dublin 1922) p. 4.

4. Moirin Chavasse, undated, MacSwiney Collection, UCD Archives, P48c/97.
5. Terence MacSwiney Diary, undated, MacSwiney Collection, P48c/98/l and 28 October 1905 to 25 August 1906, P48c/101/1.
6. Ibid.
7. Ibid.
8. Terence MacSwiney Diary, undated, MacSwiney Collection, P48c/101.
9. Eithne MacSwiney to Moirin Chavasse, MacSwiney Collection.
10. Terence MacSwiney Diary, undated, MacSwiney Collection, P48c/101.
11. Terence MacSwiney Diary, 11 November 1905, MacSwiney Collection, P48c/101.
12. Ibid.
13. Terence MacSwiney Diary, 13 November 1905, MacSwiney Collection, P48c/101.
14. Ibid.
15. Terence MacSwiney Diary undated, MacSwiney Collection, P48c/254.
16. O'Hegarty, *Terence MacSwiney*, p.3.
17. Ibid.
18. Terence MacSwiney Diary, undated, MacSwiney Collection, P48c/253.
19. MacSwiney Collection, P48c/254.
20. Terence MacSwiney Diary, 9 September 1902, MacSwiney Collection.
21. Ibid.
22. Ibid.
23. Ibid.
24. Ibid.
25. Ibid.
26. Terence MacSwiney to Mrs Murphy, undated, from 1917, MacSwiney Collection.
27. Chavasse, *Terence MacSwiney* (Dublin 1961) p. 17.
28. Sean Nolan to Máire MacSwiney Brugha, MacSwiney Collection.
29. Terence MacSwiney to Vincent McCarthy, 27 March 1909, MacSwiney Collection, P48b/165.
30. Terence MacSwiney to Cork Municipal School of Commerce, 7 March 1910, MacSwiney Collection, P48b/214.
31. Cork Municipal School of Commerce to Terence MacSwiney,

18 April 1910, MacSwiney Collection, P48b/214.

32. D.J. Coakley, Principal, Cork Municipal School of Commerce, MacSwiney Collection.
33. Letter to Terence MacSwiney, 6 June 1912, Cork Municipal Archives.
34. O'Hegarty, *Terence MacSwiney*, p. 33.
35. Ibid. p. 22.
36. Terence MacSwiney, "Address for the Emmet Centenary," 1903, MacSwiney Collection, P48b/30l.
37. "The Insurgents Farewell A.D. 1798," MacSwiney Collection, P48b/300(1).
38. MacSwiney, *Principles of Freedom* (Buffalo 1975) p. 152.
39. Chavasse, *Terence MacSwiney*, p.196.
40. Terence MacSwiney Diary, undated, MacSwiney Collection, P48c/253.
41. Ibid.
42. Terence MacSwiney, *The Last Warriors of Coole*, MacSwiney Collection, P48b/294(3).
43. Ibid.
44. Ibid.
45. Terence MacSwiney, *The Holocaust*, Manuscript Copy, MacSwiney Collection.
46. Ibid.
47. Ibid.
48. Ibid.
49. Terence MacSwiney, *The Breamers*, Manuscript Copy, MacSwiney Collection, P48b/297.
50. MacSwiney, *Principles of Freedom*, p. 116.
51. Ibid.
52. Ibid.
53. MacSwiney, *The Breamers*, MacSwiney Collection, P48b/297.
54. Ibid.
55. MacSwiney, *Principles of Freedom*, pp. 77-78.
56. Richard Davis, *Arthur Griffith and Non-Violent Sinn Féin* (Dublin 1964) p. 118.
57. Terence MacSwiney, Notes from *The Revolutionist*, MacSwiney Collection, P48a/109.
58. Ibid.
59. MacSwiney, *Principles of Freedom*, p. 40.
60. Ibid.
61. O'Hegarty, *Terence MacSwiney*, p. 25.
62. Ibid.
63. Terence MacSwiney to Margaret MacSwiney, undated, MacSweeney Collection, P48c.

Chapter II

The Writer Turns to the Gun

STRESSING THE IMPACT that Terence MacSwiney had on the 1981 Irish Republican hunger strikers, David Beresford writes that MacSwiney "was an extraordinary idealist in whose little known writings can be found the philosophical drive which foreshadowed the relish with which he would throw his life and death at England".[1] In his own time, MacSwiney sought to draw meaning from the writings of Robert Emmet as to the value of physical struggle and the importance of discipline. On the subject of "Excesses", MacSwiney quoted Emmet as giving this address to his men at the commencement of his failed 1801 revolt:

> We now speak to you and through you to the rest of Ireland on a subject dear to us and to the success of our country – its honour. You are accused by your enemies of having violated that honour by excesses, which they themselves have provoked, but which they have grossly exaggerated and which have been attributed to you. The opportunity for vindicating yourselves by action is now for the first time in your power, and we call upon you to give the lie to such assertions by carefully avoiding all appearances of intoxication, plunder or revenge.[2]

In the columns of *Irish Freedom*, MacSwiney reflected on the legitimacy of armed insurrection in the context of a just war. "At the heart of the question," he wrote, "we will be met by the religious objection to revolt ... In Ireland an army representative of the people would be largely Catholic, and much former difficulty arose from Catholics in Ireland meeting with opposition from some Catholic authorities."[3] MacSwiney contended that Dr Murray of Maynooth, one of the foremost Irish Catholic scholars of the nineteenth century, felt the Church took no definitive stance on the question of armed resistance. It is striking that in his discussion of the subject, he made no reference to classical Catholic theological works setting out conditions for a "just war", such as those outlined in Thomas Aquinas' *Summa Theologica*.

In his articles in *Irish Freedom*, later to be published collectively in a posthumous volume entitled *Principles of Freedom*, MacSwiney laid bare his sense that the Irish people would inevitably turn against British rule:

> One day the consciousness of the country will be electrified with a great deed or a great sacrifice and the multitude will break from lethargy or prejudice, and march with a shout for freedom in a true, brave and a beautiful sense ... A man who will be brave only if tramping with a legion will fail in courage if called to stand in the breach alone. And it must be clear to all that till Ireland can again summon her banded armies there will be abundant need for men who will stand the single test. 'Tis the bravest test, the noblest test, and 'tis the test that offers the sweetest and greatest victory.[4]

The theme of patriotic discipline was one to which MacSwiney would return. In the December 1912 issue of *Irish Freedom*, he wrote glowingly of Irish patriots of the past and of the example they gave. "They had still the finest appreciation," he stated, "of the finer attributes of comradeship and love." These men, he emphasised, "were ready to go on to the end, not looking for the suffrage of the living nor the monuments of the dead". Of his own day, MacSwiney wrote that "when finally the re-awakened people by their better instincts, their discipline, patriotism and fervour, will have massed into armies, and marched to freedom, they will know in the greatest hour of triumph that the success of their conquering armies was made possible by those who held the breach".[5] His romanticisation of imagined armies, to be "massed" against the enemy, showed little understanding of the kind of warfare that would actually come in Ireland.

Not unlike other Irish separatists of his time of an intellectual bent, Terence MacSwiney did not delve deeply into the divisions that separated Catholic and Protestant in Ireland. Like Pearse, Connolly, MacNeill and others, he sought to lay the problem almost exclusively on the British presence. Were it removed, according to their logic, there would evolve a natural understanding between the two sides, who would share harmoniously in the bounty of an independent Ireland. Nonetheless, unlike many of his separatist contemporaries, MacSwiney conceded the reality of the division between Catholic and Protestant, and the long-term problem it posed for the nation.

> But the men of different creeds who stand firmly and loyally together are a minority. We are faced with the difficulty of uniting as a whole North and South; and we are faced with the grim fact that many whom we desire to unite are angrily repudiating a like desire, that many are sarcastically noting this ... while through it all the most bitter are emphasizing enmity and glorifying it. All these unbelievers keep insisting North and South are natural enemies and must so remain ... By those who cling to prejudice and abandon self-restraint, extol enmity, and always proceed to the further step – the plea to wipe the enemy out; the counter plea for forbearance is always scorned as the elevating gospel of weakness and despair. Though we call ourselves Christian, we have no desire for ... that outstanding Christian virtue.[6]

For him, a resolution of the differences separating Catholic and Protestant Ireland lay actually in each side genuinely adhering to the articles of their respective faiths. "Catholics and Protestants," he wrote "instead of saying to one another the things with which we are familiar, should look to their own houses; and if in this age of fashionable agnosticism, they should conclude that the general enemy is the atheist, socialist, and the syndicalist, they should still be reminded to look to their own houses."[7]

In this vein, MacSwiney also made it clear that he was an opponent of religious sectarianism. He made his view on groups like the Catholic fraternal organisation, the Ancient Order of Hibernians, known, and characterised their members as "sincere but misguided Catholics". The organisation was "in effect, a sort of Catholic Freemasonry, but like Orangeism, it was a political and not a religious weapon".[8]

Though he was not sectarian, neither was MacSwiney an anti-cleric. "There are, it is my belief," MacSwiney wrote to P.S. O'Hegarty in February of 1904, "a few in our ranks who

seem to regard priests as if they were our natural enemies ...
I heartily wish they would show us their backs as I am
convinced they are a greater source of danger to our cause
and our ultimate hopes of success than all the power of the
British Government."[9]

But MacSwiney's defence of the clergy met with a swift
rebuttal from O'Hegarty. O'Hegarty's response shows the
difference in outlook between two young advanced nationalists: one, MacSwiney, who had remained all his life in Ireland,
and one whose experience as an immigrant in London
perhaps made him more independent.

> I don't hold that the priests are our natural enemies but I do think
> strongly that they have acquired the habit and that nothing but
> strong determined actions will break them of it. They ruined
> every movement – directly or indirectly – since the passing of the
> Maynooth Grant in 1795 and we have to put them in their places
> if we are going to do anything ... Most of the fellows here are
> anti-cleric to a greater or lesser degree ... It is only when a man
> leaves Ireland that he begins to see straight on some things ... [10]

MacSwiney, like Patrick Pearse, supported the Home Rule
bill as a practical means of gaining wider Irish authority over
the country's affairs. This decision to embrace Home Rule
was an opportunistic one; both men saw the fundamental
precepts of constitutional nationalism as bankrupt and
antithetical to the cause of an independent Irish nation. As
early as the summer of 1906, MacSwiney had written of the
inherent contradictions he found in the arguments of the
constitutional nationalists. In a diary entry from August of
that year, he acknowledged that "my ideas about politics have
developed on what is known as 'extreme lines'"[11] and
proceeded then to delineate what he saw as the fundamental
differences between the advocates of physical force and those
favouring a constitutional approach as the means to attaining
Irish nationhood. This, of course, was a theme central to
several of his plays, *The Breamers* and, in particular, *The
Revolutionist*.

> The "extremist", so-called, is one who has an ideal and strives
> to the best of his ability to aid in the realisation of that ideal. The

history of this country tells him that England got possession of this country by a combination of fraud and force, and that the power which she has usurped she maintains by force. To obtain and keep possession of this country, she has trampled on every moral law. The history of this country tells him ... that through succeeding generations, gallant efforts have been made to restore his country to her rightful position of sovereign independence. This was the highest ideal that inspired patriotism in the past; it has called for some of the grandest sacrifices ever made in the sacred cause of liberty ... And so the "extremist" keeps the ideal of nationality unsullied and adopts for his watchword "no-compromise." But what of the constitutional-constitutionalist? The very name by which he calls himself has a little history in itself. His doctrine is to "win our rights" by constitutional methods. But as it is our right to be separate from the British Empire if we wish it – and how heartily we do wish it – and to obtain this right would mean the destruction of the British Constitution in Ireland, it must be admitted that the doctrine of the constitutionalist is somewhat paradoxical. But the constitutionalist idea of our rights is a home parliament under the English flag, and if you attempt to explain to him that this is not the full measure of our rights. but that in reality our country should be raised to a position of sovereign independence, he will in all probability tell you that you are an extremist.[12]

MacSwiney's articles in *Irish Freedom* drew him to the attention of the Irish Republican Brotherhood (IRB) in Dublin. Yet according to Diarmuid Lynch, "The consensus of opinion among my fellow members of the Cork Circle was that he was not to be 'approached' with a view to membership in the IRB – not in 1911-1912 at any rate."[13] Lynch speculated that their hesitancy may have been due to a belief that MacSwiney would be loath to become a member because Catholics were prohibited from joining the organisation. A few years later, however, in the weeks before the Rising, MacSwiney did join the IRB.

At this time, MacSwiney was already in contact with some of those who would engineer the 1916 Rising. On 19 June, 1911, Sean MacDiarmada commiserated with him over what he called "the corrupt press of this country" which "would lead outsiders to believe that all Ireland is wallowing before their Britannic Majesty".[14] For young men like MacSwiney, Eoin MacNeill's article "The North Began", in the November 1913 issue of *An Claidheamh Soluis*, served as an important catalyst.[15] Here was an idea of establishing a Nationalist Volunteer Force, on the model of the Ulster Volunteers. As events would show, however, this assertion of nationalist identity by force of arms would be met by a different response from the British government than did its Orange predecessor, Ulster Unionism's threat of treason against the crown notwithstanding.

The inaugural meeting of the Irish Volunteers in Cork took place on the evening of Sunday, 14 December 1913, at the City Hall. Florrie O'Donoghue described the events of that evening:

> The hall was filled to capacity. A number of Fianna boys in uniform stood guard on the platform. In addition to the principal speakers, MacNeill and Casement, the platform party included J.J. Welsh, J.F. Fawsitt, Liam de Roiste, Sean O'Hegarty and Liam Owen. A large party of active supporters, including Tomás MacCurtain, were in the vestibule just off the platform. The reading by Fawsitt of the Provisional Committee's manifesto was received with much enthusiasm. MacNeill followed, speaking first in Irish and then in English.[16]

When MacNeill remarked, in reference to Ulster Volunteers and the Irish Volunteers, that there was "no reason why either should fear the other", he was met with cries of indignation and an attempt at disrupting the meeting by a sizeable contingent from the Ancient Order of Hibernians present in the audience. Days later MacNeill was forced to explain himself in the letter's page of the *Cork Examiner*. "I am," he said, "and have long been, a supporter of Mr John Redmond."[17]

Afterwards, the promoters of the Irish Volunteer's meeting in Cork released the names of a "provisional committee"; the group included MacSwiney and Tomás MacCurtain, along with J.F. Fawsitt, Liam de Roiste, P.S. O'Hegarty, and several others.

The meeting marked a turning point in MacSwiney's life.

He had now found a vehicle for his energy and hopes which went beyond his efforts as a playwright and Irish separatist propagandist. The study and practice of the military arts were now foremost in his activities, and he threw himself into the Volunteers' organisational efforts. Seven years later, as life ebbed from him during his final days at Brixton Prison, MacSwiney recalled in a letter to Sean O'Hegarty how the two had been among "the first eight to take the floor" of the drill hall at the Cork Volunteers' first gathering.[18]

Despite the attraction that the Volunteers came to hold for him, some of those closest to MacSwiney differed as to his acumen as a soldier. To Florrie O'Donoghue, Terence MacSwiney was "the very best kind of soldier in the circumstances of the time, the man who serves from a sense of duty", but to Sean Neeson, MacSwiney "really had not a military mind. He was an intellectual and a would-be philosopher. They seldom made good soldiers."[19]

The Irish Volunteers were organised more on political than military lines. By the summer of 1914 they had grown to a force 100,000 strong, and placed the Irish Party's John Redmond at the helm. Mitchelstown, County cork, was one of the first towns to organise, and 2,000 men enrolled in the Galtee regiment in that first year. But a crisis erupted in June between Redmond's majority and the separatist wing headed by MacNeill as to the manner for selecting an executive for the organisation. Redmond sought the addition of twenty-five men nominated by the Irish Party to the provisional committee which governed the organisation. MacNeill's provisional committee sought the election of an executive through a series of conventions covering the whole country. Trying to avoid a permanent split in the Volunteers' ranks, the provisional committee voted to accept Redmond's plan. In Cork city, as Florence O'Donoghue noted, while the local executive committee included most of the original promoters there, "it gave the Redmondite followers a less than proportionate representation".[20]

The Irish Volunteers' Cork executive, created on 21 June 1914, included Terence MacSwiney, Tomás MacCurtain, Liam de Roiste, Sean O'Hegarty, Tadhg Barry, Diarmuid Ó Donobhan, with J.J. Walsh and Denis O'Maloney to serve as chairman and deputy chairman respectively. It was especially significant that most of these names, including those of MacSwiney and MacCurtain, were included in the separate military council which the executive committee set up immediately after it took office.[21] Florence O'Donoghue's description of the realities which the military group faced is particularly useful.

> The problem of equipment and arms was formidable. Uniforms, belts, bandoleers, puttees and haversacks were made locally of Irish materials, but there was no fund from which they could be purchased in bulk and the men who were so equipped had purchased the articles themselves. The arms position was even more difficult. The so-called Peace Preservation Act of 1881, which had been allowed to lapse in 1907, had been revived by a proclamation of 4 December, 1913, immediately after the formation of the Irish Volunteers. It prohibited the import of arms into Ireland. In the Cork Companies, arms were limited to a few rifles which had been purchased by individual Volunteers and some miscellaneous small weapons.[22]

The gun-running into Howth, County Dublin, on 26 July 1914, had only a marginal impact on the arms situation of the Volunteers in Cork. Of the relatively small cargo of 1,500 outdated rifles and 49,000 rounds of ammunition brought in on the yacht, the *Asgard*, and another privately owned craft a week later, only fifty rifles found their way to Cork. The weapons were placed under the control of Tomás MacCurtain.[23]

The outbreak of the First World War in August provoked a crisis in the ranks of the Irish Volunteers. Rather than seeing this development as a chance to force the Home Rule issue, in an address to the House of Commons on 3 August Redmond instead pledged Ireland's support to the empire. But while he spoke for a majority within the Irish Volunteers, if not a majority of his countrymen, Redmond also forced the minority of Irish separatists, to whom support for the empire was anathema, to follow a radically different course of action.

A majority of the Cork executive joined the national provisional committee in endorsing Redmond's action. Still hoping to maintain the unity of the Irish Volunteers, the separatist element sought to accept a course that provided for Ireland's defence, but not for Irishmen fighting to preserve the empire. Terence MacSwiney wrote in the maiden issue of *Fianna Fáil* on 19 September 1914, that the Volunteers as a whole "are anxious, eager, almost pathetically eager, it may be said, to strengthen and support any party leader who will take the straight course for Ireland".[24] MacSwiney was very direct on the terms he sought from England:

> We make a simple proposal; we ask no restitution for plundering of the past, but this: let England as a slight compensation deliver us free a quarter of a million Lee Enfield rifles, latest pattern, with bayonets and ten million rounds of ammunition. We will provide heavy guns at our own expense, and thus armed we will hold Ireland, for Ireland, against all comers. And we guarantee to England that this country will not be used as a base against her. She is entitled to this – no more. On our side we demand the recognition of our independence. We will take no less.[25]

MacSwiney also mused on what he saw as an important harbinger on the road to Irish independence.

> What is the great new factor in the situation? The eagerness of the men called extremists – simple lovers of Ireland without qualification – no more to stand in with the men called constitutionalists. They are anxious, eager, almost pathetically eager it might be said, to strengthen and support any party leader who will take the course for Ireland. They recognise that the old party leaders are, perhaps, battle weary. They want it to be recognised that they themselves are young, full of fire and vitality and that they want a fight.[26]

Under the pressure of these opposing forces, the Irish Volunteers split. The "Volunteers" were soon formed as a separate organisation under MacNeill's leadership, though for a time they maintained "an uneasy partnership" with Redmond's forces.[27] It was soon to disintegrate, as positions further hardened.

MacSwiney's views as to why Ireland should remain outside of the war were made explicit in the pages of *Fianna Fáil*. MacSwiney published, and did most of the writing for the paper himself. While, as Florence O'Donoghue has noted, it "was not an official organ of the Executive Board on the IRB", it expressed their views.[28] It was largely financed by the sale of his own personal library. In a letter to his Aunt Kate in October, he explained his rationale for starting the paper, a development which followed the publication of his play *The Revolutionist*.

> It was quite clear Ireland's interests were being sacrificed to the new cry "England and the Empire" and we had our hands full to keep Ireland uppermost. Our ideal for Ireland was so entirely shut out of the daily press that it became imperative to find some outlet: so to help I started in Cork a small weekly paper. And now the straights [*sic*] to which I'm put to find time to write for that and money to print it.[29]

MacSwiney's undertaking represented, in his friend P.S. O'Hegarty's words, "what was best in Terry's character: his impersonality, his tolerance, his firmness and the clarity of his general ideas".[30] Its sharp attacks on British rule in Ireland combined with its regular diet of incitement to arms against the crown served to ensure its eventual suppression. That the publication was allowed to circulate for as many as eleven issues might even be seen as surprising while Britain was involved in some of the worse phases of its war with Germany. In answer to his own rhetorical question "Why have we come?" MacSwiney offered a fiery response in the paper's first issue.

> Because we believe that in Cork genuine nationalists of all parties and sincere lovers of Ireland are crying out in their hearts for a rallying point from which to declare war on the ancient enemy of our race; war on their allies within our gates, who would sell her honour openly and without shame. We have come to let them know that Ireland is not to be delivered over to serve as a prop for a decaying and tottering empire; that they have mistaken a momentary apathy for acquiescence.[31]

He laid out the historical foundations for his own separatist philosophy through his interpretation of the contributions of those whom he regarded as the champions of Ireland's quest for liberty.

Emmet, calm and confident on the verge of the grave, commanding his epitaph be not written – not till we win a partial freedom, but till Ireland stands amongst the nations; Davis' repudiating the bauble of a parliament that gives not a genuine freedom; Tone, who would strike Ireland forever clear of her ancient and treacherous foes; and Mitchell, who put Ireland's historic faith in one line: "The passionate aspiration for Irish nationhood will outlive the British Empire."[32]

The last issue of *Fianna Fáil* appeared on 5 December 1914, when the paper, along with *Irish Freedom*, and other separatist organs, was suppressed. In that edition, MacSwiney openly called for a German victory. He also mentioned as evidence of German good-will toward Ireland the favourable comments which Sir Roger Casement had received from the German foreign ministry regarding Ireland's national aspirations. Under the heading "German Manifesto to Ireland", a document described as an official wireless from Berlin appeared on page one of the paper. The text of the wire stated that "The Acting Secretary of State for Foreign Affairs, by orders of the Imperial Chancellor, officially declares that the German Government repudiates the evil inventions attributed to it, and only desire the welfare of the Irish people and their country ... Germany would never invade Ireland with a view to its conquest, or the overthrow of any Irish national institutions."[33]

In *Principles of Freedom*, MacSwiney displayed a different tone toward those larger nations involved in suppressing self-determination elsewhere. He appears to have made no effort to reconcile his acceptance of imperial Germany's stated good intentions towards Ireland, and its oppressive conduct in Belgium, for example, or its desire to expand its colonial holdings in Africa. He did, however, place heavy emphasis on the need for all parties to a conflict, Ireland included, to fight with honour.

A fight that is not clean-handed will make victory more disgraceful than any defeat. I have heard it argued that we ought, if we could, make a foreign alliance to crush English power here, even if our foreign allies were engaged in crushing freedom elsewhere. If Ireland were to win freedom by helping directly or indirectly to crush another people she would earn the execration she has herself poured out on tyranny for ages. I have come to see it is not possible for Ireland to win her independence by base methods. It is imperative, therefore, that we should declare ourselves and know where we stand. And I stand by this principle: no physical victory can compensate for spiritual surrender. Whatever side denies that is not my side.[34]

Elsewhere in *Principles of Freedom* he demonstrated an antipathy toward imperialism in general. "Where are now the empires of antiquity?" MacSwiney rhetorically asked. "Let them consider this clear truth. Peoples endure, Empires perish." Ireland, he held stoically, "shall endure; and the measure of our faith will be the measure of our achievement and of the greatness of our future place".[35]

While MacSwiney's energies were divided between his essays, his work with *Fianna Fáil* and the Irish Volunteers, he was not devoid of the usual desires of a young man in his early thirties. In a letter to his Aunt Kate, MacSwiney made it clear that he would like to get married. At the same time, he showed a great degree of playfulness in responding to her urging that he do so. "I don't know what is best to say about your hopes that I won't die in single blessedness," he wrote. "But my dearest Aunt Kate, you are very far off the mark in thinking me likely to laugh. I find no particular virtue or attraction at all in single blessedness – and now you may be disposed to laugh." He offered the view that he "wouldn't be an entire failure in the role of wedded bliss". But the run of his life to date, he cautioned, did not appear to contribute to his eligibility for marriage.[36] The letter also offered a revealing glimpse into his view of the institution of marriage and its conventions at the time.

> All the conventions that seem to go to the making of a suitable and admirable married man are just the things I can't stand. For example, the prosperity and comfort are the two chief things ... to these people to be ruled by any higher idea that might entail sacrifice for the man, trouble for the woman and destitution for the children would seem nothing short of a crime and a very great crime. Well, I disagree. If our domestic peace is to be so worshipped that we will not have it disturbed by any higher thought, don't

you think it nearer to a curse than a blessing? "What doth it profit a man to gain the whole world and suffer the loss of his soul?" Oh, but I'm actually getting preaching, though it's the revolutionist way. My dear Aunt Kate, don't misunderstand me. I'm as fond of comfort as anyone alive. If you saw me comfortably ensconced in an armchair by the fire, you'd wonder how pleasant I'd look if asked to fall into privation.[37]

In light of the eventual privation to which he was to subject himself, this last sentence is especially poignant. He did, however, apprise his aunt of the kind of girl he saw himself most attracted to. "But, dear Aunt Kate," he asked, "if a 'match' had just been made for me and I were married to a girl with a good fortune, and if the fortune were swallowed because of my patriotic activities, what do you think the people-in-law would say, not to mention the girl herself."[38] That he had weighed his marital prospects in pragmatic terms was also evident.

You may say I could surely get a girl as foolish as myself! That would be a dream, Aunt Kate. Do pray for it. I shall most heartily sympathise or more: tell me when you have begun the prayers and I shall join in ... But in all seriousness, don't think me unsympathetic to your wishes. If I were put to it I might write freely and at length about the matter and set your mind at rest as to my desires though, alas! I wouldn't say much as to possibilities. Chief difficulty: the girl is not at hand – obviously we can't get on without the girl! But if she were, a practical difficulty – though not so great – strikes me in the force-expenses. I suppose the marriage expenses would run to £50. I haven't got it. All my very little spare money is gone in my writings. The first little volume from my remembrance some years ago cost me up to £20. The recent one £30. That money could only be got by very slow and careful and even painful saving. The paper I'm running now is likely to run me to my last penny. So I'm afraid the average marrying person wouldn't think me very provident or promising. What do you think? If that hypothetical foolish girl would turn up and let me marry as the labourers do – go to the chapel and return to our work – it might be done! But I don't take to that. I'm no hero. I'd like to have a fling for a week or two anyhow. I'm sufficiently conventional to want a honeymoon. There. You can't say now that I've given the matter no thought.[39]

But his multiplicity of activities continued at the same furious pace. At the end of January 1915, as a result of the split in the Volunteers MacSwiney was elevated to the position of deputy chairman for the Cork executive committee. Five months later he became chairman, when J. F. Fawsitt was served with an expulsion order by the British government. Independence for Ireland and not Home Rule was now their open objective, but, as Florence O'Donoghue noted, "At no time prior to Easter, 1916, was the means by which the organisation was to obtain this objective entirely clear to the rank and file of the Volunteers."[40]

All through 1915 much of the new executive's activities were focused on combatting the apathy of the Irish people, the majority of whom supported England in its war against Germany. August of that year marked MacSwiney's appointment by Volunteer general headquarters as a full-time organiser for County Cork. His experience as a countywide commercial studies instructor now served him and the cause well. The vitality and sense of purpose which MacSwiney brought to the Volunteers throughout Cork is vividly chronicled by Florence O'Donoghue.

> Terence MacSwiney took up the work of organisation with enthusiasm and energy. His experience showed that it was less difficult to start companies than to keep them going. He covered most of the county by train and on a bicycle – mainly on a bicycle – working the undeveloped areas by after-Mass addresses on Sundays, speaking to students after Gaelic League classes, or to any groups or individuals he could get together anywhere, and keeping contact with the organised companies. Night and day he was on the road, starting new companies, advising, encouraging, endeavouring to push the organisation into every parish in the county, blowing to flame the spark to be found in some few men everywhere. At the end of 1915, as a result of his efforts and those of the other brigade officers, new companies had been formed and were actively training at Ahiohill, Ardfield, Ballinadee, Boherbue, Carriganimma, Donoughmore, Dungourney, Eyeries, Kilnamartyra, Kilmurray, Keale, Lyre,

Macroom, Millstreet, Mushera, Nadd, Rathduane and Reallen and Means.[41]

When the great nineteenth-century Fenian leader, Jeremiah O'Donovan Rossa, died in 1915, the leader of the Volunteers, Patrick Pearse, gave the oration at his graveside in Glasnevin cemetery, where he proclaimed famously that "Ireland unfree shall never be at peace".[42] For Terence MacSwiney the words of O'Donovan Rossa, which he quoted in a commemorative pamphlet, served as a personal credo:

> I have made no peace with England. I am at war with her, and so help me God, I will wage that war against her till she is stricken to her knees or till I am stricken to my grave.[43]

O'Donovan Rossa's time spent in English jails, and the deprivations he endured, amounted to more than mere subject matter for MacSwiney's efforts as a propagandist. They were demonstrably a source of inspiration to him.

> What we should bear in mind is that Rossa was no passing misfortune ... We have to remember the implacable savagery he was enduring for years, that for years he was trying without success to get a work of truth to the world – and suffering every failure. When we think of it, we see how just was Mitchell in paying tribute to the nobility of the man. Kickham too, among others, paid Rossa his tribute. From his estimate, as genuine as Mitchell's, we can take one word which perhaps more aptly than any other single word can be used to sum up the character of Rossa – indomitable.[44]

Although MacSwiney quoted O'Donovan Rossa extensively in his memorial essay, no mention was made of the dead patriot's severe criticism of the Catholic Church for what he saw as its willing acceptance of British rule. Indeed, O'Donovan Rossa, and such Fenian compatriots as John O'Leary and James Stephen, had been condemned by the Catholic hierarchy for their revolutionary activities. Nonetheless, MacSwiney's pamphlet provided him with an opportunity to tie the efforts of the Republicans in the later nineteenth century with the Irish Volunteer movement of his own day. It was also a vehicle for rebutting accounts published in the British and American press that O'Donovan Rossa on his death bed had expressed his reconciliation with Britain and had condemned German imperialism. And the pamphlet affords a glimpse of MacSwiney's views on the importance of martyrdom. In his conclusion he summoned readers to reflect on the image of the dead O'Donovan Rossa reunited with other Irish "martyrs of many a persecution".[45] MacSwiney can also be seen to place a greater value on heroic death than on such mundane matters as the prospect of actual victory.

> Why then, pray either to stand or fall, when either way we are happy? But pray for courage and constancy. And if we survive, we shall rejoice in putting Ireland, as Lalor dreamed, at the head of the nations; and if we fall, our spirits rising from another battlefield shall be found worthy to enter what must surely be one of the noblest companies of Heaven.[46]

At the end of the 1915 school year, MacSwiney made it known to the Joint Technical Instructional Committee that he would be taking a summer course in Irish in Ballingeary. "I have a good knowledge of the language, both spoken and written, and desire to make myself fully qualified to teach Irish as a commercial subject," he informed the committee's principal.[47] His devotion to the Irish language, the Gaeltacht, and to Ballingeary in particular, remained with him for the remainder of his life.

New Year's Day 1916 brought MacSwiney to Eyeries on the Beara peninsula, which forms part of County Cork's western boundary, to assess the progress made by the local Volunteers. According to Liam Deasy, who later served as adjutant of the West Cork Brigade, MacSwiney "was particularly struck by the fine spirit" evident among the group which by then numbered about thirty in all.[48] Two weeks later MacSwiney was arrested, and charged with having made a seditious speech, inciting young men to join the Volunteers instead of the British army at Ballynoe.

In January also, James Connolly came to Cork to deliver a talk to the Volunteers on the tactics that were likely to be used in a rising. Since neither MacSwiney nor MacCurtain were present, Connolly's lecture, O'Donoghue noted, "does not appear to have been given official Brigade sanction".[49] Connolly's remarks in Cork gave a glimpse of what would take place in Dublin just four months later, when he served at the head of the "Citizens Army" and as overall commander of the insurgents during the Easter Rising.

> Connolly commented adversely on the traditional idea in a rising of taking to the hills, maintaining that it was bad tactics by which the insurgents cut themselves off from supplies of many kinds. He was in favour of the occupation of towns and cities and of street fighting. He recommended the occupation of complete blocks of buildings, bored so that defenders could pass easily from one building to another. In this way a threatened position could be rapidly reinforced and a covered line of retreat was provided. Tools should be available; crowbars and pickaxes were essential. Provision should be made for a supply of food and water for the garrison. Street barricades should be constructed of any heavy materials available locally, anything not easily removed and providing cover from fire was suitable. This, of course, reflects the tactics employed in the rising in Dublin, and it is evident that Connolly had made a close study of street fighting problems before this date.[50]

MacSwiney's trial in Cork city for causing "disaffection" between the monarch and his subjects did much to enhance his reputation in the movement. The trial, where he was defended by the brother of Irish Party MP Timothy Healy, was a public spectacle that featured numerous interruptions from an audience sympathetic to MacSwiney and his co-defendant, Tomás Ceannt. Ceannt was the brother of Eamonn Ceannt who four months later would face a British firing squad for his role in the Easter Rising.

The crown prosecutor argued that MacSwiney had gone so far in his remarks from a public platform at Ballynoe as to state that "a bullet should be put through the brain of Mr John Redmond" owing to the Irish Party leader's support of Irishmen fighting for England. In a letter to the Cork *Evening Echo* MacSwiney vigorously denied this allegation, stating that even the police reports of his remarks indicated no such statement. "I must ask you to give this correction the same prominence as you did the report," MacSwiney wrote.[51] At Ballynoe MacSwiney had also criticised the crown for "allowing the Ulster Volunteers to be armed and equipped at the connivance of Government". In response to an interruption from a man in the crowd who suggested that the Irish Volunteers were without even the most meagre weapons, MacSwiney, according to an account appearing in the *Cork Constitution*, "put his hand into a pouch in his belt and showed a small cartridge to the crowd, saying that it was guaranteed to kill at a mile and 'there are others where that came from!'"[52]

MacSwiney was given a month in Cork Gaol and fined one shilling. Through the winter and spring of 1916, MacSwiney worked to develop an efficient Volunteer force throughout County Cork, and in a memo of 3 March he outlined a proposal for bringing "the organisation to a state of efficiency." Referring to himself in the third person, he went on: "It is proposed to retain the services of Mr. D. Barry who took up work as an organiser during Mr. MacSwiney's absence. Mr. B will continue to do the work and this will leave Mr. MacSwiney free to organise the County Corps into Battalions and draw up plans for training each Battalion area ... It is calculated a contribution of one shilling a week from each company will provide the minimum with which the work can be carried on."[53]

MacSwiney had a clear vision of the type of man that should be admitted to the ranks of the Volunteers. "If we are to have an effective army of freedom," he wrote, "we must enrol only men who have a clear conception of the gaol, a readiness to yield full allegiance, and a determination to fight always so as to reflect honour on the flag."[54] He was precise as to the damage he felt would be done to the cause by the admission of those he saw as adventurers.

> While human nature is what it is we will always have on the outskirts of every movement a certain type of political adventurer who is ready to transfer his allegiance from one party to another according as he thinks the time serves. He has no principle but to always be with the ascendant party, and to succeed in that aim he is ready to court and betray every party in turn. As a result, he is a character well known to us all. The honest man who has been following the wrong path, and after earnest inquiry comes to the flag, we readily distinguish. But it

is fatal to any enterprise where the adventurer is enlisted and where his influence is allowed to dominate.[55]

It is likely that foremost in his mind in this admonition was the danger of a takeover of the national movement by those who had been aligned with the Irish Party. For MacSwiney, such a late convert, hailed as a "man of experience", presented a source of danger.[56]

In April, one week before the Easter Rising, Terence MacSwiney told a public gathering of the Volunteers in the West Cork village of Drimoleague that "the time has come to give up forming fours, and to learn to shoot straight".[57] The lack of action by the Volunteers in Cork city during the Rising, for which he and Tomás MacCurtain were directly responsible, made these words he would grow to regret. Theorising about a rising and actually carrying out a revolt proved to be two entirely different matters.

The date of the Rising by the Volunteers, which it was hoped would draw mass support and spark off a general insurrection, was set by the supreme council of the IRB for Easter Sunday, 23 April 1916. MacSwiney, MacCurtain and the rest of the Volunteers in Cork did not know of this plan. The Munster representative on the supreme council of the IRB, Diarmuid Lynch, did not himself know of the Rising until Holy Thursday – just seventy-two hours beforehand. It is somewhat ironic that MacSwiney appears to have agreed to a request by Sean T. O'Kelly, then head of the Gaelic League, to address the Irish National Teachers Association at its annual congress in Cork during Easter Week, on the need to support the Irish language.[58]

Unlike Tomás MacCurtain, Terence MacSwiney was a late convert to the Irish Republican Brotherhood, joining shortly before the Easter Rising; he eventually left the organisation, apparently out of religious convictions. The extent of MacSwiney and MacCurtain's knowledge of the events planned for Easter Week was limited to the imminent landing of weapons from Germany off the coast of County Kerry. Whether they knew exactly when the vessel would arrive remains unclear, but a plan was devised for marshalling various Volunteer units from County Cork to meet the shipment and to link up with other Volunteer groups from Kerry and Limerick at Tralee and other points. Acting on the theory that something "was on" for Easter Sunday, MacCurtain and MacSwiney set about mobilising the Volunteers. At a meeting of battalion commandants at their headquarters in Cork city, details for a parade on Easter Sunday were provided by MacCurtain. Florence O'Donoghue notes that the Volunteer leader said nothing more definite "as to its purpose than that arms were coming and that they might have the pleasure of firing ball ammunition".[59]

Over the course of the period 10-19 April, MacCurtain and MacSwiney visited the Volunteer leaders in the principle districts in the county. They gave instructions that the Volunteers from Cork city would for the most part head for Macroom after the parade on Easter Sunday and make for the high ground north of there near Millstreet. They believed that Cork's allocation of the German arms arriving at Kerry would be routed in that vicinity.[60] The Cork city companies would then merge with the Ballingeary and Bantry companies and seize the RIC barracks in those towns. MacCurtain told Tom Hales to march his Volunteer battalion to Kilmurray but not to fight unless attacked. These preparations appear to indicate that little more than an arms seizure was planned, and that those in charge of the Volunteers in Cork knew of no other actions.

After his death, Mary MacSwiney wrote to the Republican weekly, *Poblacht Na hÉireann,* that "three weeks before Easter", MacSwiney and others in the Cork Volunteers were concerned that the German arms might be used solely "to create a diversion for Germany irrespective of the advantage to Ireland". It was this, she stated, that led her brother to consider going to Dublin "to get fuller particulars of the expected help and an assurance from Dublin headquarters that the chestnuts were for Ireland only."[61] This account is challenged, however, by Diarmuid Lynch, on the basis that the Cork Volunteer Command "had sufficient confidence in Clarke, McDermott and Pearse ... not to entertain much doubt as to conditions, if any, in which the German arms were coming to Ireland and that they were much more interested in ascertaining the details of the material expected."[62]

On Wednesday 19 April, five days before the Rising, word of a rift within the Volunteer leadership in Dublin reached MacCurtain and MacSwiney. They sent MacSwiney's sister, Annie, to establish contact with IRB conspirators Tom Clarke, James Connolly and Seán Mac Diarmada, and set up a meeting with them for the following afternoon. Clarke, the only one of the three Annie MacSwiney actually met, opposed the request outright and told her that given the security cordon which the crown, in anticipation of a revolt, had by that time imposed on Dublin, her brother would very likely be arrested if he came to the capital.

On Wednesday also, a directive from Irish Volunteer headquarters, signed by Eoin MacNeill as chief of staff, was sent to Volunteer leaders throughout the country. It warned that a government crackdown was imminent, and added to the uncertainty of the Volunteers in Cork city and elsewhere. MacNeill's initial directive, dated 19 April, stated that:

> A plan on the part of the Government for the suppression and disarmament of the Irish Volunteers has become known. The date of putting it in operation depends only on Government orders to be given.
>
> In the event of definite information not reaching you from Headquarters you will be on the look out for signs of any attempt to put this plan into operation. Should you be satisfied that such action is imminent you will be prepared with defensive measures.
>
> Your object will be to preserve the arms and the organisation of the Irish Volunteers, and the measures taken by you will be directed to that purpose.
>
> In general, you will arrange that your men defend themselves and each other in small groups so placed that they may best be able to hold out.
>
> Each group must be provided from the outset with sufficient supplies of food, or be certain of access to such supplies.[63]

MacNeill's communication had apparently been agreed to by Pearse and the other IRB men supporting him.[64] Remarkably, however, MacNeill, who was technically in command of the Volunteers, had not been informed of the Rising planned for Easter Sunday, and only came to know of it as a result of a conversation overheard by J.J. "Ginger" O'Connell and reported to MacNeill by Bulmer Hobson. MacNeill immediately confronted Patrick Pearse at a meeting on Friday morning, 21 April, and sent Ginger O'Connell to Cork by train with orders to take command of the Volunteers there and to inform them that no rising should be allowed to take place.[65] But then, persuaded by Pearse and Sean MacDiarmada's explanation that a shipment of arms was imminent, MacNeill, according to IRB supreme council member Diarmuid Lynch, agreed that "The fight is inevitable and we are all for it." With that, the military council despatched Jim Ryan to Cork with these instructions: "Commandants MacCurtain and MacSwiney are to proceed with the Rising. Commandant O'Connell is to go forthwith to Tralee as per previous advises."[66]

In the mean time, the *Aud*, disguised as a Norwegian freighter, had succeeded in running the British blockade, but it was not met on schedule by the Irish Volunteers from Tralee under the command of Austin Stack. The *Aud* waited in the bay, but was discovered by the British and escorted to Cobh. Rather than see the ship's cargo of munitions captured by the British, the *Aud's* captain scuttled the vessel. On Good Friday, 21 April, Sir Roger Casement was himself discovered after being put ashore on Banna Strand from a German submarine. His fate was sealed by incriminating documents found in his possession, among them a recent ticket for the Berlin underground.

Ginger O'Connell arrived in Cork city on Good Friday afternoon. Soon after, at Terence MacSwiney's house, he presented MacSwiney and Tomás MacCurtain with MacNeill's orders. Both men were by this point aware of the *Aud* fiasco and, in the view of MacSwiney's biographer, Moirin Chavasse, "It seems clear that this order came more as a relief than anything else ... There was no question of not obeying the order ... MacSwiney was almost silent. The urgent problem was how best to disband the mobilisation. Their decision was to let the men march towards their first objective for that night and to follow and dismiss them the next day."[67]

In Florrie O'Donoghue's estimate it was evident from MacCurtain's and MacSwiney's actions, and from their conversations with Sean O'Hegarty, that MacNeill's order represented to them "the decision of a reunited command in Dublin".[68] In the view of another colleague, MacSwiney's willingness to accept MacNeill's order resulted from both a sense of duty and a desire to see discipline maintained in the Volunteers' ranks.[69]

When the news that the *Aud* had been captured reached MacNeill on late Saturday, he issued a countermanding order to Volunteers throughout the country: "Volunteers completely deceived. All orders for special action are hereby cancelled. On no account will action be taken."[70] Jim Ryan, who had earlier brought orders to proceed with the rising, was sent back to Cork with this instruction, and the order was printed in the *Sunday Independent* the following day. Even then, the military council of the IRB persisted with plans for a Rising commencing at noon on Easter Monday, and sought to prevent further action by MacNeill.[71] But as far as Cork and south-west Munster were concerned, notwithstanding their confusion over the contradictory orders given to them, the capture of the *Aud* meant that "the efficient arming of the Volunteers in the South and West had become impossible".[72]

On Easter Monday morning, MacCurtain and MacSwiney went to Ballingeary, some forty miles from the city, to contact Seán O'Hegarty. Seán O'Hegarty was in charge of a Volunteer action to cut communications on the roads to Bantry and Glengarriff. The commandants told O'Hegarty of Jim Ryan's message, and that the rising had been called off. It was not until they arrived back in Cork later that eveing that news of actual fighting in Dublin reached them, and by that stage, "the military had taken precautions and held every exit from Cork heavily with infantry and artillery ... Cork is a city in a hollow, commanded on all sides by hills, and the military command of the hills absolutely prevented any attempt at insurrection".[73]

The confusion surrounding MacSwiney and MacCurtain is summed up neatly by George Dangelfield:

> They had received their orders to march on Easter Sunday evening and link up with the Kerry Volunteers; but they did not

know that these orders had been issued without the knowledge or consent of MacNeill. Bewildered by contradictory orders on Thursday, Friday and Saturday, by the news of the *Aud*, and by MacNeill's final order which reached them on Sunday, they recalled their march. Late on Easter Monday another message, signed by Pearse and MacDiarmada, told them to go ahead with the Rising. They were only too eager to obey; but night had fallen, the weather was dirty and when they awoke on Tuesday they found that General Stafford had invested the city with troops and artillery.[74]

Padraig Colum described the impression that MacCurtain and MacSwiney made on the wife of Arthur Griffith, who arrived in Cork during the confusion of Easter Week:

These men were in the plight of leaders whose plan had been disrupted – in their case by MacNeill's countermanding order to the Volunteers – and whose spirit might be questioned. They had not slept for nights, and now gaunt and unshaven, the desperate position that they knew themselves to be in was imprinted on them. They were not to be able to make contact with their headquarters, and now word had reached them that the Bishop was advising the Volunteers to surrender their rifles.[75]

As the fighting began in Dublin, MacSwiney's friend, Frau Fleischmann, tells of seeing him alone in the Volunteer Hall, pacing the floor, reading from Thomas a Kempis' *The Imitation of Christ*. When Frau Fleischmann asked him what steps he and MacCurtain planned to take, he answered: "We will fight!"[76] The scene was not unlike that which was unfolding in the more heated atmosphere of the General Post Office in Dublin, where Patrick Pearse was, in Michael Collins's caustic description, "writing memoranda couched in poetic phrases". The difference, of course, was that no one was actually dying in Cork.

"It was generally expected," one commentator observed after the Rising, "that Cork would rise en masse, for the Sinn Féiners had been organising the City and County for upwards of three years."[77]

Now a courier brought a message from Sean Mac Diarmada and Tom Clarke in the GPO: "For God's sake go out and do something to cause a diversion in the South, to prevent the

British troops from massing round Dublin."[78] MacDiarmada
believed that if MacSwiney could be reached, the Volunteers
in Cork would surely act, but MacSwiney and MacCurtain
reacted with frustration. It was impossible for them to mobilise
effectively, they told Kathleen Clarke. The British military
had surrounded the city and an attack was imminent. From
Bishop Cohalan, the Catholic prelate of Cork, came the exhortation that they surrender. It became clear that the Volunteers
in Cork city were not going to take part in the Rising.[79]

In an article written after her brother's death, Mary
MacSwiney sought to describe the untenable situation in
which he and Tomás MacCurtain had found themselves. In
addition to the general confusion emanating from Dublin and
the capture of the *Aud* in Tralee Bay, there was the difficulty
of the Volunteers' position:

> Cork, as everyone knows, is built in a hollow surrounded on all
> sides by hills. The Volunteer H.Q. was in the flat of the City and
> directly under one of the enemy's big guns all the week, but
> though from Easter Monday afternoon all egress was impos-
> sible, it was hard to give up hope. On Thursday afternoon, I was
> at H.Q. and some new suggestion – or an old one in a new form
> – was made, which looked worth an examination. The mere
> hope cheered them wonderfully, and to provide for contingen-
> cies I was sent to get a further supply of First Aid requisites which
> they would need.[80]

On her return she learned "that further information of the
enemy's movements had shown the impossibility of any
movement on our part and then came the further threat that
any attempt on the part of the Volunteers to take action
would result in the instant shelling of the City."[81] The
Republican command in Cork was unwilling to risk this
destruction. In desperation, the two men decided to enter into
discussions with the bishop of Cork and the city's lord mayor.

At a meeting with Bishop Cohalan on Friday, 28 April,
MacCurtain and MacSwiney agreed in principle to accept a
British offer that, if the Volunteers' arms were given up to the
possession of the bishop or to Lord Mayor Thomas
Butterfield, the authorities would not demand that the
weapons be turned over to them. The bishop and the lord

mayor passed on an assurance from General Stafford, the British commander in Cork, that the arms would be returned to the Volunteers after the crisis was over. However, he added the caveat that he was speaking only for the military and could not guarantee against possible later action by the government to disarm the Volunteers.

As part of the terms, MacCurtain and MacSwiney also agreed to go to Limerick and Tralee to gain acceptance of this agreement from the Volunteers there.[82] Accordingly, on Saturday, 29 April, with the Rising in Dublin now in tatters, MacCurtain set out for Limerick and MacSwiney for Tralee. Both men travelled on a British army permit. It was a development that MacSwiney did not make reference to in either his future correspondence or public remarks. His biographer, Moirin Chavasse, noted that even the bishop of Cork regretted the decision of the two men to travel on British permits, and the fact that "in their absence the military proposal could not be submitted to the general body of the Volunteers and unauthorised reports of the terms of peace were creating trouble in the City".[83] The message the two men carried, that the Volunteers should give up their arms, was met with disbelief in both centres. Worse still, some Volunteers had begun to accuse the two men of betrayal. The agreement almost broke down when the *Cork Constitution* of 29 April published an account which claimed that the Volunteers had handed their weapons over to the RIC; MacCurtain and MacSwiney believed the British authorities were responsible for this report.

MacSwiney's willingness to believe that the Volunteers' arms would actually be returned to them at a later date, given that their comrades were involved in an open revolt against the crown on the streets of Dublin, remains incredible. As Moirin Chavasse put it: "It is surely most improbable that any nation, not only the British, would have kept such an undertaking, and it is interesting to note that the traditional instinct of the greater number of the Volunteers told them they would never see their rifles again."[84] MacSwiney's apparent inability to grasp that the British military would in the end be unable to accede to any such agreement is characterised by Chavasse:

He was one of those rare people who credit others with their own nobility. He could speak in burning words of English treachery in the abstract, but when it came to the point of disbelieving the honesty of another man, or a group of men, he was almost incapable of thinking such a thing possible. When the police were already starting on their way to surround the house he was in, on the Tuesday after Easter Week, he refused to leave it, saying that the undertaking given by the British would not be broken. We may be sure it had never crossed his mind that an undertaking given by a local Commanding Officer could be cancelled by his Commander-in-Chief once its object had been attained.[85]

MacSwiney's willingness to accept the motives of the ecclesiastical and civic authorities in Cork is also surprising, all the more so when Bishop Cohalan was noted for his anti-Republican views. But in the eyes of such contemporaries as Florrie O'Donoghue, the actions of MacSwiney and MacCurtain were beyond reproach.

Two independent inquiries were held in 1917, into events in Cork at Easter 1916. Three officers appointed by the Volunteer executive carried out one inquiry and two members of the Supreme Council of the IRB carried out the other. Having investigated all the facts and heard a number of witnesses, each of the inquiry boards arrived at the same findings – that no blame be attached to Tomás MacCurtain or Terence MacSwiney for the miscarriage of plans for the Cork Brigade in the rising.[86]

The report adopted by the Irish Volunteer executive at a meeting on 18 March 1918 expressed its regret at "the delay in completing the investigation re action of Cork, Kerry, and Limerick during Easter Week, 1916 ... The decision "regarding Cork is that owing to conflicting orders no blame can be attached to them for their inaction."[87] Further vindication of MacSwiney's and MacCurtain's actions in Cork came from Cathal Brugha shortly before his death in 1922. Brugha had served with Diarmuid Lynch and Eoin Collins on the panel that had conducted the inquiry. "Our decision was that owing to the sinking of the arms ship and subsequent conflicting orders, Cork could not have acted other than they did," Brugha stated.[88]

While MacSwiney did not in the end participate in the fighting, he was inspired by the example of those who did, and by Patrick Pearse's remarks, uttered during his court-martial, that "We have kept faith with the past and handed a tradition to the future." Charles Townsend has written that due largely to "a lack of willing manpower and ammunition, Tomás MacCurtain and Terence MacSwiney sat through Easter Week glumly, developing a guilt complex which MacSwiney was later to expiate in the grimmest way".[89] While Townsend's analysis might seem harsh, the two men would never again be found wanting, and in the years that followed, rather than merely respond to direction from a reconstituted general headquarters in Dublin, they would try to initiate action themselves.

On 3 May 1916 MacSwiney was arrested at the home of Robert Hales near the village of Ballinadee. This came as a surprise to him: he had taken the British authorities at their word when they said they would take no further action if the Volunteers surrendered their weapons. One week later Tomas MacCurtain was also arrested. At 7:30 on the morning of 22 May, the two Cork leaders were handcuffed in pairs with 139 other Volunteers at Cork Gaol and sent to Richmond Barracks, Dublin. They remained there for a week before being placed on a cattle boat bound for England. Their first facility was Wakefield Prison, where the two men arrived on 1 June. Ten days later they were bound for the prison camp at Frongoch, Wales, which had served previously as a German prisoner-of-war camp.[90] In all, there were 1,800 men interned.

At Frongoch with MacSwiney and MacCurtain were men who were also to play prominent parts in the different kind of revolution soon to be waged against British rule in Ireland. The list included Michael Collins,[*] Gearoid O'Sullivan,[†] J. J. O'Connell,[‡] Sean Hales,[**] and Seán O'Muirthile.[††] Any

---

[*] Michael Collins: minister of finance in Republican government, member of Dáil Éireann for Armagh and Cork; IRA director of intelligence with service also as adjutant general and director of organisation for the IRA, as well as head simultaneously of IRB executive. A signatory to the 1921 Anglo-Irish Treaty; later commander-in-chief of Free State army and head of Provisional Government; killed in Cork during Irish civil war.

[†] Gearoid O'Sullivan: Protégé of Michael Collins; served as director of organisation (adjutant general IRA); member of IRB executive.

[‡] J. J. "Ginger" O'Connell: hand delivered Eoin MacNeill's order counter-

anger felt by those who fought in the Rising towards Tomás MacCurtain and Terence MacSwiney appears to have dissipated by the time the two men entered Frongoch. On 21 June they were chosen as executive officers of the camp and were soon active in strengthening the Volunteer organisation there.

But MacSwiney's time spent at Frongoch was not without its difficulties. A curious dispute occurred between Terence MacSwiney and Gearoid O'Sullivan over a "bucket strike" which O'Sullivan ordered. The strike dealt with the refusal on the part of the inmates to clean out latrines and slop-buckets for the soldiers at the camp. MacSwiney opposed the protest, largely on the basis that it was proper that, when incarcerated, prisoners should obey reasonable orders.[91] In the end, O'Sullivan's action prevailed. On another occasion during his term at Frongoch, MacSwiney was placed in solitary confinement. Life in prison was something with which Terence MacSwiney was about to become all too familiar.

As this chapter concludes, the behaviour of Mary MacSwiney in the aftermath of the Rising requires mention, particularly in light of the closeness of the relationship between her and her brother. She was no doubt defensive about his actions in Cork during Easter Week and anxious to emphasise that his conduct was nothing but appropriate to the circumstances. At the same time, her comments concerning the leaders of the Rising in Dublin after their execution received severe criticism from Kathleen Clarke, the wife of Tom Clarke, whose name appeared as the first signatory to the Easter Week Proclamation.

> I was surprised and shocked when Mary, without any preliminary, started to denounce the men who had been executed. She said they were nothing short of murderers. I said, "Come back

---

manding the Rising from Dublin to Cork to MacCurtain and MacSwiney; director of training for IRA after death of Dick McKee, November 1920; later general of the Free State army.

** Sean Hales, Cork IRA leader, commandant of First Battalion of Cork No. 3 (West Cork) Brigade; killed during Irish civil war (his brother, Tom Hales, was a member of the original party that set in motion the ambush of Michael Collins at Béal na mBlath).

†† Seán Ó Muirthile: member of supreme council of the IRB.; replaced Collins as secretary of IRB executive.

to the house and explain what you mean ..." In the house she
repeated her accusation. She asserted that all the arms had been
kept in Dublin and that Cork was left unarmed ... I knew that
Cork City and part of Kerry were well armed ... Cork county and
other counties were to be supplied with arms from the landing
in Kerry and with arms captured from British military police
barracks which it had planned to raid. No matter what I said,
she persisted in her accusation and denunciation.[92]

Despite being told by Kathleen Clarke of the pain her
comments caused her, Mary MacSwiney persisted in delivering virtually the same attack during a visit to the widow's
sick-bed months later.[93] Miss MacSwiney's actions in Cork
city before and during the Rising were also criticised in the
years following Terence MacSwiney's death by Bishop
Cohalan of Cork. He went so far as to argue in one public
statement that she actively urged her brother and the Cork
Volunteers not to join the revolt. These and other charges
levelled by Cohalan against Mary MacSwiney will be
discussed later.

Notes
 1. David Beresford, *Ten Men Dead* (London 1987) pp. 17-18.
 2. Terence MacSwiney, "Emmet: Irish Fundamentalist,"
    Handwritten notes, MacSwiney Collection, UCD Archives,
    P486/329.
 3. *Irish Freedom*, December 1912.
 4. Terence MacSwiney, *Principles of Freedom* (Buffalo 1975) pp.
    228-30.
 5. *Irish Freedom*, December 1912.
 6. MacSwiney, *Principles of Freedom* pp. 46-7.
 7. Ibid.
 8. Ibid.
 9. Terence MacSwiney to P.S. O'Hegarty, 4 February 1904,
    MacSwiney Collection, P48c/295.
10. Ibid.
11. Terence MacSwiney Diary, 17-18 August 1906, MacSwiney
    Collection, P48c/l0l.
12. Ibid.
13. Diarmuid Lynch, *The IRB and the 1916 Rising* (Cork 1951).
14. Florence O'Donoghue, *Tomás MacCurtain* (Tralee 1971) p. 25.
15. Ibid.
16. Ibid.

17. *Cork Examiner*, 19 December 1913.
18. Terence MacSwiney to Sean O'Hegarty, 24 September 1920; cited by Chavasse p. 175.
19. O'Donoghue, *Tomás MacCurtain*, pp. 27-28.
20. Ibid. pp. 34-35.
21. Ibid. p. 36.
22. Ibid. pp. 37-38.
23. Ibid.
24. *Fianna Fáil*, 19 September 1914.
25. Ibid. 10 October 1914.
26. P.S. O'Hegarty, *Terence MacSwiney* (Dublin 1922) p. 48.
27. O'Donoghue, *Tomás MacCurtain*, p. 48.
28. Ibid.
29. Terence MacSwiney to Aunt Kate, 20 October 1914, MacSwiney Collection, P48c/288.
30. O'Hegarty, *Terence MacSwiney*, p. 56.
31. *Fianna Fáil*, 19 September 1914.
32. Ibid.
33. Ibid. 5 December 1914.
34. MacSwiney, *Principles of Freedom*, pp. 2-3.
35. Ibid.
36. Terence MacSwiney to Aunt Kate, 20 October 1914, MacSwiney Collection, P48c/288.
37. Ibid.
38. Ibid.
39. Ibid.
40. O'Donoghue, *Tomás MacCurtain*, pp. 57-58.
41. Ibid. pp. 61-62.
42. Patrick Pearse, oration at burial of Jeremiah O'Donovan Rossa, 1915.
43. Terence MacSwiney, memorial pamphlet on O'Donovan Rossa, MacSwiney Collection.
44. Ibid.
45. Ibid.
46. Ibid.
47. Terence MacSwiney to Joint Technical Instructional Committee, June 1915, MacSwiney Collection, P48/a.
48. Liam Deasy, *Towards Ireland Free* (Dublin 1973) pp. 20-21.
49. O'Donoghue, *Tomás MacCurtain,*.p. 69.
50. Ibid.
51. Ibid.
52. *Cork Constitution*, March 1916.
53. Terence MacSwiney, 3 March 1916, MacSwiney Collection, P486/202.
54. Ibid.

55. MacSwiney, *Principles of Freedom*, p. l07.
56. Ibid.
57. Deasy, *Towards Ireland Free*, p. 36.
58. O'Donoghue, *Tomás MacCurtain*, p. 70.
59. Ibid. pp. 74-75.
60. Ibid.
61. Mary MacSwiney, *Poblacht na hÉireann*, 20 April 1922.
62. Diarmuid Lynch, *The IRB and the 1916 Rising*, p. 116.
63. MacNeill, Directive to Irish Volunteers, 19 April 1916, MacSwiney Collection, P48c/256.
64. O'Donoghue, *Tomás MacCurtain*, p. 77.
65. Chavasse, *Terence MacSwiney*, p. 51.
66. Lynch, *The IRB and the 1916 Rising*, p. 51.
67. Chavasse, *Terence MacSwiney*, p. 55.
68. O'Donoghue, *Tomás MacCurtain*, pp. 72-78.
69. O'Hegarty, *Terence MacSwiney*, p. 68.
70. Lynch, *The IRB and the 1916 Rising*, p. 51.
71. Ibid.
72. Ibid.
73. O'Hegarty, *Terence MacSwiney*, p. 68.
74. George Dangelfield, *The Damnable Question* (Boston 1976) p. 204.
75. Padraig Colum, *Ourselves Alone* (New York 1959) p. 172.
76. Chavasse, *Terence MacSwiney*, p. 87.
77. L.G. Howell, *Six Days*, (Boston 1916).
78. Kathleen Clarke, *Revolutionary Woman* (Dublin 1991) p. 80.
79. Ibid. p. 81.
80. Mary MacSwiney, "Easter Week in Cork", undated, MacSwiney Collection, p48a/407.
81. Ibid.
82. Chavasse, *Terence MacSwiney*, pp. 63-64.
83. Ibid. pp. 65-66.
84. Ibid.
85. Ibid. p. 87.
86. O'Donoghue, *Tomás MacCurtain*, p. 120.
87. Ibid. pp. 120-121.
88. Cathal Brugha Statement, 1922, Cork Municipal Archives.
89. Townsend, *Political Violence in Ireland*, p. 300.
90. O'Donoghue, *Tomás MacCurtain*, pp. l22-23.
91. Sean O'Mahoney, *University of Revolution* (Dublin 1987) p. l21.
92. Kathleen Clarke, *Revolutionary Woman*, p. 124.
93. Ibid.

Chapter III
Imprisonment and Love

TERENCE MACSWINEY entered "outstanding dates" in his diary covering the period between May-December 1916, chronicling his arrest and imprisonment after the Rising.

May 3, arrested at the house of Robert Hales, Knocknacurra, Ballinadee, and brought to Bandon Military Barracks.
May 4, removed from Bandon to Cork Gaol.
May 9, removed from Cork Gaol to Richmond Barracks, Dublin.
June 1, deported from Richmond Barracks, Dublin.
July 11, removed from detention Frongoch Internment Camp, to Reading Prison called "a Place of Internment"!
July 24, taken before Advisory Committee at Wormwood Scrubbs Prison and brought back to Reading the same day.
December 23, received notification of impending release.
December 24, released Christmas Eve – left Reading 5 o'clock train.
December 25, arrived home Christmas Day about 5 p.m.[1]

But the keeping of a diary proved something of a sporadic exercise. An entry for 3 August 1916 noted: "It had been my desire to keep some sort of a diary during my captivity in England. In the other prisons, I did not find it possible ... Since coming here [Reading], where there is more facility, I have resolved to make the attempt."

The same date also marked the execution by hanging of Sir Roger Casement for his role in attempting to bring arms to Ireland at the outset of the Easter Rising. MacSwiney described the events in the prison compound at Reading Gaol on the evening of Casement's death. He wrote as if Sir Roger's demise amounted to an actual "victory".

The English have immortalised another day in Irish history. Today they executed Casement for his attempt to restore

Ireland's independence ... He died in a manner worthy of our comrades who have already failed in the same Cause and worthy of the long heroic line of martyrs to English misrule ... When we read of the execution in the evening papers it was a consolation to learn how splendidly he faced death with a reverence with which the Irish people always like their leaders to die. We had the details before evening prayers and we said the Rosary for him again. But there was nothing sad in our prayers. The note of victory was struck on rising from our knees when Arthur Griffith asked someone to sing God Save Ireland, and at once Peadar Sweeney started it and we all chorused in with the greatest spirit as one man. At the conclusion, O'Connell called for three cheers for Casement and three cheers were given such as I suppose were never before in Reading Gaol. They were cheers of triumph and it was well. For they celebrated a victory.[2]

MacSwiney's own increasingly regular periods of incarceration during the years 1916-20 were readily accepted by his brothers and sisters. On 12 July 1916, following his transfer from Frongoch to Reading Gaol, Mary MacSwiney informed Terence that "Katie C. came down last eve with the news. Dick and Oonah were with her. I asked Dick where Uncle Terence was and he told me, quite happily, 'In gaol.'" She also made her brother aware of the latest children's rhyme making the rounds in Cork:

> "Here's to the Sinn Féiners. The Sinn Féiners are men. If I were a boy I would Sinn Féin with them. As I'm a girl, I must lead a girl's life. But I'll do my very best to be a Sinn Féiner's wife!"

On more weighty matters, she sought to keep Terence aware of developments on the political front, particularly in regard to the Home Rule Bill, which Asquith wished to amend in order to make provision for Ireland's partition. She also hinted at efforts undertaken by the British and American governments to stem the flow of arms to Ireland.

> Did you see the Bill? It is comique [*sic*]. I should like to be listening to America just now. It would be interesting. I heard lots of imports here have been stopped by the US Government ... Have you any idea why you were changed? Who has been charged with you? Give us the names when you write. When are

you going to be charged and for what? If they trot you about a
bit and show you the scenery it will be no harm – I hope they
take you to the Lake District next. The shades of Wordsworth
may explain their incomprehensible methods ... We'll have a lot
of interesting literature in the near future from "Irish Rebels in
English Prisons".[3]

In addition to providing assistance to Terry, Mary Mac-
Swiney played a direct role in supplying necessary provisions
to Irish prisoners in the various camps and prisons in Britain.
In a correspondence of 3 July, she was told by the head of a
support committee she had helped get underway in Liverpool
that they would be able to supply the internees at Frongoch
with a portable altar, a harmonium, washing utensils, soap,
various items of clothing and a football, among other things.[4]
One Catholic clergyman of Irish origin who took a particular
interest in the welfare of the Irishmen incarcerated in the
various camps and prisons in England was Fr Thomas
McGarvey. He became a central part of the efforts set in
motion by Mary MacSwiney to aid the internees. McGarvey
frequently visited the men, and while he worked principally
to ensure that their spiritual needs were met, he also took
them money, clothing and foodstuffs. In addition, he wrote
letters for publication in newspapers in Britain and Ireland
decrying the poor conditions found in many of the facilities.
In a letter to Mary MacSwiney of 9 June 1916, Fr McGarvey
made reference to what he saw as the dichotomy in the situation of the Irish prisoners, and offered an assessment of the
attitudes towards the men by some of his fellow Irish-born
priests in England.

> Those as a rule from the South have too many visitors, as they
> themselves say, while others have no one. This arises from the
> fact that most of the priests and sisters in this diocese are from
> Munster. We are organising help for them in various parishes. I
> cannot do much as my boss is a German ... but my fellow curates
> have lost their nationality and their feelings as far as these unfor-
> tunates are concerned. The worst word that the slums of an
> English city has familiarised them with is good enough for their
> own countrymen.

The cleric noted that he found the prisoners from the West of

Ireland at Wakefield Prison "have no one to visit them, and as a rule are poor and would require some things for a 'change' besides money to buy eatables ... When I go home," he stated, "I will start a kind of a fund for those from the north. As a rule they are poor except a few from Derry City who are shopkeepers' sons."[5]

MacSwiney penned some verse while imprisoned, and made a number of entries in the log kept by the internees at Frongoch. "No country can be conquered whose sons love her better than their lives," he wrote in one.[6] In another, MacSwiney entered this quotation from scriptures: "Cease to complain, consider my passage and the suffering of my saints; you have not yet resisted unto blood."[7] Like Patrick Pearse and Thomas MacDonagh before him, MacSwiney inclined toward religious imagery in political discourse.

At Frongoch, MacSwiney was allowed only one visit from his sister, on 27 June at 2 p.m., and this was limited to just fifteen minutes. She was also allowed to visit Tomás MacCurtain for a quarter of an hour.[8] A subsequent attempt by Mary MacSwiney to visit her brother was rejected outright by the home office, though she had enlisted the assistance of Irish Party MPs JC. Dowdall and Timothy Healy, who petitioned on her behalf. Healy, in fact, raised the matter of visitation rights for MacSwiney in a question to the home secretary in the House of Commons on 6 July. The reply offered by the home office was that Frongoch had become "overwhelmed with visitors" and that since she had already visited her brother once, the home secretary would rather not ask for any exception to the rule.[9] One official whom Mary MacSwiney dealt with at the home office was Edward Troupe, who would later be involved in shaping and communicating the home office's position to the MacSwineys during Terence's hunger strike at Brixton Prison.

Although restricted to only one visit with her brother at Frongoch, Mary MacSwiney endeavoured to meet Irish prisoners in other prisons and to help organise support groups to meet as many of their material needs as possible. The persistence she demonstrated on the men's behalf may well have encouraged the government's decision to minimise her direct contact with her brother. By now, her open involve-

ment with matters concerning prisoners' rights and with
Cumann na mBan in Cork, undoubtedly figured in her
removal from her teaching position at St Angela's in Cork.
Her personal actions on her brother's behalf ranged from
tracking down the location of his Volunteer coat and hat,
seized by the RIC after Easter week, to arranging for other
visitors less controversial than herself to see him in prison.[9]
During each point in his incarceration, from Richmond to
Wakefield, from Frongoch to Reading, Mary MacSwiney
tried to do everything possible to help maintain her brother's
morale. She was kept apprised of his situation by the letters
he sent her as well as by reports from friends who had seen
Terence while visiting other inmates. One account of him sent
to her during his internment at Frongoch, sometime between
June and July 1916, stated that "Terry got your last two letters.
He pulled them out to show me." Although MacSwiney
appeared "well and in good spirits", he was also "a little
grave and probably chafing at confinement. I think he is
suffering a bit from the heat or nerves," the author surmised.[10]

Yet not all the letters to Mary MacSwiney referring to her
brother's imprisonment were possessed of such a spirit of
concern for the Corkman. Some were layered with a note of
sarcasm, hinting at the bitter memory of his and Cork's non-
involvement in the events of Easter Week. One writer, who
had seen MacSwiney during his initial incarceration at
Richmond Barracks, made these remarks to his sister in a
letter of 30 July: "It is strange how some who were in the
thick of the fight are released and others who were not at all
are detained. Of course a lot of the latter did more as non-
combatants than those who had the opportunity of being in
the scratch. Did many Cork men get out?"[11]

Among the communications sent to Mary by her brother
were instructions about the publication of his literary works
by the Maunsell Publishing Co. "Terry said to tell you," one
source informed her, "that five percent of the gross profits is
better than five percent of the net profits ... He also said to tell
you, that his claim would be before the cost of printing and
publishing and the price of the books sold ... The five percent
is in reference to the copyright of plays that some Australians
are treating for."[12]

On 5 June 1916, Michael Savage, a recently released inmate who had served with him at Wakefield, wrote to Mary MacSwiney to tell her that he had "promised your brother when leaving Wakefield Prison I would call on you to ask you not to send any parcel to him without registering it and if the registry is not taken to send them to a lady friend who visits the prison twice a week and brings tobacco and everything to the prisoners ... Up to a fortnight ago, we had hard times, but now it is not too bad since the help came from friends outside ... Your brother is well and hopes to be soon home," Savage ended.[13]

On 11 July, MacSwiney was transferred from Frongoch to Reading Gaol, where those the government regarded as the leading Sinn Féiners were held. Among them was Arthur Griffith, who had been transferred to Reading immediately after the Rising, in the mistaken belief that he had been involved directly in the occurrences of Easter Week. The improved conditions in Reading may have been responsible for an improvement in MacSwiney's physical and mental health. One visitor to Reading informed Mary MacSwiney that the prisoners there "are certainly interred in a lovely spot ... The air from the river is beautiful," and added: "I trust your brother will feel in better health there."[14]

By the time he had reached Reading, MacSwiney had perfected a rather ingenious method of getting round the vexing problem of the censor's blotter. A useful insight into his persuasive powers is provided by Sean T. O'Kelly, a fellow internee who would later serve with him in Dáil Éireann, and who would go on to become president of Ireland. O'Kelly described MacSwiney's success in bribing a prison official into allowing the prisoners to read their mail prior to its being censored of controversial contents.

> He had to swear that the keeper would get back every single page of every letter after the prisoner had read it. It was MacSwiney himself who used to give out the letters every day. We used to read them in a half hour. Then they would be back in the hands of the censor and ready for sending to the censor of Posts in London. When the letters arrived back to us, quite often the letters had been heavily censored, with full pages missing and

sometimes with nothing but the edge of the page left, purely to show us that there had been a page there and that the censor was serious about his work. But it didn't matter to us since we had the letters read. This was a fine piece of cajolery on MacSwiney's part. It was a good test of his mettle and evidence of the talent for coaxing that was in him. And it cost us, who derived so much pleasure from it, the price of two bottles of beer a day.[15]

At Reading, MacSwiney was also credited by Ginger O'Connell – who was probably the originator of the plan of guerrilla warfare followed by the IRA during the War of Independence – as having been "the main inspiration in insisting on the continuation of theoretical military study". At Mac-Swiney's instigation, the internees were given instruction in the prison yard in drilling and at other times in signalling, history, and analysis of fighting techniques then current in the Great War. During his time at Reading, he was also adamant that above all a unified front be presented to Ireland and the outside world, and was severe in his criticism of sections of O'Connell's prison diary for "tending to reveal divergence of views among the pre-Easter Week leaders".[16]

MacSwiney kept in touch with news of his family, and with the publication of his written work. Peter MacSwiney wrote to his brother to inform him that "Minnie's* school is to be in Belgrade Terrace on the Wellington Road ... It is a good centre," he noted, and added that "the school venture is an undertaking that requires character and courage to make it succeed but Minnie has both."[17] Two weeks later, MacSwiney heard from his long-time friend, the aspiring writer, Daniel Corkery. In a letter of 10 September 1916, Corkery wrote to MacSwiney and offered great praise for an article of his that had appeared in the July issue of the *Catholic Bulletin*.

> I wouldn't change a word in it. I read it through and through. I read it through with anxiety lest it should not prove thorough in every way – and up and up it went in word, thought, and style – every way. It has in it everything that I – earth lover that I am – failed to find in earlier things of yours. You have made the earth your own, and the skies urge you always.[18]

---

* Mary MacSwiney was also known within the MacSwiney household as Minnie, while Annie MacSwiney was sometimes called Nan.

MacSwiney was greatly concerned about the survival of the Irish language at this time. In October, he wrote a lengthy essay in Irish in which he argued that "the time has come for us to do definite diligent work to further the cause of our language. If this work is not done it is hard to say if Irish will survive." MacSwiney held that "the language that isn't written doesn't survive." One approach he recommended for making the language more popular involved the promotion of Irish through the award of a substantial monetary prize each year for a new book in the language. He also suggested that attempts to revive the use of Irish should go beyond traditional language groups.[19]

MacSwiney was released from Reading Gaol on Christmas Eve 1916, and arrived in Cork in time to enjoy Christmas Day with his family. Almost immediately, however, he threw himself into organisational and recruitment activities for the Volunteers. One fellow Volunteer officer in Cork noted that MacSwiney was now "tireless in the procuring of arms", and that he "felt keenly the failure of the Rising in Cork and the false position he was placed in through it".[20] Ironically, since the Cork Volunteers had not participated in the Rising, their basic structure was still intact and their discipline was soon restored by MacCurtain and MacSwiney after their release from internment. Ginger O'Connell, who served as adjutant general for the IRA, remarked that "The good military quality of the Cork Volunteers was amply proved in the renewed fighting of the Black and Tan period, 1919-1921. Their exceptionally good work then afforded an index of what they might have done in 1916."[21]

Many years later, Bridget Walsh, a friend who may have been MacSwiney's first love, recalled "how thoughtful the man was at this time". She noticed the change that had come over him after his return from internment. "One big thing that struck me rather forcibly was how he withdrew from ordinary intercourse as he was getting deeper into the meshes of his country." The Terence MacSwiney she had known before was one who "joined the family tea parties, was quite bright, most talkative and argumentative", but as his work with the Volunteers increased, he withdrew from such functions. Thereafter, Bridget Walsh remarked, "I hardly ever remember seeing him at tea in that house on Old Blackrock Road and still less seldom on Victoria Road."[22]

Whether Terence MacSwiney had at one time entertained the hope of marrying Bridget Walsh remains unclear. His sister, Mary, speculated after his death that had he wanted in fact to marry her "the obstacle would have been a monetary one. Terry had not much of an income, and a good share of it went in expenses for national matters. He would not care to invite a wife to poverty ... Anyhow," she added, "I am sure he never felt the real thing 'till he met his wife-to-be."[23]

His "wife-to-be" was Muriel Murphy, daughter of one of Cork's most prominent families. Owners of the Cork distillery and brewing concern which produced Paddy's whiskey and Murphy's stout, they were amongst Cork's wealthiest Catholics. The youngest of the six Murphy children, Muriel, like all of her family, was educated in England. Many years later, Máire MacSwiney Brugha, the only child born of Muriel's marriage to Terry, noted that: "The Murphy family were very 'Anglo', possibly to maintain their position in the Cork of the time which was an English Garrison town."[24]

MacSwiney first met Muriel at a musical *soirée* held by Tilly Fleischmann at her home during Christmas 1915. MacSwiney, who went to the party with his friend Sean Neeson, read poetry to the gathering; Muriel, who took piano lessons from Mrs Fleischmann, displayed her accomplished musical skills. The twenty-three-year-old Muriel and her girlfriend Geraldine O'Sullivan would both in fact meet their future husbands that evening.

By this time MacSwiney was a commandant in the Irish Volunteers. He represented a set of beliefs with which Muriel Murphy had had little prior contact: "I did not get the opportunity to meet Republicans when I was a child," she later recalled.

She was taken with the handsome young man, twelve years her senior. She admired his dark complexion and the one big lock of black hair that "was always getting over his face". She also admired his ambition and his commitment to Ireland. His account of his study habits equally impressed her, particularly when she learned of how, when preparing for university exams, he would come home to his evening meal, go to sleep for a few hours and awaken at 2 a.m. to study until daybreak and a new work day. "I thought that a man like that could do anything," she remarked.[25]

Soon after their first encounter, MacSwiney was arrested and imprisoned for the first time for making a seditious speech. In their married life MacSwiney would spend more time in prison then he would with her.

Muriel was a rebellious young woman. As a teenager she was a source of consternation at home, demonstrating a lack of respect for authority in general, as well as opposition to organised religion.[26] MacSwiney's courtship of her caused consternation in the Murphy household. A dalliance with, let alone marriage to, a would-be Irish rebel was the last thing a family at the centre of Cork's Catholic mercantile aristocracy desired. Such was their opposition to the relationship that Muriel was unable to receive permission to marry Terry until after her twenty-fifth birthday. She was by then also able to take what her daughter described as a "very extensive" dowry with her.[27]

Terence's letters to Muriel prior to their marriage, often written from a jail cell, portray a man of some sensitivity who appeared able to separate his personal self from the cause to which he had dedicated his life. In a 25 July 1916 letter to her from Reading Gaol he mentioned that he had just left his last "lodgings", and expressed his displeasure that a recent letter she had written to him "was packed back with the others to the important supervisor of such things and I haven't seen it since ... Oh, if you knew how cross I was at not having my contriving faculty at work to secure it," he wrote. "Could there have been any hint about local happenings in that missing letter – that could have got on the nerves of the supervisor?" Combining a desire to know more about the progress his young love had been making in her study of the Irish language with a wish to confuse the prison censor, he asked Muriel to consult with Minnie about "my suggestions for sending a harmless letter, to be followed if need be (am I not kind to myself?) by another in which you can tell the supervisor what you think of him". Advising her where best to pursue her language and artistic efforts, he told her that

"Ballingeary is the spot for you – Irish of the first and a glorious place for sketching".[28]

A postscript to the 25 July letter showed his concern at the attempts Muriel's family were making to end their relationship. He asked her to "tell me would you prefer ... my writing direct to save time or under cover to Minnie?"[29] MacSwiney's prison environment did not help their correspondence: "the inch of candle is burnt to a quarter of an inch, if I don't hurry I will soon burn the paper". In another letter from prison, he expressed his dissatisfaction at being unable to write "a decent letter" with others all around him.[30]

In December 1916 he wrote a lengthy letter from Reading almost exclusively on the subject of art. It came in response to a letter Muriel had sent some seven weeks earlier.

> I think I said already that we can't discuss art today without raising the greatest questions of life ... The ordinary person who has no particular talent, and goes a hum-drum round, takes life as it comes without any particular thought, but the artist should have a philosophy of life, and direct life to some great purpose. You said the divine gift was art and the use of it the vocation. You wrote very clearly and might well write at least as clearly as I on the whole subject ... When I urged that the artist should take his work as a vocation and let the word art refer merely to excellence in technique, you objected rightly that technique is simply mechanical facility, and you said the deeper thing within us is art.[31]

His letter reveals a line of reasoning which he developed further in his published essays on the relationship between art and spirituality: "The priest approaches truth from its ethical and moral side: he preaches the good. The artist approaches it from the beautiful side: delineates the beautiful. But they approach not different things, but the same thing – only in different ways according to their inspiration."[32] His reflections on art and beauty, however, were interrupted by the reality of his confinement.

> I cannot write a decent letter while there are others around to interrupt me. I'm now burning the midnight candle. It will be dawn soon if I don't hurry up ... After this expect a long silence from me. I pray your Christmas and New Year may be happy.[33]

Their engagement was rumoured at Christmas-time, when MacSwiney returned home, but the news was by no means joyously received by Muriel's mother. Nonetheless, the couple continued with their courtship, and neither MacSwiney's commitment to the Volunteers nor his frequent periods in detention interrupted their plans.

> I feel today was one of our most beautiful days. That walk over the hills was the best yet. You are so beautiful in your love and so sensible in your business talks. It is so rare and perfect. Oh, my darling, you will be such a perfect wife. I feel more the wisdom of God is keeping us waiting. Your people in trying to draw you away from me, only discover for me more beauties in your love. I bless them for the coldness that is the cause of my finding the depths and sweetness of your heart ... If my article of faith made you happy, your praise is like a perfect song to me, the purest of hymns.[34]

MacSwiney was now touring County Cork, a full-time political activist who "lived with the intensity of one who cannot fill his scanty hours with sufficient work to satisfy him".[35] Like other Republicans, he was subject to close police attention and frequent arrest. Despite his uncertain life, MacSwiney wrote in Irish to Muriel, assuring her that "the banns will be on the way in time". The letter was written while he was very much on the move: "I will do the business this week. I wrote to Aunt Kate in time ... She will have the letter tomorrow. You will have an answer on Friday. She will tell you if you can come. I hope that you will go. I will go and visit you on Friday or Saturday. I hope I will find you well. I am fine, thank God."[36]

But towards the end of February, MacSwiney was arrested again and re-imprisoned, this time in Bromyard Gaol, near Worcestershire. When he wrote to his sisters Mary and Annie on 9 March, however, his enthusiasm for Muriel was undiminished. "I hope to write enough to make you understand that this is entirely and beautifully a happy thing for me," his sixteen-page letter began.[37] "I know that you'll be happy in hearing from me that a prayer of mine has been answered." He returned to a theme that he had dwelt on three years before with his Aunt Kate: the loneliness of a bachelor's life. He pondered on some of the fears he had had at that time, as well as on the loss of his most prized possession – his books.

> When friends criticised and blamed me for not getting married, they never realised how they touched the most intimate part of my feelings; and that sympathy rather than abuse would have been more to the point. I always kept the hope close to my heart ... I'm sure you never suspected that the modest property my books made had a value for me besides their use value or their literary value. They had in a secret corner of my heart a sort of link with the future ... that would make a modest beginning, with perhaps a trifle of distinction all their own for the foundation of a home. When I sold them to carry on *Fianna Fáil*, I felt I had cut my anchor, and cut definitely with that hope. Do you remember that evening the books were gone, and the place was bare, how we felt as if someone had died and the funeral was over? But you had no suspicion at all that something else had been buried for me ... But then the situation was beginning to grow more critical, and we looked as if we might be in peril of our lives before long. And I questioned to myself if I really had the courage to go through with whatever might be in front. And I felt I should pray for that courage. Then the prayer I used to say was replaced by one that I might subordinate my personal desires to the service of Ireland, and never fail in my duty.[38]

It was around this time he had met Muriel. "She began to take an interest in me, and it made me wonder, but it did not make me change my prayer ... I was attracted by Muriel," he wrote, but, "she did not come at once to occupy that entire hold of my heart that is now the case." He expressed particular delight "when she came down to us and we could stay listening to her music for hours."[39]

In the end, though, it was her interest in his political activities that won him, particularly during the week of the Rising. "When Muriel came so much to the Hall," he wrote, "and was so concerned in everything for us, our doing the right thing, and getting the support of our friends, and her anxiety to enlist support – that week she brought me a few pounds collected from friends of her own – one of many little signs, I was set thinking." He noticed on his part what he described as "a certain curiousness that fear was a thing that never seemed to touch her".[40]

His desire to avoid what he saw as a "conventional" marriage continued, however. In his description of these feelings, MacSwiney may have been burdened by a certain priggishness, tied outwardly to an expression of duty. "I never would make approaches to any girl in the way of marriage where marriage might be assumed to mean only a comfortable settling down," he wrote. He felt that "while many worthless men sought this themselves for any easy selfish life, it also tied the hands of some good men". But rather than extolling his own virtues, MacSwiney claimed that this attitude was a means of protecting himself from what he described as "my weaknesses". These sentiments led him to another conclusion, one which he feared might be seen as "extreme".

> The feeling took shape definitely that if I was to be married, the girl should make the approach to me rather than I to her. That was so much the reverse of the natural course of things that it seemed to remove the possibility of marriage for me altogether. But the more unusual the point of view seemed, the more fixed I became on it. It was as clear a thing as ever felt. Because it looked that anyone united to me would have to follow the hard path. I wanted her to advance to that path, rather than I should ask her to come to it. And that is why Easter made a change.

He described Muriel at that time as having been "just full of enthusiasm for the cause". In reaching out to him willingly, MacSwiney wrote, Muriel at the same time "never suspected then what was coming. She did not feel anymore than I did what we both feel now." He also described his own less than warm conduct towards her. "I was almost cold to her at times, expostulated with her for staying out late, and treated her without any sign of particular interest ... I think it would be almost a tragedy for me if I loved anyone who cared for me only a little less than I cared for her," he reflected.[41]

But MacSwiney also reassured his sisters that "marriage will in no way lessen what you are to me". He would continue, he emphasised, to assist in looking after their welfare and pursuits. "No matter what our family tiffs might have been from time to time, there were never brothers and sisters more loyal to one another".[42]

Muriel had visited MacSwiney during his imprisonment at Richmond and later at Wakefield. "Even in the difficulties of our position," he wrote to his sisters, "we managed to talk a good deal privately while she was there ... She told me so much of her home troubles." In his view, Muriel had "become a woman, yet her family treated her like a child and she lived in a continued state of opposition ... From her attitude, I feared she would break away altogether and I got really concerned on her account."

> She made me entirely her confidant, and spoke to me as freely as a woman could speak to a man. There was no part of her mind that she did not open to me – and that was having its own effect. I did everything I could to persuade her to make things up at home, and restore friendly relations ... I saw that when she was in trouble with them, she was apt to fly off on her own account, here, there, and everywhere, without any of the restrictions which protect a fire. I felt it was dangerous for her who was accustomed to being tied down. She saw that I was upset on her account, and she had remorse of conscience for worrying me about her affairs; and she promised to do all I told her. The result was quite happy at the time.[43]

It appears from this narrative of their relationship that MacSwiney had developed a certain controlling influence over Muriel. When the young woman returned home, after visiting MacSwiney in prison, she wrote regularly to him. "But then matters came through that seemed to point to other ways and then the trouble pressed on me," he wrote. Expressing his own frustrations, he noted bitterly that, "I was locked up and couldn't speak to her." In a reference that offers some insight into his own attitudes, he wrote that Muriel "took a notion of going to some art centre, and I knew that such places abound with adventurers, and feared all sorts of dangers ... I could do nothing but pray and pray and hope for the best." At the same time, he acknowledged, "That is how she came into my heart."

"No one but myself," he told his sisters, "knows how much of the mature woman is hidden below Muriel's open, almost child-like eagerness." At first, he had "treated her like a big brother, or perhaps even more of a guardian," but he "soon found out that she was no child – that she had more than the fully developed brain power of her 25 years".

He described his exchanges with Muriel over art and music:

> I didn't want to bore her. But she replied with considerable force, protesting against my pain in the head assumption. I had written rather loosely and she quite pulled my clumsy phrases to pieces and set me the task of collecting my thoughts and calling my philosophy to my aid to state my case.[44]

The couple sought Bishop Cohalan's permission to marry. MacSwiney wrote to him from prison, referring to a letter Muriel was sending. "I wish to write to you about the matter which is the subject of Miss Murphy's letter to you ... She wishes to inform her mother that she and I are engaged to be married, and she feels she could make the announcement later this year, if you would be so kind as to do her the service."[45] He elaborated on the haste involved in their decision in a letter to Muriel's parents.

> I wish to add a few words on my own account. The circumstances in which I am suddenly unexpectedly placed and the difficulty surrounding our position is the explanation for the letter to you. Were matters normal we both would naturally wait and we could arrange our marriage in a quiet manner that would not hurry our families on either side. But the situation is not normal. I do not know what may happen from day to day. There is the possibility of our being separated indefinitely and for that reason wish to be married at the earliest possible moment – not months however, but weeks.[46]

On 8 June 1917, the day after Muriel's twenty-fifth birthday, they were married in the Catholic Chapel in the English town of Bromyard. MacSwiney's IRB colleague, Richard Mulcahy, served as best man. The groom turned out for the occasion in the full regalia of an Irish Volunteer, specially tailored and smuggled over for the occasion. The priest officiating at the ceremony, Fr Augustine, a friar of the Capuchin order, which had been openly identified with ministering to the spiritual needs of Irish Republican men and women since the Easter Rising. On their wedding day, MacSwiney wrote directly to Muriel's mother to reassure her about his intentions in marrying her daughter. But a letter to the matriarch of a long established merchant family, written from the confines of a prison cell, was probably not the most promising beginning in any case.

The bridegroom told Muriel's mother that "Because of the reverence in which I hold my mother's memory ... and understanding a mother's anxiety for her daughter's future at the time of her marriage, I would like you to know I am truly conscious of a husband's responsibility." The letter, however, would not be finished that day: a postscript adds that he was "interrupted writing this Sunday. Muriel will write soon."[47]

One week later came a general release and return with Muriel to Ballingeary in the Cork Gaeltacht. It was her first time in this part of the country, which was closest of all to her husband's heart, and the following three months were among the most joyous of their married life. Mrs Murphy, however, continued to harbour doubts about her daughter's marriage. From Ballingeary, on 8 August, an evidently upset MacSwiney wrote to her again.

> In reply to your request in your letter to Muriel, I hoped what I wrote at the time of our marriage covered everything. That you ask me now not to consent to her doing anything rash makes me feel I have already written in vain. Were such a thing possible it would be my simple duty to prevent it. Having said so much, I must say – thought I do not wish to hurt you – that you are unjust to Muriel. She is more sensible than you seem to think and in every way careful ... She is not an impulsive child. She is a responsible woman. This may come to you as a surprise. But I hope it will afford you happiness and relief.[48]

In September Terence and Muriel MacSwiney set up what they hoped would be a permanent residence at Douglas Road in Cork city. Though their expectations were short-lived, the importance MacSwiney attached to marriage is shown in his advice to Richard Mulcahy, best man at his own wedding and later the IRA's chief of staff. Writing to Mulcahy in May 1920, MacSwiney told him, "I always believed in marriage and experience has confirmed my belief."[49] By this time he and

Muriel had been married almost three years, and the difficulties imposed upon their life together by MacSwiney's
frequent periods in prison and his time spent on the run, did
not prevent him from urging Mulcahy to marry. Indeed,
whatever Muriel may have felt about the strains her
husband's obligations as a revolutionary imposed on their life
together, to MacSwiney they offered an incentive for
marriage. "I could never understand," he wrote, "the man
who hesitated to marry because his life might be in danger
and he'd consider it unfair to the woman to ask her to share
it. The risk is a common duty and should be regarded as such.
In sharing it and helping each other to meet it is the highest
form of personal happiness one can have at a time like this."[50]

Nearly one half of the last four years of Terence MacSwiney's
life were spent in prison. In all, he was arrested six times
between 1916 and 1920. He was never to be at home, even
when not incarcerated, for more than a few days at a time,
and this was the only life with him that Muriel ever knew. Yet
Terence's letters to her, written while on the run, or from one
of the several prisons that held him during the three years of
their marriage, were not lacking in tenderness. Writing from
St Ita's, his sister's new school, on the night of Sunday, 22 July
1917, he promised Muriel that "for once I will not be
verbose. But I must admit," he added, "I write just to tell you
what I'm doing – and wonder what you're doing – and to say
I'm thinking of you and keeping the sweetest picture of you
in my mind."[51] Travelling County Cork rebuilding old
Volunteer companies and training new ones, Terry informed
her that he had been "moving all day – had a good run to
Macroom – got to Cork in time for Mass nicely – day's
business all done". He went on to describe an evening spent
with a friend, and assured Muriel that his health was good.

> Dick invited me to dinner – such a happy thought – when I had
> that problem to solve, and sweet I had a good dinner. Are you
> satisfied I am not neglecting myself? We had a rest and a talk and
> all and I invited Dick to tea at Turner's Hotel and solved that
> problem! ... I keep wanting to talk and write and dream of my
> darling. My own Muriel, I talk to my heart and hold you there
> and place your cheek to mine and kiss you goodnight.[52]

Using St Ita's as an address, he wrote on 24 July 1917 with plans to see his wife the following morning. He was not "travelling on the 5:15 a.m. as I want to get confession in the morning. Otherwise ... I'd take that first train ... But a Ruin [*a rún*, my love], when my duty is done, there can be no rest till I reach you."[53]

MacSwiney's need to reassure Muriel of his love comes through in a hurried letter to her one week later:

Oh, my darling, I will put peace in your heart. It is in all my prayers. Don't fear that we shall grow slack, either you or I. You will make me do good work and I will make you do it. Together sweet, we shall yet accomplish something. Pray for me always ... one small sweet prayer in particular and my own beloved I will pray for you a prayer that I know must be heard.[54]

He wrote again the following day, echoing sentiments expressed in *Principles of Freedom* on the role of women.

I won't rest till I have you at your music and even your painting again and make you realise you are doing something creative yourself. My wife, my own, there is a dream of dearer things close to both our hearts too sacred almost to write about – the divinest creation of all. For that I pray to God every night for you and me. But I believe that a wife should be helped to develop the music and art that is her and not merely be a second to her husband.[55]

The reference to "the divinest creation of all" is probably an allusion to their mutual desire to have a child. During this time, Muriel told him of her innermost hopes in the event the Troubles ended:

I love you so much and oh, my darling, if all this blows over I'm going to hold on to you and hug you and to have my own lovely man all for myself. Am I selfish about your love? I think I am. I want to take you away from everything ... You won't mind a Ruin will you: You know you're not like anyone, darling, not a soul in the whole world. I never can forget all you've done for me".[56]

But "the Troubles" were nowhere over. On 6 November 1917, Terence MacSwiney was tried under the Defence of the

Realm Act for "wearing a uniform of a military character" while leading a body of some 700 to 800 men "marching in military formation". The charge against him included evidence from three local RIC men who were in the arresting party. One Sergeant Patrick Kenny stated that "I arrested Terence MacSwiney this morning, the 31 October, about 2 a.m. I charged him with illegally wearing a military uniform. He made no statement."[57]

MacSwiney was sentenced to six months penal servitude in Cork Gaol, but on 17 November he began a hunger strike in protest at his sentence. Four days later he was released, along with a large number of other prisoners who had participated in the protest.

During the winter of 1917 Muriel became pregnant, and in a letter written during a rare period of freedom, MacSwiney conveyed to her his hopes for a son: "I must do your Irish letter, so I will have an Irish speaking house when Terence Óg comes." The letter also had more immediate concerns. He asked Muriel to inquire about the price of a pair of field glasses, no doubt for military use. "Those glasses are good." he said, "I'd be delighted to have them if they go cheap."[58]

"My own darling boy," Muriel wrote to him. "I am tired and I want to come into your arms. Oh, darling, ... you know how I love coming right into you." Fearing for her husband's safety, she added: "If you are in the brightest place in heaven which I am quite sure you will be, I'll try to be as near you as possible here by being good, my own love."[59]

But in March 1918 MacSwiney was arrested again while visiting Dublin with Muriel, and imprisoned in Belfast until 4 April, when he was removed to Dundalk. Here he found himself in the company of Oscar Traynor, Dick McKee and Sean Treacy, each of whom would play vital roles in a renewed military campaign the following year. Treacy served as the catalyst for the campaign, when Dan Breen and he led an attack on an RIC convoy transporting a shipment of gelignite in County Tipperary in January 1919, on the same day Dáil Éireann held its first session. While Treacy and MacSwiney developed a bond as comrades in arms, a difference in outlook became apparent during their incarceration at Dundalk. MacSwiney's effusive praise for a development

which he saw as a moral victory, led a somewhat less enthusiastic Sean Treacy to comment: "Damn it! I'd rather take one
peeler's barrack than all your moral victories!"[60]

MacSwiney spent six weeks in Dundalk, and was transferred to Belfast again on 15 May. Muriel wrote to him
frequently, often in a quite fawning tone. "The little baby
loves you very much," she wrote, "but darling – she is only a
weak little thing with the most unbounded confidence in
you."[61] Many of her letters during this time include references
to "baby Terry", the name they both attached to their child
before it was born: Muriel hoped to present her husband with
a son. In one letter she told him that "baby Terry says its time
to go to bed. He's moving in such a funny way, the little
darling." Her unending devotion to her husband was profusely
expressed:

> My lovely, perfect, perfect husband, you know baby Terry and I
> will be all right no matter what happens. We always want *astóir*
> [my love] to do what is right because we know it will be the most
> right thing in the whole world, and we are very proud of *astóir*
> and want to help him in every possible way. My own perfect
> husband, I do love you so very much, five minutes of you would
> be far more than a hundred years of somebody else. My own
> angel Terry, try to make me a little like you, even if its only a
> little. I'd simply love to feel just ... all your religious feeling ...
> Baby Terry can't understand like *astóir* and never will be able to,
> only my own perfect angel can really do it for me. Oh, my own
> lovely Terry, you said God understands better than any of us, but
> you will have to make me understand God.

In that April letter she goes on to ask her husband to "write me
a long letter and tell me all about what is going to happen once
there's conscription".[62]

On another occasion she alludes to a belief that the unborn
child was reading *Imitation of Christ*, a book which was an
important spiritual catechism for MacSwiney. Her description of the child's preference for the location of its birth is
rather poignant: "He rather wants to see the world first in
Dublin. It's because of his being able to pay a visit to *Athair*
[father] very soon and because of the rebellion having been
in Dublin. I told him that of course his wishes would be

considered in the matter but that he must do what *Athair* told him, and he understood this all right."[63]

MacSwiney indulged this makebelieve with Muriel. He told her that "I am building my dreams and hopes of T. Óg [little Terry]. But there is always," he added, "in the inner-most shrine of my heart one special place for my darling wife that is hers and no other's ... A world full of beautiful children couldn't fill it, though I'll love all our children most wonder-fully."[64] Some letters written by Muriel were signed "little Terence", written in Irish. One such letter had "Little Terence" telling his father that he was going "to try to do all the wonderful things you do *Athair* when I am old enough ... I don't expect to be as perfect as you but I'll try and *Máthair* [Mother] has promised to help me all she can to be as good and great an Irishman as *Athair*."[65] The tone of the letter made clear Muriel's tacit acceptance of the possibility that the offspring might one day be without a father, and she without a husband.

MacSwiney, in turn, wrote back to "Little Terence", and Muriel responded: "Your letters are perfectly beautiful; I think most especially your ones to T. óg. If you knew how delighted the little darling is when he gets them, you would be so happy. He says his lovely baby prayers every night and every morning for *Athair* to be there when he is born, he loves *Athair* oh so much, I couldn't tell you. He'll have to explain himself."[66]

In a letter of 14 April 1918, the unborn child "tells" Terence of his reading activities.

> I forgot to tell you in my other letter that I read a chapter of *The Imitation* every night for mother when we're in bed. We began No. I and are doing the third tonight. We're going through them regularly like this in order that you may know ... what chapter we're at, and that you may read the same one yourself. I would love so much to be a man like you and fight with you and help you, but I'm too small yet, though I am complete as you are, now ... I don't make any noise yet, but that's only because I'm perfectly comfortable and have nothing to complain about. I don't think I'd ever cry though ... it's too unlike a man."[67]

But there were other concerns on the couple's minds, too.

On 4 April 1918, Muriel cautioned Terry against the wisdom of their over-reliance on St Ita's as a receiving point for correspondence and packages. "I don't think it is a good place to have things going down regularly ... It will be raided in time surely and the school will have to stop." Muriel asked her husband whether he wanted "your *Battle Cries* and *Ethics of Revolt* sent in openly and if so how many of each".[68] In prison, MacSwiney was busy communicating his military ideas to his fellow inmates.

There were times, though, when Muriel protested during his imprisonment, over his lack of response to her numerous letters. Describing herself as "baby *beag*" (or "little baby"), Muriel wrote that what she wanted from him was a letter "full of love from you and all that sort of thing and no business". Using the third person, Muriel told him how "she felt sort of lonely when she got your letter yesterday. She and T. Óg ... will come to see you in the afternoon if you like ... Even if you are all right," she added, "baby *beag* must have those letters answered". On the matter of the family finances, she informed her husband that she had given his sister Annie £15. The amount translated into "10 for St Ita's and 5 for the rent and a few small things".[69] Some of their correspondence was interrupted by the prison censor's work:

> I got your letter this morning – censored. This was the first time anything you wrote to me was scratched out. So while we must suffer ... you outside must not be allowed to say what you think. However, keep on saying it. It won't reach me – but it will let all whom it concerns know what the outside public are saying.[70]

Though she longed for her husband's release, Muriel accepted the path he had chosen. In one letter she touched on the delicate subject of his not having participated in the Easter Rising.

> I loved your letter and baby Terry did too, the little love. Although he got two, I think mine was the nicest. Darling, I know it is the best that have to make the sacrifice, that's why you always had to do so ... but my own angel, I don't believe what occurred last time will this, I feel just like you, if it has to come I'd mind just as much as you're not being in it. And darling, think how

different it would be this time with baby Terry to come after you in case anything did happen.[71]

An appendix which Muriel added to a letter from "Terence Óg" on 18 April took on an even more sombre note, when she speculated as to how she might dispose of her own resources in her will.

> I thought it best to leave the £5,000 15 shilling shares and the next £1,000 or whatever will be necessary to make up £6,000 for him. Then the £2000 each for Minnie and Annie to come next ... Then Peter, John, and Ada, the £5,000 if it's there ... for Irish literature to be left to Terry Óg for that purpose, not for himself ... what about Eoin MacNeill?[72]

As her pregnancy advanced, Muriel wrote that she did not feel "good enough to be baby Terry's mother. Think of all your mother was, ... just think and then think of your poor little baby *beag* – write to her about this because it's worrying her awfully and you are the only person in the whole wide world who can make her better."[73] She still hoped for a baby boy, but in a note of 8 May 1918, she noted that "if it's baby Maire, of course she ought to have a bonnet but I don't think she will mind wearing a hat for once. She couldn't well be a pronounced suffragette at that age."[74]

On 23 June 1918, Muriel gave birth to a baby girl. She was named Máire, apparently after Terence MacSwiney's sister. The birth of a daughter was a clear disappointment to both of them. One biographer described how in the weeks leading up to the child's birth, MacSwiney made plans for the proper training of a boy in such areas as "duty". Muriel's apparently desperate need to bear her husband a son was made painfully clear in a letter to her husband in the weeks before she gave birth, though by now the couple had already agreed to the name Máire, in the event of the child being a girl.

> Oh darling A Ruin, do pray hard – hard that it is baby Terry. I wouldn't tell anyone else in the whole world, no, not for anything, but I'd mind it if it wasn't now I really would. I didn't feel this before. I wanted baby Terry and would have preferred him, but now I feel I must have him. Oh A Ruin, I'm not good enough for either him or baby Maire, not a hundredth parts good enough, pray to make me better, do A Ruin."[75]

In an effort to console Muriel and to assure her of his happiness, MacSwiney wrote to her from Belfast Gaol soon after Maire's birth. The letter is especially tender.

> I look forward to your being up and about and quite strong enough to write to me about her and everything relating to her ... Before now you will have got mine saying how much better it is that baby Máire came first ... I remember also your saying to me that it is easier to bear a girl than a boy which is another reason for it being better that baby Máire came first. I feel confident darling her baby brother will be coming. But if God chose to send us no more children, I would be full of gratitude for a little angel of a girl alone. We three would be a perfect family, complete in ourselves. I take a deep and quiet joy in thinking how the seed has come to life at last, and that our baby girl is a visible reality, that I am actually a father and that you, beloved, are happily a mother at last.[76]

A few days later, he told her of his longing to be with his new family.

> I'm thinking just now of how happy we'll be when alone together for the first time. I look forward to it, I live in it, I pray for it. I have a picture of you, sweetheart, showing me how lovely our little love is, and I'll take both of you in my arms in the way I used to tell you of. You will have baby Máire on your breast and you will lean on mine. And then surely I will be the happiest man on earth."[77]

Three weeks after the child's birth, a letter from MacSwiney showed that, while expressing affection for his wife and daughter, his thoughts also centred on politics and the uncertainty of the times, with the prospect of his imminent deportation foremost among them.

> Since I wrote to you about deportation one or two others have been deported and the danger for me remains. The worst of it is I won't know what's going to happen till time for release comes. So I must mention it that neither of us may be taken by surprise. Darling, let us pray hard to avert it, and if it comes, let us make it an offering for baby Terry's coming. If our reunion is short let's wish it will be all the sweeter in the end.[78]

Already his thoughts turned to the need for the new child to learn Irish. "Darling, I'm keen about the Irish for baby Máire. Tell me how it will be with you, for study now. Is this time from now on good or bad for you? If as soon as you can get a teacher you can start, it will be excellent. I know you have application and with that a good teacher, we'll make our little darling an Irish speaker between us. And we'll have an Irish speaking home."[79]

Muriel brought the new baby when she visited her husband in prison, and on 3 August he penned the following verse, with the introduction: "For Máire – Two months old – a memory of her first visit to Belfast Gaol."

> Baby. Baby. Sweet and wise
> Deeper than the morning skies
> Is the wonder of your eyes.
> Where we pause before this wonder –
> All life's cares just drop asunder
> In the spell you hold us under.
> Ah, we had been sad reviewing
> Barren years and fruitless doing
> Lo! You give our lives renewing.
> Insight had flashed to us a warning –
> Ah, we prayed, and God coming
> In your eyes restored the morning.[80]

"I'm dying to see our little angel again," he wrote to Muriel. "I suppose she won't give me a cry at all now. She's a sweet little dear to sum it up till I go home. You must take great care of yourself and eat and exercise well."[81]

Given his obvious affection for his wife and child, how did Terence MacSwiney, the husband and father, rationalise the position in which he had placed his family? Fundamentally, he believed that his obligation to the cause of Irish freedom rendered considerations such as family secondary. He admired Sarah Tone's willingness to accept her husband's travelling far from home and family, risking life and limb: "The woman can learn from it how she may equal the bravest man; the man should learn to let his wife and children suffer rather than make of them willing slaves and cowards."[82] His analysis appears callous, and brutally honest. "For there are some honest men," he wrote, "who are ready to suffer themselves but cannot endure the suffering of those they love, and a mistaken family tenderness blinds and drags them down."[83]

MacSwiney's candour can be interpreted as the sentiments of a man oblivious to the obligations he owed to his wife and child, or as the stoical expressions of a patriot so committed to what he saw as his duty to his country that all else had to be put aside. Perhaps MacSwiney's most extreme expression on the need to subordinate family considerations to the national struggle was his admonition that "no man be afraid that those he loves may be tried in the fire, but let him, to the best of his strength, show them how to stand the ordeal, and then trust to the greatness of the Truth and the virtue of a loyal nature to bring each one forth in triumph, and he and they may have in the issue undreamed of recompense".[84]

MacSwiney clearly believed in the likelihood of providential intervention, owing to the truth and justice implicit in the Irish cause; this belief was underscored by his own religious mysticism. "For that battle that tries them will discover finer chords not yet touched in their intercourse," he wrote.[85] The individual's sacrificing of his family's interests would yield a higher reward. MacSwiney's later actions would match his words. His vision served as a script to be played out, one which ultimately involved the most hideous of ends for the central figure: death by the body's slow consumption of itself.

MacSwiney's desire to follow Pearse and his other dead comrades was also shaped by his view of the role played by the hero. "When we need to hearten ourselves, or others for a great enterprise," he wrote, "we instinctively turn to the examples of heroes and heroines who, in similar difficulties to ours, have entered the fight bravely, and issued heroically, leaving us a splendid heritage of fidelity and achievement."[86]

In 1916 Pearse had willingly faced an English firing squad, and in the following year Ireland had seen another example of self-sacrifice by Thomas Ashe, the first Republican prisoner to die on hunger strike. A National School teacher in Dublin and a native of County Kerry, he fought with Richard Mulcahy as a Volunteer officer at the successful attack on Ashbourne Barracks during Easter Week. After his surrender, Ashe was court-martialled and sentenced to death, but like other prominent participants in the Rising, including Eamon de Valera, his sentence was commuted to penal servitude for life. Ashe was released in the general amnesty granted in June 1917. After his arrest in September 1917 for delivering a seditious speech in County Longford, he was sentenced to one year in prison.

Joined by other prisoners, Ashe demanded that he be treated as a political prisoner. Following the British government's outright refusal of this demand, he went on hunger strike on 20 September. Five days later he died in a prison hospital from pneumonia contacted as a result of the dampness of his cell and forced feeding by prison authorities. Ashe's death caused indignation throughout Ireland, and his funeral served as an occasion for national protest. Under the direction of a young Volunteer of rising prominence named Michael Collins, there was a strong IRB presence at Ashe's obsequies. Speaking briefly at the graveside, Collins gave the order for the firing of a volley of shots by an honour guard of Irish Volunteers. Two days later the British government granted political status to the dead man's comrades, who in turn ended their own hunger strikes. Terence MacSwiney was saddened by Ashe's death, but he was also inspired by it, and impressed by the fact that the protest had forced the British to capitulate to the demands of the Republican prisoners.

While he was in Belfast Gaol, MacSwiney learned from Muriel that she had "signed the old will leaving everything to you ... I asked about the war bonds, and Edward said there was £500 in them and he'd write about it ... I didn't think there was any use in asking him about the land question – we can't do it till you get out."[87] On 14 July 1918, MacSwiney told her that he wanted "to say a word about money". Evidently he wished to plan the family's budget as far as possible within the context of the uncertainties imposed by his imprisonment and political activities.

> Has anything come in yet and have you any idea how you stand? You might be able to tell me this is in a special letter. Make up amount of debts and whatever cash in hand. Miss B. and Doctor will be pretty big and Munster Academy which is very big may

send a request for payment. Then you can predict your own expenses will be higher than before. I think last of this half year's cash amount comes in before September and so some judgment will be required in handling cash on hand. You'd want to take stock of this too, if you wish to give Min and Nan anything.[88]

MacSwiney was scheduled for release in September, but he was immediately re-arrested on suspicion of involvement – along with hundreds of other Sinn Féin activists and Volunteers – in the so-called "German Plot." The "plot," in which the British government alleged that Sinn Féin leaders had "entered into treasonable communications with the German enemy," was a pretext for the arrest and deportation of Republicans. Though the charge was never substantiated, MacSwiney was sent to Lincoln Goal. He related the details of his deportation to a friend.

> I was taken to the boat about 2:30, but to my disgust was put in a dirty sort of hold, you couldn't call it a cabin. It was full of sick soldiers and they nearly all got sick the moment the boat cleared the harbour. The sea was running very high and the boat pitched very much. Notwithstanding the dirt and the sick soldiers, I didn't get sick. I kept a porthole open and kept my head to it. The air was refreshing and the sea was fine. It tumbled in on me frequently and I got more than one good ducking, but I landed fresh and in good form.[89]

He wrote to Muriel from Lincoln, urging her not to think that he was "despondent". "God has been very good to us," he wrote, and added that he felt "all will be right in the end".[90]

Despite the continuous harrassment and arrest of its activists, by late 1918 Sinn Féin had reached a point where it was ready to challenge John Redmond's Irish Party at the polls. MacSwiney was one of many imprisoned Republicans whose name was put forward in the general election in December. He was nominated for the mid-Cork constituency, a seat held by the Irish Party. On his nomination paper, MacSwiney described himself as a "teacher by profession."

The election was a landslide for Sinn Féin. When the results became known, the young Corkman was one of the seventy-three Sinn Féin candidates elected. Their success resulted in nothing less than the decimation of the Irish Party, but it was not at Westminster they sought to serve. Instead, the young abstentionists founded Dáil Éireann, the parliament of the Irish Republic which had been proclaimed at Easter 1916.

Mary MacSwiney kept her brother abreast of developments in Ireland. On 6 December, she told him that she had "motored out to your constituency last Sunday – a few of the backward places wanted waking up and I was invited to wake them". And she asked him whether there were any other graduates of the National University of Ireland "in Lincoln besides you and Dev?"[91]

Notes

1. Terence MacSwiney Diary, MacSwiney Collection, UCD Archives. P48/a.
2. Ibid. 3 August 1916.
3. Mary MacSwiney to Terence MacSwiney, 12 July 1916, MacSwiney Collection, P48b/8.
4. Joseph Barrett to Mary MacSwiney, 3 July 1916, MacSwiney Collection, P48a/109 (10).
5. Thomas McGarvey to Eilish Murphy, 9 June 1915, forwarded to Mary MacSwiney on 12 June, MacSwiney Collection, P48a/l09(3).
6. O'Mahoney, *University of Revolution* (Dublin 1987) p. 2, citing Thomas a Kempis' *Imitation of Christ*, a volume which would feature prominently during MacSwiney's later protest at Brixton prison.
7. Ibid.
8. Permit forwarded to Mary MacSwiney from commandant at Frongoch, 25 June 1916, MacSwiney Collection, P48a/109 (9).
9. Royal Irish Constabulary district inspector for Macroom to Mary MacSwiney regarding inquiry made into Terence MacSwiney's clothing, 12 July 1915, MacSwiney Collection, P48a/109 (20).
10. E. Sheehan to Mary MacSwiney, undated, MacSwiney Collection, P48a/ l09 (33).
11. Letter to Mary MacSwiney, 30 July 1916, MacSwiney Collection, P48a/109 (24).
12. Letter to Mary MacSwiney, undated, MacSwiney Collection, P48a/109 (l7)
13. Michael Savage to Mary MacSwiney, 5 June 1916, MacSwiney

Collection, P48a/109 (2).

14. Letter to Mary MacSwiney, 16 August 1916, MacSwiney Collection, P48a/109 (27).

15. Sean T. O'Kelly, *Sean T.* (Dublin 1963) pp. 238-39.

16. J. J. "Ginger" O'Connell to Etienette Beuque, 13 August 1930, MacSwiney Collection, P48c/42.

17. Peter MacSwiney to Terence MacSwiney, 25 August 1916, MacSwiney Collection, P48b/9.

18. Daniel Corkery to Terence MacSwiney, 10 September 1916, MacSwiney Collection, P48b/206.

19. Terence MacSwiney essay, written in Reading Gaol 30 October 1916, Cork Municipal Museum.

20. Fred Murray to Etienette Beuque, 23 July 1936, MacSwiney Collection, P48c/91.

21. J.J. O'Connell to Etienette Beuque, 4 March 1933, MacSwiney Collection, P48c/87.

22. Bridget Walsh to Etienette Beuque, undated, MacSwiney Collection, P48c/97.

23. Mary MacSwiney to Etienette Beuque, 13 August 1930, MacSwiney Collection, P48c/42.

24. Máire MacSwiney Brugha to author, 10 November 1990.

25. Testimony of Muriel MacSwiney before US Commission on Conditions in Ireland, Washington, DC, 8-9 December 1920, as published in *The Nation*, 20 December 1920, p. 752.

26. Máire MacSwiney Brugha to author, 13 March 1992.

27. Ibid.

28. Terence MacSwiney to Muriel Murphy, 25 July 1916, MacSwiney Collection, P48b 6/15.

29. Ibid.

30. Terence MacSwiney to Muriel Murphy, 16 December 1916, MacSwiney Collection, P48b/16.

31. Ibid.

32. Ibid.

33. Ibid.

34. Terence MacSwiney to Muriel Murphy, 28 April 1917, MacSwiney Collection.

35. Moirin Chavasse, *Terence MacSwiney* (Dublin 1961) p. 98.

36. Terence MacSwiney to Muriel Murphy, 1917, MacSwiney Collection, P48b/19.

37. Terence MacSwiney to Mary and Annie MacSwiney, 9 March 1917, MacSwiney Collection, P48c/290/1.

38. Ibid.

39. Ibid.
40. Ibid.
41. Ibid.
42. Ibid.
43. Ibid.
44. Ibid.
45. Terence MacSwiney to Bishop Cohalan, 6 March 1917, MacSwiney Collection, P48b/209(1).
46. Terence MacSwiney to Mr and Mrs Murphy, 8 June 1917, MacSwiney Collection, P48b/186.
47. Ibid.
48. Terence MacSwiney to Mrs Murphy, 8 August 1917, MacSwiney Collection, P48b/187.
49. Terence MacSwiney to Richard Mulcahy, undated 1920, MacSwiney Collection, P48b/187.
50. Ibid.
51. Terence MacSwiney to Muriel MacSwiney, 22 July 1917, MacSwiney Collection, P48b/21.
52. Terence MacSwiney to Muriel MacSwiney, undated, MacSwiney Collection, P48b/2l.
53. Terence MacSwiney to Muriel MacSwiney, 24 July 1917, MacSwiney Collection, P48b/23.
54. Terence MacSwiney to Muriel MacSwiney, 30 July 1917, MacSwiney Collection, P48b/24.
55. Terence MacSwiney to Muriel MacSwiney, 31 July 1917, MacSwiney Collection, P48b/25.
56. Muriel MacSwiney to Terence MacSwiney, undated, MacSwiney Collection, P48b/135.
57. British charge sheet in arrest of Terence MacSwiney, 6 November 1917, MacSwiney Collection, P48b/365.
58. Terence MacSwiney to Muriel MacSwiney, undated letter 1918, MacSwiney Collection.
59. Muriel MacSwiney to Terence MacSwiney, undated, MacSwiney Collection, P48b/131.
60. Desmond Ryan, *Sean Treacy and the Third Tipperary Brigade* (Tralee 1945) p. 41.
61. Muriel MacSwiney to Terence MacSwiney, undated, MacSwiney Collection, P48b/132.
62. Muriel MacSwiney to Terence MacSwiney, 10 April 1918, MacSwiney Collection, P48b/124.
63. Muriel MacSwiney to Terence MacSwiney, 22 March 1918, MacSwiney Collection, P48b/111.

64. Terence MacSwiney to Muriel MacSwiney, 18 March 1918, MacSwiney Collection, P48b/Bl(1).
65. Muriel MacSwiney to Terence MacSwiney, 13 April 1920, MacSwiney Collection, P48b/127.
66. Muriel MacSwiney to Terence MacSwiney, undated, MacSwiney Collection, P48b/l30.
67. Muriel MacSwiney to Terence MacSwiney, 14 April 1918, MacSwiney Collection, P48b/128.
68. Muriel MacSwiney to Terence MacSwiney, 4 April 1918, MacSwiney Collection, P48b/119.
69. Muriel MacSwiney to Terence MacSwiney, 11 April 1918, MacSwiney Collection, P48b/125.
70. Terence MacSwiney to Muriel MacSwiney, 23 June 1918, MacSwiney Collection, P48b/42.
71. Muriel MacSwiney to Terence MacSwiney, undated, MacSwiney Collection, P48b.
72. Muriel MacSwiney to Terence MacSwiney, 18 April 1918, MacSwiney Collection, P48b/139(1)
73. Muriel MacSwiney to Terence MacSwiney, 4 May 1918, MacSwiney Collection, P48b/120.
74. Muriel MacSwiney to Terence MacSwiney, 8 May 1918, MacSwiney Collection, P48b/123.
75. Muriel MacSwiney to Terence MacSwiney, 8 May 1918, MacSwiney Collection, P48b/130.
76. Terence MacSwiney to Muriel MacSwiney, June 1918, MacSwiney Collection, P48b/46.
77. Ibid.
78. Terence MacSwiney to Muriel MacSwiney, 14 July 1918, MacSwiney Collection, P48b/55.
79. Ibid.
80. MacSwiney Collection, P48b/302.
81. Terence MacSwiney to Muriel MacSwiney, 30 August 1918, MacSwiney Collection, P48b/80.
82. MacSwiney, *Principles of Freedom* p. 129.
83. Ibid.
84. Ibid.
85. Ibid.
86. Ibid. p. 119.
87. Muriel MacSwiney to Terence MacSwiney, 8 May 1918, MacSwiney Collection, P48b/123.
88. Terence MacSwiney to Muriel MacSwiney, 14 July 1918, MacSwiney Collection, p48b/55.

89. Terence MacSwiney, 23 November 1918, MacSwiney Collection, P48b/ 384.

90. Terence MacSwiney to Muriel MacSwiney, 13 December 1918, MacSwiney Collection, P48b/984.

91. Mary MacSwiney to Terence MacSwiney, 6 December 1918, MacSwiney Collection, P48b/13.

Chapter IV
Serving the Republic

OWING TO HIS imprisonment through the winter and spring, MacSwiney missed the Dáil's opening session on 21 January 1919 at Dublin's Mansion House. He was released on humanitarian grounds in March, to attend to Muriel who was stricken with severe influenza, and on 1 April he entered the Dáil for the first time. He quickly became involved in a wide range of activities. He served as a member of the Dáil's foreign affairs committee, and, despite further time spent in jail and on the run, he was active in matters relating to trade and commerce, vocational education, and forestry development. In June 1919, he spoke in the debate on the forthcoming Paris Peace Conference, and suggested to the Dáil that they should ask the conference to support Ireland's national rights. He called for the establishment of a select commission "to inquire into the national resources and present conditions of Manufacturing and Productive Industries in Ireland, and to consider and report by what means those natural resources may be made fully developed, and how those industries may be encouraged and extended".[1] This last was an area where his background in business and his experience as a commercial studies instructor could be put to practical use.

At both national and local levels, MacSwiney lent his commercial experience to helping Michael Collins put the Dáil Loan on a firm financial footing. MacSwiney and Collins's involvement on the question of finances, vital to the success of the national effort, dated back to the work they had done in 1917 to set up the Irish National Aid and Volunteer Dependents Fund, which had been established by the IRB to assist those men whose lives and families had been affected by internment in the aftermath of the Rising. In addition to its charitable work, the National Aid Association served as an important organisational tool for a Volunteer movement that had become fragmented after the failed Dublin revolt.

Collins, who was elevated to the IRB's supreme council soon after his release from Frongoch, became the association's secretary. On 11 December 1917 he wrote to MacSwiney – using the spelling "MacSweeney" – at his address at 5 Eldred Terrace, to thank him formally for £29 he had raised for the association. "On behalf of the Executive," Collins stated, "permit me to offer you our sincere thanks, and appreciation of your action, in returning this amount."[2] This exchange of correspondence between the two Corkmen marked the beginning of what would be a cordial and productive relationship. Collins was phlegmatic, young and energetic, MacSwiney more sombre, intellectually inclined and romantic, but both men possessed a keen capacity for hard work and an adherence to sound financial practices. Each man also possessed a degree of ruthlessness.

In Frank O'Connor's view, men like Terence MacSwiney were "the last of the romantics;" MacSwiney was "the greatest" of the idealists in the service of the Republic during the Black and Tan war.[3] He painted a stark contrast between MacSwiney and the more pragmatic physical force adherents, such as Collins.

> It is hardly likely that Collins cottoned on to MacSwiney, (how could he have liked anyone whose letters had first to be translated into English for him?). His view of life, as expounded in *Principles of Freedom*, he would certainly have regarded as priggish. Neither did MacSwiney cotton to him. His friendship he reserved for Mulcahy, whom he thought "the only great man among the leaders." Each drew different types to himself, and within the revolutionary organisation there were already two worlds, two philosophies, running in very doubtful harness.[4]

Richard Mulcahy, the IRA's chief-of-staff, had been best man at MacSwiney's wedding; later he served as godfather to MacSwiney's daughter. MacSwiney and Mulcahy bore a physical resemblance to one another, each possessing what one writer described as "the thin face of the monk" and piercing blue eyes. Mulcahy, too, was to prove himself loyal to

Michael Collins, with whom he worked for the better part of four years in Dublin.

The Dáil Loan represented the single most important undertaking on the part of the fledgling Republican government to obtain public support for the independence movement in the form of subscriptions from the Irish at home and abroad. The project was launched at a session of Dáil Éireann in the autumn of 1919, and was placed largely in the domain of Michael Collins as minister for finance. In all, from the initiation of the loan's funding drive until its completion in July 1920, some £400,000 was raised in support of the Republican government. Over half of that amount came from the United States through the efforts of the Irish Self-Determination League and the work done there by Eamon de Valera and Harry Boland.

In a prospectus for subscriptions co-signed by Michael Collins and Arthur Griffith, acting president of the Republic, the purposes for which the loan were to be applied were explained:

> The Loan, both internal and external, will be utilised solely in the interests of Ireland – an indivisible entity. It will be used to unshackle Irish Trade and Commerce, and give them free access to the markets of the world; it will be used to provide Ireland with an efficient Consular Service; it will be used to end the plague of emigration, by providing land for the landless and work for the workless; it will be used to determine the industrial and commercial resources of our country and to arrange for their development; it will be used to encourage and develop the long neglected Irish Sea Fisheries, and to promote the re-afforestation of our barren wastes; it will be available for, and will be applied to, all purposes which tend to make Ireland morally and materially strong and self-supporting.[5]

Early in their communications regarding the loan, Collins provided MacSwiney with official receipts from the Dáil's department of finance, to be administered to subscribers on the basis "that it gives a good impression and is also much more convenient for ourselves from a recording point of view".[6] Communications between the two men on matters of finance were never easy, however. The effect of British raids on Collins's offices was made clear in a letter of 25 September 1919, in which he explained that "you will forgive me for not replying sooner, but I have been extremely rushed as a result of raids and seizures of correspondence and prospectuses in various parts of the country ... The Head Office ... seems to be the only place where no documents were got."[7]

A week later, MacSwiney conveyed to Collins evidence of the pressure that he was under because of the loan effort and other duties in Cork. "Anything may happen to us here," he wrote. "I had a narrow shave yesterday – district police held me up and searched bag – got nothing." MacSwiney speculated that the RIC "probably had instructions to lift me if any excuse". He gave an account of how he and Sean Nolan had organised subscriptions in mid-Cork. "We are laying our lines so well that if anything happens to the two of us the work will go on successfully." The system they developed was comprehensive and thorough: they oversaw personally the creation of five sub-executives, in Macroom, Millstreet, Kilnamartyra, Donoughmore and Crookstown, designed "to look after the work of the clubs in their particular areas, giving special attention to any part of their areas where no clubs at present exist ... In these backward parts of their areas, ... it is hoped incidentally to establish Volunteer and Sinn Féin cumanns."[8]

MacSwiney's detailed programme for raising the loan in mid-Cork included the printing of large numbers of special circulars which were distributed prior to a door-to-door canvass, in order to ensure that "everyone visited by deputation will have the Loan explained in advance". He told Collins that "we have discouraged well meaning people from asking for subscriptions lest they get smaller amounts than might be forthcoming when we approach them later". Two weeks later, MacSwiney told Collins that 5,000 more copies of the official loan prospectus were needed in order to enable his team "to work the whole constituency ... We need them at once," he emphasised, "as we are about to begin the house-to-house canvass."[9]

"It was very refreshing to have such a satisfactory account from you," Collins answered on 11 December 1919. "It shows what work and energy will do." Collins added that while he didn't like "drawing comparisons" with other areas, he believed that "some will suggest themselves at once". Nonetheless, at this early stage in the loan's subscription, he expressed the view that "places that are now backward will ultimately do well".[10] Yet three weeks later, though assuring MacSwiney that the subscription lists from mid-Cork were acceptable "in the circumstances", he went on to say in relation to other areas that "if you saw some of the particulars we were supplied with they would simply drive you mad".[11]

Sean Nolan, who had joined MacSwiney in mid-Cork, won particular praise from Collins. "From what I hear," Collins told his colleague on 25 October 1919, "everybody is very high in their praise of the work done by Sean Nolan ... Even in the difficult town of Thurles, he seems to have done very well, and from what I hear to have been treated pretty shabbily."[12] Nolan was so successful that, some ten months later, Collins told MacSwiney he planned to use Nolan's knowledge to develop an income tax system for the Republican government. "I intend putting to him a proposal," Collins wrote, "about our Income Tax Scheme ... You could give him a hint of this," Collins said, "but for the moment there need be nothing further."[13]

An analysis in MacSwiney's own hand reveals that from the inception of the drive until 12 February 1920, a total of £5,317 had been raised and sent to Dublin. Of that amount £4,817 had been received in pound notes while £500 had been collected in gold.[14] The total included proceeds from some twenty-nine districts, including Cork city. MacSwiney's analysis compared the amount targeted for each village and town with that actually received: almost every locality either reached its target or came within a few pounds of doing so.

At one Dáil Loan meeting MacSwiney narrowly escaped detection by the crown. It was a point Collins made note of in a 16 March 1920 communication to his colleague. Expressing his gladness that a British raiding party had arrived on the scene too late, Collins remarked, "Let us be thankful it was, for if you yourself had been absent, I don't know what would have happened in Mid-Cork." In that letter, however, Collins made clear to MacSwiney the importance of his

securing the public support of Dr Cohalan, the bishop of
Cork, for funding in Cork city. "I think," Collins stated, "it's
an awful pity that Dr. Cohalan has not been seen long ago,
and I do hope that the interview will take place during the
next week."[15] The following week, however, events took a
dreadful course.

MacSwiney, like other members of Dáil Éireann, was
constantly under threat of arrest. Despite the burden which
living on the run imposed on him and his family, he took an
almost whimsical view of things. "I'm living a modified sort
of tramp life just now," he told a friend in March.

> We went in for the great adventure of getting a new house before
> Xmas ... but the attention of old "friends" became so overpow-
> ering we had to evacuate again before Xmas. The "friends" were
> so pressing quite a number of them followed me to the old house
> with an invitation to go on another "holiday" presumably over
> the water. Having spent really too much time on holidays these
> last five years, I had to deny myself this time. I escaped their
> entreaties by the simple, tho' rather impolite, expedient of not
> waiting to receive them. Their desire for familiarity bordered on
> the rude and I had to adopt the distant manner and leave them
> standing directions that to all such uncouth callers I am "not at
> home".[16]

A few days later, the home of MacSwiney's great comrade,
Tomás MacSwiney was raided. The lord mayor's household,
located above his business on Thomas Davis Street, was
awakened in the early hours of the morning by intruders with
blackened faces. MacCurtain fell dead from two shots that
hit him as he stood at the top of his stairs, while other
members of the raiding party held his wife. He was murdered
on his thirty-sixth birthday.

Florence O'Donoghue, who served under MacCurtain in
the Cork No. 1 Brigade, wrote that his death "was the first
though not the last deliberate and premeditated murder of a
Republican public representative holding a post of high
honour, and even, for the abnormal conditions of the time,
the circumstances surrounding it were unusual and
shocking."[17]

MacCurtain's death thrust new responsibilities on Terence

MacSwiney. He succeeded his comrade as commandant of the Cork No. 1 Brigade, and on 30 March 1920 a special meeting of Cork Corporation elected him lord mayor of the city. Fellow alderman and lifelong friend Liam de Roiste proposed MacSwiney's name; the nomination was seconded by Tadhg Barry and supported by Sir John Scott. As MacSwiney left his seat in the chamber to receive his chain of office, the audience broke into sustained applause and cheering.

Terence MacSwiney assumed the mayoralty of his native city in the worst possible circumstances. MacCurtain had been his closest colleague in the Republican movement; they had been friends for almost two decades. Together they had helped launch the Irish Volunteers in Cork. Before that they had been active in Irish cultural and language projects. Together they bore the burden of having made the decision that Cork would not participate actively in the 1916 Rising, and faced the innuendo levelled at them as a result. They had served as mayor and deputy mayor of Cork city, and at the same time continued to act as the leaders of the IRA in Cork. Terence MacSwiney was also godfather to MacCurtain's infant son, Thomas Jr.

MacSwiney's inaugural speech as lord mayor proclaimed his determination not to be deterred from the Republican ideal despite MacCurtain's death. In it he uttered the comment that would follow him to eternity:

> I wish to point out again the secret of our strength and the assurance of our final victory. This contest of ours is not on our side a rivalry of vengeance, but one of endurance – it is not they who can inflict the most, but they who can suffer the most, who will conquer – though we do not abrogate our function to demand and see that evil doers and murderers are punished for their crimes ... Those whose faith is strong will endure to the end and triumph.[18]

MacSwiney demonstrated his intent to carry on unimpeded with the work of the Republic on the day of his election, by appointing a panel of five judges for the Sinn Féin district court for his own Mid-Cork constituency. The panel included his friend and fellow writer Daniel Corkery;

Callaghan McCarthy, chairman of the Macroom Board of Guardians; MCCs J.J. Crowley and John J. Murphy along with Paud O'Donoghue, Chairman of the Macroom Urban District Council.[19] Ensuring the establishment of the Republican courts as an institutional fact of Irish life was a matter that greatly occupied MacSwiney, both as lord mayor and as a member of Dáil Éireann.

MacCurtain's death struck a deep sense of sadness in Michael Collins. "I have not very much heart," he wrote to MacSwiney on 22 March, "in what I am doing today, thinking of poor Tomás ... It is surely the most appalling thing that has been done yet."[20] As well as evoking remorse, MacCurtain's murder must also have reminded the two Corkmen that their lives, too, could be cut short at any time. Rather than recoil, however, their response was to inflict further violence on their adversaries. Within days of his letter to MacSwiney, Collins followed up with another in which he told him of his satisfaction with MacSwiney's "intention of carrying on". Appreciating the pressure that would now be on MacSwiney, and the increased element of danger, Collins remarked, "I know what this means."[21]

Collins praised MacSwiney's intention to see a detailed report written into the circumstances of MacCurtain's slaying. "We did it here in the Ashe case and it has been of the greatest value on many an occasion since," he stated. Soon after he sent a personal check for £10 to the new lord mayor towards the memorial fund for MacCurtain: "I regret it cannot be larger." Collins's expectations for the success of the memorial, and his assessment of its importance, were also candidly stated.

> It is to be hoped that this fund will rapidly run to very large dimensions. Every subscriber who gives his or her contribution gives proof that he or she knows that the late Lord Mayor of Cork died for Ireland, and signifies belief that he was murdered by the agents of England. This memorial is in no way a private matter. It is fully a national one, and it is more than that – it is the answer of our people to the enemy people who are slandering our dead comrade.[22]

On 31 May 1920, MacSwiney wrote that he had not "forgotten report of the inquest ... I had it all together as I thought, but took the precaution of having it composed with a file here and found there were some points missing. I have got a full file together now, but for convenience of anyone who has to use it, am getting it set up and pasted on foolscap to have it in a handy form."[23]

An inquest into the lord mayor's death, conducted at Cork's old City Hall, lasted for more than a week, and drew hundreds of spectators each night. For many it was an outlet for venting their anger at MacCurtain's slaying. The crown's chief attorney at the inquest, W.E. Wylie, suggested that "twenty five percent" of the "300 or 400 toughs", which he believed to have been Sinn Féin members, attended the proceedings "with guns in their pockets". On one particularly intense evening during the inquest, Wylie and a companion required the assistance of Bishop Cohalan to ensure their safety. At the time, the crown's attorney did not realise that his protector had been the bishop himself, but some years later, Cohalan recounted to Wylie how he had been "in bed and at 10 o'clock the phone rang and I was told that I should hurry up to the City Hall as murder was about to be done that night. I dressed and drove down, and I think I was just in time to save you."

The coroner's jury, which had been chosen by the RIC, held that MacCurtain had been "wilfully murdered, under circumstances of most callous brutality", and contended that "the murder was organised and carried out by the Royal Irish Constabulary officially directed by the British Government".[24] Prime Minister Lloyd George, the Lord Lieutenant of Ireland, Lord French, the head of the RIC in Munster and three RIC inspectors were officially cited by the coroner's jury in connection with MacCurtain's death. Some months later Lloyd George, a staunch defender of his government's reprisals policy in Ireland, expressed his shock before the cabinet that he had been found culpable in MacCurtain's murder by a body constituted under the king's writ. His government later remedied that fault. It passed the Coercion Act which abolished coroner's juries and provided for the system of martial law which was soon used to convict MacSwiney. Officially sanctioned acts of murder and terror could now be carried out with impunity.

One who fared worse in relation to MacCurtain's murder
was RIC District Inspector Swanzy, who had also been named
in the jury's verdict. Transferred to the Unionist stronghold
of Lisburn, County Armagh, the inspector was shot dead on
the orders of Michael Collins some months later. During the
Anglo-Irish truce Collins explained the reasons for this and
other actions to one British general:

> As I was in command I decided to collect my evidence and play
> them at their own game. This was the start of the vicious circle
> – the murder race. I intercepted all the correspondence. Inspector
> Swanzy put Lord Mayor MacCurtain away so I got Swanzy and
> all his associates wiped out, one by one, in all parts of Ireland to
> which the murderers had been secretly dispersed. What else
> could one do?[25]

Collins appears to have been exaggerating somewhat as, in
fact, MacCurtain's killing did not result in a wholesale series
of killings by the IRA of RIC members. Despite District
Inspector Swanzy's murder, apparently at the hands of IRA
Belfast Commandant Joe McKelvey, no one else connected to
the assassination of the lord mayor was attacked in retaliation.
Years later, ex-IRA officer Florence O'Donoghue wrote:
"Unfortunately our information on the individual men
involved, apart from Swanzy, was never sufficient to justify
any other executions. You may take it that Swanzy's case was
the only one in which a decision was made and carried out."[26]
    MacSwiney's own anger toward what he saw as the
government's involvement in MacCurtain's death is apparent
in a letter of 24 April 1920 to a subscriber to the memorial
fund in the dead lord mayor's name. He rejected outright the
story advanced by the government and the British press that
MacCurtain might have actually been murdered by a group
of disgruntled IRA members. "If they had material evidence
to put forward, the place to do so was before the Court," he
argued. "We, on our side, would not permit of any rejoinder
to the slanders because the matter was Sub Judice, and we
were most anxious nothing should be said that would in any
way impair the strictest and most impartial inquiry."
MacSwiney also emphasised that if British officials had been
"in a position to verify the story, they could destroy the

Republican movement in Ireland in this generation ... The lie has come home to them," he added, "and helped to lay the guilt at their own door."

MacSwiney's view was that "two things stand out clearly: l) that the murder was carried out by the police; 2) that it was organised officially – the latter making the government responsible." The evidence against the RIC was conclusive:

> The men who formed the murder party were seen by independent witnesses marching like trained men in King Street, on St. Patrick's hill and in Blackpool area. Policemen in uniform were seen with them on St. Patrick's hill by Nurse Daunt ... Two police in uniform held up witness McCarthy in Blackpool close to the late Lord Mayor's house when the murder was about to take place. The murder party was seen marching through King Street before the murder, and they passed two patrols. The police did not accost them or report to King Street Police barracks which was in sight. Obviously if the raiders were Sinn Féiners, the Military and Police would be called out at once. After the murder a group of the murder party was seen entering King Street police barracks. Here is the evidence of Lamplighter Desmond, as quoted by Counsel. "Whilst standing there at twenty minutes to two o'clock, he saw a body of men in single file and advancing at quick march and carrying rifles, enter King Street Barracks. He saw them go up the steps. They were admitted after a light knock..."[27]

MacSwiney's support for the killing of members of the RIC must be considered in the context of MacCurtain's murder. On 1 August 1920, at a meeting in Dublin of commanders of the South Munster brigades with defence minister Cathal Brugha, Michael Collins, director of intelligence, Dick Mulcahy, chief of staff, Rory O'Connor, director of engineering, Diarmuid O'Hegarty, director of organisation, and Gearoid O'Sullivan, adjutant general, MacSwiney voiced his opposition to a general headquarters' directive concerning the practice of ambushing. Mulcahy had recommended that the enemy should be called upon by the IRA ambushing parties to surrender before opening fire, and Brugha also favoured that approach. The bulk of the South Munster commanders emphasised that given the superior firepower of the British military, such a policy, in the words of Liam Deasy, "would be disastrous". Deasy writes that "the main objection to the plan was voiced by MacSwiney in whose area, Macroom, the Manchester Regiment was stationed". According to Deasy, MacSwiney stated, "that he could provide the men to carry out the plan suggested but that he could not supply them with sufficient arms".[28]

Earlier that year, MacCurtain and MacSwiney, frustrated by what they saw as the slow pace of IRA activity in Cork, and anxious also to put the memory of their inaction during Easter Week behind them, had suggested to general headquarters a plan of multiple risings around the country, but Collins had shot this down. There were also moments which were plainly embarrassing for MacSwiney as IRA leader in Cork. A planned attack on a British airfield at Ballyquirk on 4 July 1919, was aborted after the car transporting MacSwiney, Florrie O'Donoghue and others, along with most of the arms needed for the operation, went astray on a by-road and broke down. O'Donoghue stated that the group "did not get to Ballyquirk until after most of the assembled Volunteers had scattered."[29]

MacSwiney made clear his support for the killing of RIC members, their Irishness notwithstanding, in an interview with the *New York Herald*. He fully supported the IRA's policy of shooting policemen in cold blood, whenever and wherever the opportunity presented itself.

> Just because they [the police] have been such capable servants of the British we must get rid of them ... Once destroyed as a force, the British will never be able to organise another such. Revolutionary Ireland has too much at stake to spare them because they are doing their duty by England.[30]

These sentiments are perhaps removed from the image of MacSwiney the poet, the romantic, the Catholic mystic. But he was all of these things, as well as possessing a capacity for ruthlessness that would ultimately justify the taking of his own life, as well as the lives of others.

He received encouragement for his revolutionary activities from his wife, Muriel. In a letter of 15 April 1919, she told him that she would "fight in any case as you know, but of course I'd rather be with my own perfect love and look after him in other ways ... Darling, I don't think I'm brave really, only cool, that's all." Three days later she told Terry that "there is no one like you in the whole world ... I don't care for or even consider anyone except you, but you know, love, I want you to do more than anyone else in the coming trouble ... I am so terribly proud of my *fear* [man]."[31]

MacSwiney showed himself to be both innovative and industrious in his new role as lord mayor. While holding what was in reality a ceremonial office, he tried nonetheless to address commercial and civic issues which complemented his work in Dáil Éireann.

Soon after he took office the Labour movement in Cork city sought his support for workers who found themselves imprisoned or unemployed because of their active involvement in the Irish independence struggle. On 25 May 1920 Cork labour leader James Fitzgerald made a direct appeal for funds to supplement the Prisoners' Dependents Fund for workers in Cork incarcerated for Republican activities.* Fitzgerald also sought to impress upon MacSwiney the need to make "suitable arrangements" with the labour bureau in Cork, to provide work for what he described as "our out-of-work soldiers ... The drain on our Prisoners, Dependents Fund is £20 pounds weekly," he stated, "and as you can imagine, such cannot continue..." Fitzgerald outlined for MacSwiney a specific case:

> For example, the bearer of this note is one Sean O'Connell, just released from Wormwood. He organised and carried out successfully the capture of six rifles at Rushbrooke last February and his arrest was accomplished soon after. This resulted in his dismissal from Haulbowline Dockyard. Although we allow himself and his people 3 pounds per week, we cannot do so for

---

* This letter was actually released by the British government along with other captured documents at the time of MacSwiney's death some five months later in an apparent attempt to discredit him. In an internal memorandum from Dublin Castle to the cabinet following the documents' seizure by the authorities, it was emphasised that Fitzgerald's letter revealed the severe financial situation which the Republicans faced. "As a result of the vigorous efforts of the police and military, a great number of Irish Republican Leaders are on the run with the result that they and their families are dependent on Republican funds for maintenance."

long more; and to keep his family (a large one) in comparative decency, his aged father (65 years old) is intending going to sea before the mast in a week's time. His brother was out in Easter Week with himself and our small section and surely his case deserves our attention.

Fitzgerald concluded his letter by soliciting MacSwiney's assistance in seeking gainful employment for the man in Cork city, suggesting specifically the Ford Motors Co. He added that O'Connell's situation "is but one of many similar cases, and where we suffer in common for the cause, we might also unite in helping each other".[32]

Despite the sympathy for those living in squalid conditions evident in his play, *The Holocaust*, MacSwiney's political stance on the provision of public housing by the municipality was quite conservative. At a meeting of the City Council on 23 April 1920, he held to the moderate line being followed by Dáil Éireann on social issues, as part of their attempt to present Sinn Féin as a "responsible" movement emphasising national independence rather than class conflict. In a response to a new public housing proposal for Cork city, "the Lord Mayor said under the scheme they could provide houses at a rent of about 9 shillings per week. 'Such houses,' he said, 'could be occupied by the working classes, who are fairly well paid at present and who could pay nine shillings, or ten shillings, or eleven shillings per week for them, and the cheaper houses that they vacated could then be made available for the poorer people.'"[33]

At the same time, MacSwiney's plan caught the attention of his counterpart in Limerick city, William O'Callaghan. "This is very interesting," he wrote to MacSwiney, "as I find that we cannot do houses at anything like that rent." But the effort became sidetracked, as MacSwiney informed O'Callaghan: "Since our decision to build a limited number of houses (about 150) as a beginning was made, a further increase in wages in the building trade here has been given; and that of course will upset all our calculations."[34]

While MacSwiney may been sympathetic to those living in poor housing conditions, the record of his short tenure as lord mayor also indicates a concern with less material matters. As one of his first official acts, he proposed sending a delegation from Cork Corporation to Rome for the beatification of Blessed Oliver Plunkett, the 17th century Catholic prelate and martyr.

MacSwiney's ability as an educationalist, and the depth of his desire to develop Ireland's commercial and human potential, were well illustrated in a report he submitted to the Dáil following an inspection he conducted of the Limerick Technical Institute on 22-23 June 1920. The school, which had been taken over by the Dáil, was seen as an important model for the development of technical education throughout the country, and it provided an opportunity for the Republican government to demonstrate its ability to conduct the affairs of the nation in a constructive way by revitalising an area that had been neglected under British rule. MacSwiney's interest in the school went back to the previous year, according to a letter from Michael Collins: "The enclosure regarding the Limerick Technical Schools I have sent on to Mr. Griffith. There is nobody specially looking after this activity at the moment, but between us we shall deal with it."[35]

MacSwiney's report was unsparing in his criticism of what he saw as the shortcomings of the school's administration and the Dáil's responsibility in this regard. He was particularly critical of the institute's principal.

> In approaching the work of this report, I keep in view the position of Dáil Éireann in taking over control of the Limerick Technical Institute ... from the standpoint of establishing Technical Education on a more satisfactory basis than it had been under the English Department ... In making the new departure, I would have looked for an educational ideal in the Principal who, realising that Technical Education under the English Department had been largely a failure, would also realise that the Dail, in taking over the Limerick Technical Institute, should aim at a higher standard and should achieve that success in the educational sphere which the Administration of the Republic has already won in other spheres. I also would have expected the Principal to have realised the opportunity given to him of showing what a free Ireland might do for education, and his responsibility in making use of that opportunity.

In MacSwiney's analysis, this ideal opportunity "was
completely missed", while the "secondary position of at least
maintaining the English Department's standard had not been
maintained – unless the standard of the Limerick Technical
Institute was lower than any of which I have had experience".
Among the many deficiencies he cited, was the principal's
practice of inflating the school's enrolment with ill-equipped
students from the ranks of "backward adults and very young
students of day-school standard", for the purpose of having
more students than were in attendance under the British
administration of the institute. MacSwiney found an even
more serious fault in the lack of qualifications of the teaching
staff to teach certain subjects: "I gave Chemistry as an
example in my preliminary report. The teacher of this subject
was qualified in his own special subject; he was given
Chemistry to teach because he had done well in it in his
examination. But he had not specialised in Chemistry and
could not be expected to teach students who wished to make
Chemistry a profession." Of the principal himself,
MacSwiney stated that "we who went to inspect the Institute
last year were led astray by his cheerful assumptions of new
classes to be formed ... I mistook him then ... to be a man of
initiative and enterprise."

While he took issue with the institute's administration,
MacSwiney also demonstrated concern over what he saw as
the "inadequate" pay given the teachers. "I think there should
be a standard salary for full-time teachers of £250 a year," he
contended. Whether the additional funds to support a wage
increase were to "be obtained by increasing the Dáil grant or
organising local assistance, I feel strongly that the Institute
should not re-open and ask the staff to work for the very low
salaries that prevailed as a whole". MacSwiney stated
emphatically that "it is not to the credit of the Dáil that an
educational institution should be conducted under its
auspices and the teachers paid on a scale below a living
wage". In all, he offered a fifteen-point proposal for invigo-
rating the institute through the provision of "competent
guidance" along with a combination of measures including
more rigorous standards for admission to the school,
additional funding, and reform of the curriculum. His

concluding remarks were reserved for what he saw as the Dáil's own obligation to make the Limerick Technical Institute a model of success:

> I regret that I should have to write so severely but I feel it a matter of duty. The administration of the Republic has hitherto been so efficient in every Department as to win the admiration not only of friends, but of enemies. The taking over by the Dáil of the Limerick Technical Institute was our first notable advance to control in the Educational sphere; to fail conspicuously there would be disastrous to our prestige – particularly as Education is the most important of all departments and fundamental to success in every sphere. We have a failure to retrieve in Limerick, even though the Dáil grant should be not only renewed but increased. Because I urge that course very strongly, I urge the need for a complete reorganisation of the Institute and the appointment of the most highly qualified and efficient Principal available. To that end I have been unsparing in my criticisms as a duty I owe in conscience to the Administration of the Republic.[36]

MacSwiney's analysis of the need to develop an advanced system of Irish technical school education came less than two weeks before his final arrest. The document stands as testimony to his intellectual vigour. Favourable comment on his report came from Alfred O'Rahilly, then registrar of University College, Cork, and a man who would himself emerge as a major force in Irish education, particularly as a champion of an advanced vocational school system.

"I have read with great pleasure and sympathy your report on the Limerick Technical Institute," O'Rahilly wrote to MacSwiney on 26 July. He shared many of the lord mayor's concerns, and had "noted in more places than one the tendency, which constitutes such a danger to our nascent Republic, to undervalue technical and scientific proficiency and to accept, in lieu thereof, political enthusiasm". O'Rahilly held that "competency in such matters should be our first aim". In his only note of criticism, he pointed out to MacSwiney that "you say nothing of equipment and of library facilities". However, MacSwiney wrote on O'Rahilly's letter: "this covered in first report, building and equipment fund".[37]

Shortly after MacCurtain's murder, Collins had again emphasised to MacSwiney, now lord mayor, the urgency of securing the commitment of Cork's Bishop Cohalan to the Dáil Loan: "You will also appreciate my desire that you should lose no opportunity of having that interview with his Lordship. The point I already made about the moral value we may get from same is becoming more and more obvious as the days go on."[38]

The importance of Cohalan's endorsement of the loan was not lost on MacSwiney, but neither was it lost on Cohalan himself, who continued to ignore MacSwiney's representations. Other Catholic bishops, such as Dr Fogarty of Killaloe, County Clare, openly embraced the Dáil Loan: Fogarty was listed on the loan's prospectus documents as one of its three principal trustees, along with Arthur Griffith and Eamon de Valera. Cohalan, however, had a record of being less enthusiastic about the cause of Irish independence. On 9 April Collins suggested to MacSwiney that "If you have not seen His Lordship by this time, I wonder if you would make it your special business to interview him in priority to any other engagement whatever ... You will forgive me ... if I have been unduly stressing this matter with you, but I have given up hope of Liam [de Roiste] going to see him." Collins reminded MacSwiney that the bishop had in fact been "interviewed" by Erskine Childers regarding the Republican land bank. "Mr. Childers took an introduction from me," Collins pointed out, "and had no difficulty at all in seeing him."[39]

After months of seeking an appointment with the bishop, MacSwiney met with him formally on 13 April. In a letter to Collins describing the encounter, he characterised Cohalan as having been "very unsatisfactory". While the bishop had promised a subscription, "It has not come yet, however." MacSwiney was not particularly sanguine about Cohalan's attitude towards the viability of the Irish Republic.

His line is that he would be quite ready to support "our representatives," but he does not see any possibility of "The Irish Republic" in our time; and he does not want to be taken [as a supporter] if we asked as the people's representatives for money for industries, etc., but to issue a loan as the Government of the

Republic he does not believe in. I argued the matter up and down with him for an hour and a half. All he could say was he couldn't see it, though he'd be as glad to see it as myself. If his subscription doesn't turn up I'll get on to him again.[40]

Collins responded immediately, "I think I understand his Lordship's point of view, but frankly I am surprised that he did not meet you more readily ... However, I have not the slightest doubt that he will be as good as his word, or – if I may use the expression – better than his word."[41] But Collins's optimism was not met by the bishop's public support for the loan. Three months later, MacSwiney addressed this correspondence to the bishop, still seeking his endorsement:

> I wrote to you before you left for Rome about your promised subscription to Dáil Éireann Loan. It was then about to close. In response to representations from Dublin we were given a further extension of time, and the closing day was fixed at July 17 – Saturday last. This precludes us from accepting new applications now, but we are collecting the subscriptions promised before 17th instant. For that reason I write to you again before we finally close our accounts.[42]

In his letter to Dr Cohalan, MacSwiney highlighted the gains made by the Republican government in establishing its legitimacy in Ireland. "The outstanding notable achievement," he wrote, "is the establishment and successful functioning of the Dáil Éireann Courts." He noted that "representatives of the foreign press are coming specially to see our courts in session as they see in them the evidence of the de facto existence of our own Government which we had already established de jure ... The Courts of Dáil Éireann to them really mark the end of English authority in Ireland – for the justice of their decrees is acknowledged and their judgments are enforced where English writs have ceased to run."[43]

Despite MacSwiney's latest appeal, Cohalan still proved less than forthcoming. MacSwiney's frustration with Bishop Cohalan may have led to the advocacy of a remedy quite at odds with a man of considerable religious piety. Two months earlier, MacSwiney had outlined a proposal to P.S. O'Hegarty

which, O'Hegarty recorded, "seemed to me then to be
fiendish, and indefensible and inadvisable from every point of
view". O'Hegarty's allusion may refer to a threat to use the
IRA to put pressure on Dr Cohalan.[44] If indeed this was the
case, then the incident reveals a contradictory dimension of
MacSwiney's personality, for it was precisely at this time that
he was also completing an inquiry into the murder of his
comrade Tomás MacCurtain at the hands of the RIC.

Neither MacSwiney nor Collins were satisfied with the
level of work done by Liam de Roiste in gaining subscriptions
for the Dáil Loan in Cork city. As early as 29 January 1920,
impressed with MacSwiney's work in Mid-Cork, Collins
suggested to MacSwiney that, in addition to Sean Nolan,
"perhaps you, too, would be able to give some assistance in the
City". While expressing his understanding of the obligations
already heaped on MacSwiney, Collins concluded nonetheless: "It is my experience that people who are very busy are
never so busy that they cannot do something extra."[45]

But five months later MacSwiney was still frustrated by the
response from Cork, owing to what he saw as de Roiste's lack
of commitment. "I wrote to him very strongly about the
matter," MacSwiney told Collins.[46] MacSwiney did not let
personal friendship get in the way of his work, even when it
concerned someone who had been involved with him ever
since they had formed the Cork Literary Society some twenty
years earlier.

> I would not have interfered in this matter at all but you asked me
> some time ago to bear a hand, and this naturally I was anxious
> to do. When, later, I was made Lord Mayor, I felt I had a direct
> responsibility for the City Loan, and did my best to help it on –
> addressing meetings of various city Cumainn and Executives to stir
> them up on the work of canvassing and appointing deputations. S.J.
> Moynihan has been very attentive to his work, and the canvassing
> was started at the eleventh hour with good result. There is now
> collected in case (including what you have in Dublin)
> £8,713:10:0. These are the figures I got from S.J.M. this
> morning. Liam has over £5,000 of his in hand, and he may have
> small sums in hand, paid to himself, which are not included in
> above figures. We are satisfied now that the Loan in the city will

1. Terence MacSwiney *c.* 1907

2. Terence MacSwiney (second row, second from left) with his classmates at the North Monastery, Cork

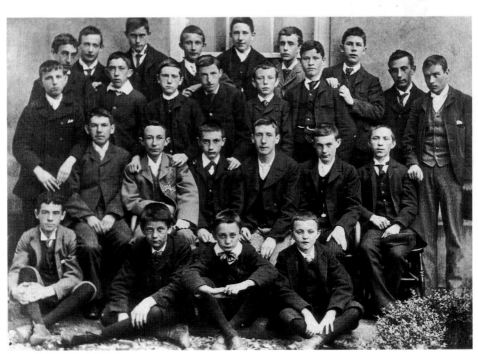

3. Muriel MacSwiney and Máire, 1920

4. Terence MacSwiney and daughter, Máire

5. Terence and Muriel MacSwiney, Cork 1919

6. MacSwiney's wedding to Muriel Murphy at Bromyard: *back* Mary and Anne MacSwiney, Fr Augustine, Josephine and Richard Mulcahy.

7. MacSwiney, first row, first from left, with a company of volunteers prior to the Easter Rising

8. Pearse surrenders to
   British officers, 1916

9. Michael Collins: as minister for finance, he and
   MacSwiney worked
   closely to raise the Dáil
   Loan.

10. A memorial issued in the
form of a postcard after
MacSwiney's death

11. The lord mayor's office,
Cork City Hall

TERENCE MacSWINEY. M.I.P.
Lord Mayor Of Cork.

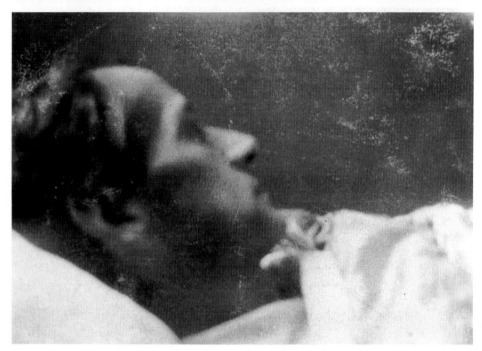

12. On hunger strike in Brixton, this photograph was smuggled out of the prison

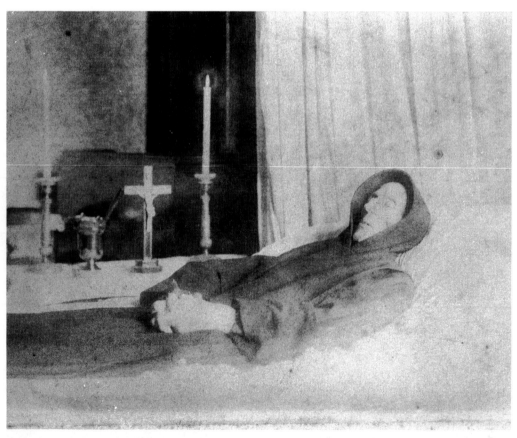

13. The body of Terence MacSwiney, Brixton Prison

14. MacSwiney's body is brought to Cork, surrounded by Auxiliaries
(George Morrisson Collection)

REMAINS BEING BORNE TO THE GRAVE.

15. Terence MacSwiney's funeral procession, Cork

16. Mary MacSwiney

17. With his mother at the turn of
the century

18. Terence and Muriel MacSwiney

reach £10,000. I am equally satisfied it would have doubled that figure if the work were taken in hand vigorously and earnestly six months ago. What has been done lately was done concurrently with the collection for Memorial Fund which naturally was a drawback. I spoke to Liam more than once about the City in the early stages of the work. It was his responsibility, not mine, and I had no desire whatever to interfere having more than enough work on my own shoulders. I am writing to you plainly about it now so that you may write to him direct yourself.[47]

Collins took MacSwiney's comments to heart. He took particular care in a reply sent four days later to praise MacSwiney's lionhearted efforts concerning the loan. "You will be glad to hear," he informed the lord mayor, "that the entire total is now assured and is, in fact, actually oversubscribed ... I have, in cash, £240,000 solid, representing applications amounting to £255,000." MacSwiney's mid-Cork constituency was among the heaviest contributors in the country, with a total of £6,025 at that juncture. As for de Roiste, Collins noted that "Liam has written me to say that you sent him a copy of the letter you wrote me and I am glad you did this ... I was feeling very strongly in the matter for a long time, but I must admit that I am somewhat softened now owing to the success of the entire venture." Collins admitted to MacSwiney, however, that "were it not for that, I should be out probably with a scalping knife ... Certainly the progress in Cork City has been remarkable at the last moment, but as I said in my letter to Liam, I don't think the total can be said to compare favourably with other places."[48] Collins's earlier frustrations with Cork city and Liam de Roiste would return, however. Praising MacSwiney for making mid-Cork "a place apart among the rural Dáil constituencies", he made less than complimentary comments about de Roiste's efforts. "For what it is worth," he wrote, "when I sent an acknowledgement to Liam de Roiste of the last payment from the City, he wrote to me saying that he knew nothing about it ... There are people who have always to be complaining about something," he concluded.[49]

As the drive for the Dáil Loan scheme was brought to a close in July 1920, the net total received from mid-Cork compared favourably with many larger and more populous areas. The level of dedication and organisation which MacSwiney brought to the loan drive was met by further expressions of appreciation from Collins. "At this closing stage," Collins wrote to MacSwiney that month, "I would mention that I am of the opinion the prompt response in mid-Cork was the greatest factor in making the Loan a success ... It had the effect, not only of urging neighbouring constituencies to a sense of their duty, but all the constituencies all over Ireland ... Mid-Cork and West Limerick made a headline at a time when it was badly needed," the publicity conscious Collins wrote. He praised MacSwiney by telling him that "the promptness and the faith which that promptness showed, deserve well of Ireland."[50]

In the end the loan effort exceeded the initial target. On 31 July 1920, in what was one of Collins' last letters to MacSwiney as a free man, he told him that "at the time of writing, the entire total exceeds £355,500." The total receipts from MacSwiney's constituency stood at £7,095. "Mid-Cork is thus," he noted, "almost £1,000 higher than any other constituency in the County."[51]

Satisfied with their success, MacSwiney told his sister Peggy that "we are all in good form, notwithstanding the pressure of the present times. I'll say nothing of the latter," he added. "Everything will come out right in the end, please God. Pray hard, ... for us all and for Ireland ... We are near the end of that long lane that has no turning back."[52]

On the contrary, MacSwiney was moving ahead with further projects. After having established the loan scheme on a relatively firm footing in the spring of 1920, MacSwiney, with Collins apparent approval, had embarked on a drive to publicise the success of the Republican courts. This entailed arranging opportunities for representatives of the foreign press to view the courts at first hand, and was a significant part of the Republican government's propaganda drive. Of the impact made by the courts, MacSwiney wrote: "The justice of their decrees is acknowledged and their judgements are enforced where English writs have ceased to run."[53] Indeed, the credibility attained by the Republican courts, and MacSwiney's role in enhancing their effectiveness, may have been the most important reason behind the British government's determination to arrest him.

As lord mayor of Cork, MacSwiney used the platform provided by that office to expand the jurisdiction of the courts beyond the confines of the city. On 12 June 1920 he announced the resolution through a Dáil Éireann arbitration court of a strike at Kinsale involving the local branch of the Irish Transport Workers Union and a local employer. The findings of the court were accepted by both sides and resulted in gains both in pay and holiday time for the workers. Sitting with MacSwiney on the arbitration court were Deputy Mayor Donal O'Callaghan and Father Eamon Fitzgerald, a local cleric.[54]

Though he did not hold a ministry, MacSwiney's judgement was valued, and on 19 July 1920 came a request from Ernest Blythe in his capacity as head of Dáil Éireann's trade department, that MacSwiney "suggest any man suitable for the American consulate ... You will understand that we must have a man of a superior type, as our American consulate is the most important of all."[55]

While MacSwiney generally supported the Belfast boycott initiated by the Dáil during the summer of 1920, including a provision that Belfast banks be deprived of deposits from the south of Ireland as a means to bring pressure on Unionist employers who sought to deny work to Catholics unless they signed an oath repudiating Sinn Féin, he emphasised that a more "constructive" approach would have to be taken in order to deal with the problem in the long term. In the Dáil, MacSwiney proposed the "establishment of co-operative factories to provide employment for Republicans who could be induced to settle in Belfast".[56] It seemed that, if Protestant settlers could be used by Britain to maintain the crown's footing in Ireland, an increase in the number of Catholics could apparently be used, in his view, to change the composition of Belfast.

He also spoke on the need to develop forestry throughout the country. In an effort to gain a better understanding of where Ireland's timber resources stood, he suggested that the department of agriculture describe "the value of woods at different stages as timber and give information generally as to the value of certain classes of woods from all points of view".[57]

By this time, MacSwiney had begun to consider ways in which the Dáil system of local government could be strengthened, and how these bodies could be financed. He made useful recommendations in regard to the Dáil's bid to attract additional sources of revenue; in the Dáil session of 6 August, he noted the potential monies which could be raised from the collection of licenses. He pointed out that "people had applied to him for auctioneers' licenses and offered to pay the tax on them to the Republic". A proposal, however, to finance local government through the collection of rates became a cause for concern to the Dáil. MacSwiney, who supported the move, gave the Dáil an optimistic assessment, and argued that southern Unionists "who sought the protection of the Republican courts, would pay the rates and an extra tax for protection if required ... The farmers would be quite willing to pay their land purchase annuities to the Republican Government."[58]

Despite MacSwiney's many political obligations, he continued to find time to write. His extensive writings in the realm of politics and government show an individual well read in the classics. In the 6 April 1920 issue of *An Réalt*, MacSwiney outlined the obligations of the public man: "To be an able politician, a man should study and master the principles of government – should study the ideas underlying the various politics, the Republic, the Kingdom, the Empire; should study the actual existing examples of such politics contrasting two of a kind where they exist, as for example the French and American Republics, the German and British Empires." Consistent with his own diverse interests, he argued further that "The politician should be a master of the science of political economy, should be an expert in the laws, government, finance, education, agriculture, industry, labour, capital; he should not only be versed in the principles governing these in general, but also as they affect Ireland in particular."[59] MacSwiney's hopes in this regard were highly idealistic, if not simply unrealistic.

The same article also discusses matters of economic concern in a manner consistent with Sinn Féin's vagueness on such questions. "The politician," he declared, "should be a thorough master of all Ireland's resources – having exact knowledge both of her limitations and potentialities." It was the politician's duty, likewise, he contended, to have "studied closely political and industrial history and to understand from precedent where and how some systems succeeded and others failed entirely."[60] MacSwiney, the commercial studies instructor, was a practical man given to systems analysis, but at the same time he had an overly idealistic set of expectations for those who would seek to be public men in an independent Ireland.

Even though pressure of other duties had forced him to resign the leadership of the Gaelic League in Cork two years earlier, the summer of 1920 saw MacSwiney reiterating the importance of the Irish language. He delivered an upbeat speech in Kilkenny on 27 June, on the gains the independence movement had achieved up to that point, before returning to a theme he had stressed over the years: the need to preserve the Irish language as a means of assuring Ireland's national identity.

> Our language is the boundary wall between Ireland and England. Irish freedom cannot be permanent ... unless we succeed in saving Irish from extinction.[61]

But the overriding consideration for the present was the practical one of how to gather more resources to underpin the independence drive. He lobbied Michael Collins's department of finance for the implementation of a fee and licensing system regulated by the Dáil. "Inquiries have come to me," he told Collins in a letter of 5 July 1920, "as to the renewal of licenses for different purposes." Among the possibilities he cited were drivers' licenses and licenses to sell tobacco and spirits. "The previous practice," he noted, "was through the police ... I don't know what revenue might be made in this way, but it ought to be appreciable if a General Order were issued, as most people would obey it."[62]

On 9 July, Collins told the lord mayor that on the question of a proposed income tax to be instituted by Dáil Éireann, it was "very likely we shall ask you to come up from the Country occasionally on this question".[63] That letter also expressed concern on Collins's part over a lack of prior information on an order issued by the Cork city Sinn Féin executive requiring local merchants to cease providing information to the British income tax authorities. The order stated that "any breach of this order will be severely dealt with". One newspaper account stated that order had left the merchants of Cork "greatly perturbed."[64]

"Could you please let me have a copy of this order," Collins wrote, "and you might also state whether any suggestion accompanied it about action, in accordance with our discussion at the Dáil Meeting."[65]

Throughout their communication, MacSwiney was determined to conduct his official correspondence, with Collins as with other members of the government, in Irish. Although Collins responded in Irish, keeping an English translation as a file copy, it appears that MacSwiney's reliance on Irish as a medium and his insistence that others correspond with him in that language was at times an irritant for one so harried.[66] On 20 July 1920, Collins wrote to MacSwiney telling him: "I am just writing you this note in English as there is no time to get it typed in Irish." The correspondence related to a summary of a letter from MacSwiney's brother Sean in Southampton, which had fallen into the hands of the British. "I only got this particular note yesterday evening, although I was already aware of the general contents of the letter." The ever security-conscious Collins cautioned MacSwiney not to mention the information "to anybody else, however, and destroy this note".[67]

On 8 August, only days before his arrest, MacSwiney wrote to Collins in Irish, telling him that "people here are asking me to do something to procure Republican Stamps in place of English ones". While it might not have been practical to use the stamps for letters, the lord mayor suggested that "they could be used for receipts and the like".[68]

The letter was the last personal contact between two men.

Notes
1. Padraig Colum, *Ourselves Alone* (New York 1959) p. 205.
2. Michael Collins to Terence MacSwiney, 11 December 1917, MacSwiney Collection, UCD Archives, P48b/358.
3. Frank O'Connor, *The Big Fellow* (Dublin 1965) p. 91
4. Ibid. pp. 91-92.
5. Dáil Éireann Loan Prospectus issued by the Department of

Finance, SPO/Dáil Éireann Files.

6. Michael Collins to Terence MacSwiney, 19 December 1919, SPO/Dáil Éireann Files.

7. Michael Collins to Terence MacSwiney, 25 September 1919, SPO/Dáil Éireann Files.

8. Terence MacSwiney to Michael Collins, 2 October 1919, SPO/Dáil Éireann Files.

9. Terence MacSwiney to Michael Collins, 19 October 1919, SPO/Dáil Éireann Files.

10. Michael Collins to Terence MacSwiney, 11 December 1919, SPO/Dáil Éireann Files.

11. Michael Collins to Terence MacSwiney, 5 January 1920, SPO/Dáil Éireann Files.

12. Michael Collins to Terence MacSwiney, 25 October 1919, SPO/Dáil Éireann Files.

13. Michael Collins to Terence MacSwiney, 4 August 1920, SPO/Dáil Éireann Files.

14. Terence MacSwiney, analysis of Dáil Loan Collections in Cork city and surrounding areas 12 February 1920, MacSwiney Collection, P48b/358.

15. Michael Collins to Terence MacSwiney, 16 March 1920, SPO/Dáil Éireann Files.

16. Florence O'Donoghue, *Tomás MacCurtain* (Tralee 1971) p. 166-67.

17. Ibid. p. 167.

18. MacSwiney Collection, P48b/400.

19. Terence MacSwiney to Dermot O'Hegarty, 31 May 1920, State Papers DE2/80.

20. Michael Collins to Terence MacSwiney, 22 March 1920, SPO/Dáil Éireann Files.

21. Michael Collins to Terence MacSwiney, 30 March 1920, SPO/Dáil Éireann Files.

22. Michael Collins to Terence MacSwiney, 15 April 1920, SPO/Dáil Éireann Files.

23. Terence MacSwiney to Michael Collins, 31 May 1920, SPO/Dáil Éireann Files.

24. Moirin Chavasse, *Terence MacSwiney* (Dublin 1961) p. 125.

25. Frank Crozier, *Ireland Forever* (London 1932) p. 218.

26. Florence O'Donoghue to Moirin Chavasse, 12 July 1958, MacSwiney Collection, P48c/169.

27. Terence MacSwiney, 24 April 1920, MacSwiney Collection.

28. Liam Deasy, *Towards Ireland Free* (Dublin 1973) p. 132.

29. Florence O'Donoghue, *Tomás MacCurtain*, p. 88.

30. *New York Herald* as cited by *Toronto Globe and Mail*, 27 October 1920.
31. Muriel MacSwiney to Terence MacSwiney, 15 and 18 April 1919, MacSwiney Collection, P48b/124-30.
32. Captured letter of James Fitzgerald to Terence MacSwiney, 25 May 1920, CO 904/168.
33. *Cork Examiner*, 24 April 1920.
34. William O'Callaghan (mayor of Limerick) to Terence MacSwiney, April 1920, Cork Municipal Museum.
35. Michael Collins to Terence MacSwiney, 1 January 1920, SPO/Dáil Éireann Files.
36. Terence MacSwiney to Dáil Éireann on Limerick Technical Institute, 23-24 June 1920, MacSwiney Collection, P48b/391.
37. Alfred O'Rahilly to Terence MacSwiney, 26 July 1920, MacSwiney Collection, P48/391.
38. Michael Collins to Terence MacSwiney, 29 March 1920, SPO/Dáil Éireann Files.
39. Michael Collins to Terence MacSwiney, 9 April 1920, SPO/Dáil Éireann Files.
40. Terence MacSwiney to Michael Collins, 13 April 1920, SPO/ Dáil Éireann Files.
41. Michael Collins to Terence MacSwiney, 21 April 1920, SPO/Dáil Éireann Files.
42. Terence MacSwiney to Bishop Cohalan, 21 July 1920, SPO/Dáil Éireann files.
43. Ibid.
44. Richard Bennett, *The Black and Tans* (London 1959) p. 68.
45. Michael Collins to Terence MacSwiney, 29 January 1920, SPO/Dáil Éireann Files.
46. Terence MacSwiney to Michael Collins, 25 May 1920, SPO/Dáil Éireann Files.
47. Ibid.
48. Michael Collins to Terence MacSwiney, 29 May, 1920, MacSwiney Collection, P48A.
49. Michael Collins to Terence MacSwiney, 26 July 1920, SPO/Dáil Éireann Files.
50. Michael Collins to Terence MacSwiney, 21 July 1920, SPO/ Dáil Éireann Files.
51. Michael Collins to Terence MacSwiney, 31 July 1920, SPO/Dáil Éireann Files.
52. Terence MacSwiney to Margaret MacSwiney, 22 July 1920, MacSwiney Collection.

53. Margery Forester, *Michael Collins: The Lost Leader* (London 1971) p. 155.

54. Findings of Dáil Éireann Arbitration Court, 12 June 1920, MacSwiney Collection, P48b/399.

55. Letter of Ernest Blythe to Terence MacSwiney, 19 July 1920, MacSwiney Collection, P48b/389.

56. Proceedings of Dáil Éireann, Private Session, 6 August 1920, SPO/Dáil Éireann Files.

57. Ibid.

58. Ibid.

59. *An Réalt*, 6 April 1920.

60. Ibid.

61. Terence MacSwiney, address at Kilkenny, 27 June 1920, Cork Municipal Museum.

62. Terence MacSwiney to Michael Collins, 5 July 1920, SPO/Dáil Éireann Files.

63. Michael Collins to Terence MacSwiney, 9 July 1920, SPO/Dáil Éireann Files.

64. *Freeman's Journal*, 9 July 1920.

65. Michael Collins to Terence MacSwiney, 9 July 1920, SPO/Dáil Éireann Files.

66. Frank O'Connor, *The Big Fellow*, pp. 91-92.

67. Michael Collins to Terence MacSwiney, 20 July 1920, SPO/Dáil Éireann Files.

68. Terence MacSwiney to Michael Collins, 8 August 1920, SPO/Dáil Éireann Files.

Chapter V

The Last Arrest

B Y AUGUST 1920, it was clear to those close to MacSwiney that he was under great stress. He planned a short holiday, scheduled to begin on 14 August, at the urging of his doctors who feared he was on the verge of a breakdown.[1] He led a hunted existence at this time, unable to spend a night at home.

Indeed, in their brief married life together, the MacSwineys never knew a single home in Cork. As a young mother, Muriel MacSwiney found herself alone with baby Máire in various temporary houses, while Terence remained on the run. It was a faith she was reconciled to, though she suffered numerous bouts of illness, in all likelihood as a consequence of this difficult lifestyle. After her husband's death, Muriel related to a public tribunal in the United States how "he really could not be with me at all. He could not be where they might find him at night. I hardly ever saw my husband at all, to tell the truth."[2]

Likewise, their child went without a father. "She was awfully fond of him," Muriel MacSwiney said, noting that the telephone in his office at Cork City Hall was more often than not the sole source of contact between MacSwiney and his daughter. "Sometimes I was speaking to other people," she recalled, "but whoever I was speaking to on the telephone, the baby would snatch the receiver out of my hand and think it was her father, and she would whisper, just whisper to him."[3]

In a conversation with a long-time friend a few days before the arrest that would point him on the road to Brixton Prison, MacSwiney laughed off rumours that he had been shot dead on the steps of his local church: "All I can say is, to quote Mark Twain on a similar occasion, 'the report of my death was grossly exaggerated'".[4]

MacSwiney's planned holiday with his wife and daughter

was to be preceded on the evening of 12 August by a meeting of the staff of the Cork No. 1 Brigade at City Hall, with MacSwiney presiding. Florrie O'Donoghue notes that this "was not a normal venue for such meetings."[5] It was arranged to suit the lord mayor.

> Except on the occasions when his public duties required his presence elsewhere, Terence MacSwiney had spent most of his days and nights at City Hall in the previous four months. Various onerous duties fell upon him as T.D. for mid-Cork, Lord Mayor of the City and Commandant of Cork No. 1 Brigade. In the two last posts he had succeeded his friend and colleague Tomás MacCurtain, who had been brutally murdered by Crown forces in March. His brigade maintained an armed guard around him day and night as a means to guard MacSwiney against the threat of assassination.[6]

MacSwiney had no knowledge apparently that IRB officers from another area had also scheduled a meeting for the same night. Neither was he directly involved in the Republican court proceedings being held in the hall. When MacSwiney entered City Hall that evening, Liam Lynch was among those waiting to meet him. Lynch "after some difficulty and with the assistance of Joe O'Connor and Brigade Quartermaster, Paddy McCarthy ... saw Terry and arranged that he would be available to meet Liam ... at 7 o'clock".[7] But while these proceedings were going on inside City Hall, the building was being surrounded by some two to three hundred regular troops. When the troops were spotted, MacSwiney set about leaving the building by a rear exit, but was arrested on the spot. Lynch and a number of other key IRA officers were also arrested. MacSwiney was taken to Victoria Barracks where he was charged some time later with possession of a police cipher code. He refused outright to remove his chain of office: "I would rather die than part with it". The chain was left to him, while other personal effects, save for his clothes, were removed by the military. After protesting his initial accommodation, MacSwiney was taken to a private room where he was given an officer's bed. He was also assigned an officer to guard him, rather than an enlisted man.

MacSwiney's arrest, along with the others captured that evening, represented "the most important capture of the war in Munster". It included, "almost the entire staff of the Cork No. 1 Brigade as well as two of the ablest and most active of the Battalion Commandants, the OC.'s of the First and Fourth Battalions".[8] However, on 16 August all prisoners except MacSwiney were mistakenly released, owing most likely to the fact that the British authorities had not involved the RIC in the raid, and were themselves not fully aware of the importance of the detainees. Prior to the group's release, O'Donoghue records that MacSwiney proposed "to his fellow prisoners that they should commence a hunger strike from that moment ... It was clear," he wrote, "that MacSwiney had determined his own line of action".[9] Whether this action on MacSwiney's part was spontaneous or the result of some long-held personal commitment remains unclear – there is evidence that the use of the hunger strike as a weapon was a matter of disagreement among even the strongest advocates of physical force at that time.[10] Nonetheless, MacSwiney went on hunger strike right from the moment of his arrest.

In Dublin, Collins, rather than make any gesture of compromise to the British, proceeded to "offer war". As MacSwiney lay in prison, he called out his handpicked assassination squad "to shoot half a dozen active G-men as they left [Dublin] Castle".[11]

The British raid on Cork City Hall was the result of what O'Donoghue called "an accident of war", in which a notice of the meeting was intercepted through the mails.[12] No cipher code, he contends, was in MacSwiney's possession at the time of his arrest. O'Donoghue was commandant adjutant and intelligence chief for the Cork No. 1 Brigade and "The police cipher key," he wrote, "was normally in my custody."[13] O'Donoghue's account was echoed in a dispatch Collins sent to Art O'Brien in London concerning MacSwiney's possession of the police cipher. An IRA source for Collins in Cork, informed him that the cipher "was not in Terry's possession at any time".[14] Collins's source continued:

> When I was leaving town I gave it to one of the Brigade Officers, and he had it on him at the City Hall that night. Not wishing to

destroy it if possible, he hid it outside at the back behind a partition. One of the soldiers saw him hide it and drew the attention of the officer in charge to the matter. Terry was one of the number of men who was in the vicinity of this place at the time. It was the code in Terry's desk. The code and the message were together in the back yard and were not found in anybody's possession.[15]

However, the police codes found that night probably had, in fact, been supplied to MacSwiney by Michael Collins, in the latter's capacity as director of intelligence for the IRA.[16] This view is backed up by Sean Kavanagh, one of Collins's main informants in Dublin Castle. So thorough was Collins's intelligence-gathering network that he regularly forwarded RIC messages, decoded, to IRA brigade intelligence officers before many RIC inspectors had decoded their despatches. Here, a copy of the RIC's most recent cipher key was found in MacSwiney's desk, though the RIC in Cork had not yet received the code.[17]

Muriel MacSwiney was in the County Cork seaside town of Youghal when word reached her the following morning of her husband's arrest. "What could I do?" she said later. "There was nobody to mind the baby except myself. I had nobody to take her except strangers and she would not go with them. My sister-in-law came down to take care of the baby."[18]

Muriel returned to Cork two days later, and caught the first glimpse she had had of her husband for many weeks, as he sat in the middle of a military lorry surrounded by soldiers, en route to his trial. He was the only prisoner in the vehicle, his protest by hunger strike now more than four days old. "I think that was one of the worst times for me," she stated. "From the morning that I heard my husband was on hunger strike, I believed that he would die. I felt terribly on that day when I saw him, because I knew he was in pain, and it was an awful thing that I could not give him anything to eat."[19]

The Dublin Castle administration became directly involved in the drafting of the government's explanation of the events surrounding MacSwiney's arrest and imprisonment. On 25 August, Sir John Anderson, principal Under Secretary at Dublin Castle, forwarded to the cabinet a statement for their consideration; the memorandum rebutted press reports that the lord mayor had been arrested while presiding over a Republican arbitration court. The fact that Anderson was not willing to criticise the arbitration court openly is noteworthy, and may have been due in particular to the fact that the court session involved the Prudential Insurance Company of London as the plaintiff. Such was the legitimacy the Republican courts had by this stage garnered in the eyes of establishment interests. In Anderson's view, the press accounts in question

> conveyed a false and misleading impression that military authorities originally set out to arrest organisers of a peaceful, if unlawful, Sinn Féin arbitration court, presided over by the Lord Mayor, but that on finding from nature of business before the court it was conceivable to proceed under that lead, they charged him instead with offences of a technical nature which had little or no connection with the purpose of the meeting ... The facts are that in this instance no interference with a Sinn Féin arbitration court was premeditated or contemplated by the authorities. Police and military forces visited City Hall because it had come to their knowledge that persons holding important positions of command in Cork brigade unit of the Republican Army had received "official" summons to attend a meeting in City Hall at that date and time. It was with a view to making investigations as to the nature of these proceedings that the ... persons arrested and documents seized ... A meeting of Commandants of Cork Brigade ... Republican Army was being held either simultaneously or under cover of an arbitration court. These documents also showed the nature of the activities of the Republican Army.[20]

The statement from the Irish secretariat made no effort to deny that a Sinn Féin court was sitting. By emphasising that MacSwiney had been arrested for reasons other than participation in a peaceful, though unlawful, arbitration court, Dublin Castle sought to deny the charge that the government itself had acted as an agent of lawlessness. At all events, the arrest of the lord mayor of Cork soon appeared to have a more single-minded objective.

The government's decision to arrest, court-martial, and in the end imprison MacSwiney was a matter of controversy in the pages of the British press. Stephen Gwynn, writing from

Ireland for the London *Observer*, offered this viewpoint: "To possess a police cipher may be illegal; but the police are doing things so strange that it is not unjustifiable to seek means to be informed as to what orders they are getting. Are the acts of reprisal, for instance the burning of creameries, undertaken by the police of their own motion? An Irish representative is entitled to ascertain."[21] In a lead article a few weeks later, the *Observer* argued that MacSwiney's continued imprisonment was a source of encouragement for Sinn Féin in Ireland and abroad and held that "the Lord Mayor of Cork ought to have been released ... But he lingers into a sixth week, to lengthen the anti-British feeling."[22]

Defending the basis on which the lord mayor of Cork had been arrested, without any specific charges having been brought initially, also proved a contentious issue for the government in the House of Commons. The attorney general for Ireland, James Gordon, explained when questioned as to what statute had actually been used that "MacSwiney and the others knew perfectly well the charge on which they were arrested, and that it was at the instance of the competent military authority."[23] In the end, the lord mayor was charged under Regulation 224 of the Defence of the Realm Act of having a cipher under his control, and under Regulation 27 for having in his possession two documents, the publication of which "would be likely to cause disaffection to his Majesty".[24]

Britain had begun to adopt a harder line in Ireland by August 1920, and it is possible that the government wanted to make an example of MacSwiney, due to the high military and political posts he held in the Republican movement. Nonetheless, "Lloyd George made anxious inquiries of the Castle executive as to the possible outcome were MacSwiney released."[25] He was not, however, encouraged by the answer.

The British authorities may also have hoped to arrest Terence MacSwiney on charges more serious than the possession of a police cipher code. In an account given after her brother's death, Mary MacSwiney described an incident that occurred earlier on the day of his arrest.

> On the night that my brother was arrested ... a letter came to my house addressed to Lord Mayor MacSwiney or Miss Mary

MacSwiney. I opened it and found it to be an anonymous letter calling on my brother to have a certain spy in Kilkenny shot. They gave his name and address. They gave him the names of the Irish Volunteers whom they said had been arrested by him. They gave him particulars as to those he had spied on and they said should be shot immediately. I put that letter in the fire. I knew perfectly well from the experience which others of my friends had had, that it was an English agent's letter and that it probably preceded a raid. That night at 7 o'clock my brother was arrested. They searched the City Hall, probably for that letter, until 10 o'clock. At half past 11 they came to my house and spent 3 hours looking for that letter. They did not find it. If they had found that paper this is what would have happened. One of their men would have been sent to shoot the policeman and my brother would have been accused of getting that man murdered and would have been sentenced on that charge and probably hanged.[26]

Whether or not the crown's representatives would have gone so far as to permit the killing of a member of the RIC by a member of the British military, or to encourage such a killing by the IRA in order to build a case against the lord mayor of Cork, it is clear that the British greatly desired his arrest and conviction. Terence MacSwiney had shown himself to be a particularly dangerous man in the eyes of the British government. His multiplicity of Republican activities, together with the platform he occupied as lord mayor of Cork, had contributed greatly to the breakdown of the king's writ in Cork and in the country at large, which was now a hotbed of rebellion. In July the IRA had assassinated the divisional commander of the RIC, Colonel Smyth, in a private club in Cork city, following published accounts of his attempts to incite the police in Munster into reprisals against the local population. The blame for this action was laid at MacSwiney's door.[27]

On 16 August, the court-martial of Terence MacSwiney began, presided over by a Lieutenant Colonel James. In all, four charges were proferred against him, including the possession of a numerical cipher of the type issued to the RIC. MacSwiney's inaugural speech as lord mayor of Cork was also used against him, and a copy of it introduced into the record. Another document, which was in fact an amended version of a resolution adopted by the Cork Corporation proclaiming allegiance to Dáil Éireann, was presented against MacSwiney as "likely to cause disaffection to His Majesty".[28]

Evidence characterised by the prosecution as "typewritten notes by the Lord Mayor for a speech" was in fact the text of MacSwiney's speech given in the aftermath of MacCurtain's murder, and an expression of the Cork Corporation's determination not to be intimidated by any such future acts of official terror.

> Our first duty is to answer the threat in the only fitting manner by showing ourselves unterrified, cool, and inflexible for the fulfilment of our purpose – the establishment of the independence and integrity of our country, the peace and happiness of the Irish Republic. To that end I am here. If the present aggravated persecution by our enemies could stop us voluntarily in the normal discharge of our duties it would help them materially in their campaign to overthrow the Irish Republic now established and functioning according to law ... Facing our enemy we must declare an attitude simply. We see in their regime a thing of evil incarnate. With it there can be no parley, no more than there can be a truce with the powers of Hell. This is our simple resolution – we ask for no mercy and we will make no compromise."[29]

As he entered the barracks where his court-martial was to be held, Muriel MacSwiney was able to communicate briefly with her husband in Irish, a medium they would also use during breaks in the proceedings. He told her that he would be sentenced and that in all likelihood would be deported to England, while the others arrested with him would probably be released. "But of course, he was pleased with that," Muriel MacSwiney recalled. "He wanted to suffer for everybody else's wrongs."[30] Clearly Terence MacSwiney's determination to die heroically was not unknown to her. "I always knew what my husband's motives and intentions were," she remarked later in the United States. "He had no other idea but to die for his country if need be."[31]

As the charges against him were proferred, MacSwiney sat in an armchair between two armed soldiers. Weakened already from the effects of his hunger strike, now in its fifth day, he received moral support from an audience which in addition to Muriel, included his sister Mary, Fr Dominic O'Connor, who would serve as his personal chaplain for the duration of his protest, and Donal O'Callaghan, chairman of the Cork County Council and deputy mayor of Cork. When called to answer whether he was represented by counsel, the lord mayor answered, giving his view of the proceedings: "The position is that I am Lord Mayor of Cork and Chief Magistrate of this City. And I declare this court illegal and that those who take part in it are liable to arrest under the laws of the Irish Republic."[32]

The military prosecutor, Captain Glover, told the court that the gravity of the charges brought against MacSwiney were exacerbated by the position "held by the accused". He went on to outline the crown's case against the lord mayor. The *Cork Examiner* reported:

> He proceeded that on August 12th a party of military, with officers in charge, went to the City Hall, arriving there between 7:30 and 8 P.M. They surrounded the Hall, and an officer would give evidence that he went to the back of the Hall, and there climbed a wall with a private. When this officer got over that wall he saw eleven men coming out of the back door of the Hall. These men went over into a hut – a workshop – and the officer, going there, put a guard over them. One of this guard – a private – said three or four of them were tearing up papers, and one of these men was the accused. This fact was reported to the officer, who came and put accused and other two men away from the others. A private searched the hut, and found behind the corrugated iron, near the place where the accused was standing, an envelope, addressed to the Commandant First Cork Battalion, IRA ... Shortly after that accused and other two men were put under arrest and brought to Victoria Barracks ... After that another party of military went to City Hall and completed the search. The officer in charge of that party went to the Lord Mayor's room. It was locked, but he got it open. A roll top desk in that room was rolled down, but not locked, and in that desk there were found the papers which were the subject matters of the four charges ... Other documents in the desk were letters addressed to the Lord Mayor, Mr. Terence MacSwiney; or to Mr. Terence MacSwiney, Lord Mayor ... The cipher was that used by

officers of R.I.C. The papers found behind the corrugated iron included a telegram form, and written on the back of it were messages in cipher, which had only then been sent out actually the day before by the police."[33]

Owing to the fact that there were no RIC members present when the police cipher was removed from MacSwiney's desk, the military at first did not recognise the importance of this code. "The key for the code," was also, according to Captain Glover, found "in the Lord Mayor's desk". The text of the cipher message which MacSwiney was accused of possessing dealt with a communication marked as designated for "Cotter", the telegraph address in Dublin for the inspector general of the RIC. The message stated, "Re: cipher – yesterday the Admiral can do nothing till he knows the number of prisoners, whether hunger strikers, number of escort, date and place of embarkation and destination." It was signed by County Inspector Maunsell in Cork.[34]

During Glover's questioning, MacSwiney remained entirely uncompromising. "The only thing relevant about a code is this," he said: "Any person in possession of such a code who is not a member of the Irish Republic is evidence of criminal conspiracy against the Irish Republic."[35] Soon after, rising weakly to his feet to make closing remarks, MacSwiney's contempt for the proceedings was no less evident than it had been at the outset: "Anything I have to say is not in defence ... You have got to realise, and will have to realise it before very long, that the Irish Republic is really existing. I want to remind you of the fact that the gravest offence that can be committed by any individual is an offence against the head of the state. The offence is only relatively less great when committed against the head of a city."[36] The lord mayor, in an effort to turn the tables on those who sought to imprison him, then proceeded adroitly to raise the issue of the murder of his predecessor by the agents of the British government:

> One of the documents seized is a resolution relating to our allegiance to the Government of the Republic. There was quite a similar document drawing attention to the verdict and inquest on my predecessor, in which the jury found a unanimous verdict

that the British government and its police were guilty of murder. And now it must be obvious to you that if that were an invention, it would be so grave a matter that it would be the chief charge today, even in this illegal court. But that document is put aside, and I am gratified to be here today, notwithstanding all its inconveniences and other annoyances, to have that brought out, because this action in putting that document aside is an admission, an assent to a plea of guilty on behalf of those who committed the murder.[37]

Pointing to MacCurtain's death in relation to his own situation, MacSwiney told the tribunal: "You must know that holding the office I do is absolutely grave for me, in view of the way my predecessor was sent to his death ... I cannot say ... but that the same will happen myself, at any moment."[38] The lord mayor also noted that among the documents seized from his files by the authorities were copies of correspondence in connection to his municipal duties, such as a letter he sent to Pope Benedict on the "occasion of the beatification of Oliver Plunkett," and a communication from the president of the Municipal Council of Paris seeking information from him on Cork harbour. Seized also were the business cards MacSwiney had received from visiting foreign journalists. The lord mayor concluded by stating that he asked "for no mercy."[39]

During the fifteen minutes in which the tribunal met in private to deliberate, MacSwiney sat and conversed with his wife in Irish. The president then returned and announced a finding that he was "not guilty on the first charge, and guilty on the second, third and fourth".[40] The following exchange then took place between the lord mayor and the president of the tribunal:

The Lord Mayor: I wish to state that I will put a limit to any term of imprisonment you may impose as a result of the action I will take. I have taken no food since Thursday, therefore I will be free in a month.
President: On sentence of imprisonment you will take no food?
Lord Mayor: I simply say that I have decided the terms of my detention whatever your government may do. I shall be free, alive or dead, within a month.[41]

A sentence of two years' imprisonment was then imposed on Terence MacSwiney. Thus had begun the battle of wills that would soon command worldwide attention, pitting a determined individual against the greatest empire of its time. Unlike the issues which would drive the IRA hunger strikers of six decades later, MacSwiney's protest was not about political status. Fundamentally, what he objected to was the right of a British court to pass judgment on him at all.

But why did MacSwiney choose to protest against British authority by sacrificing his life through the awful device of a hunger strike? Had he, in fact, willed himself to die as a martyr for the Republican cause long before his arrest in August 1920?

MacSwiney may have been driven to his second and fatal hunger strike by a feeling of guilt at not having been among those who "came out" in 1916. One views the extensive references in his literary works to the cleansing effects of sacrifice, reminiscent of the ideas of Patrick Pearse. When Pearse remarked during his own court-martial that "We have kept faith with the past and handed a tradition to the future," it was men such as MacSwiney who accepted the burden of this inheritance.

An insight into MacSwiney's feelings is provided by a letter he sent from Brixton prison to Cathal Brugha on 30 September 1920 – the thirty-ninth day of his hunger strike. In that emotional and affectionate letter to the Republican minister for defence, MacSwiney made plain his feeling that his sacrifice had a purpose:

> If I die I know the fruit will exceed the cost a thousand fold. The thought makes me happy. I thank God for it. Ah Cathal, the pain of Easter Week is properly dead at last.[42]

Brugha, like the other comrades named in MacSwiney's letter, would be dead within the next two years, casualties for the most part of a civil war the lord mayor would not live to see. MacSwiney's letter to him is the most important evidence tying the apparent "pain" caused him by his non-participation in the events of Easter Week to his subsequent action in waging a heroic hunger strike. A poem written by MacSwiney from his cell at Reading Gaol on 26 June 1916, entitled simply "A Prayer", had earlier expressed his regret at not having participated in the Easter Rising, and his desire to belatedly join his fallen comrades.

My soul, oh God, Thou has greatly blessed
With high baptism of desire
But, oh I pray the further test,
A boon, oh God, baptism of fire.
Behold me in my prison cell,
Not for the things I have essayed;
But that they charged me set - and well -
For one great deed for which I prayed.
Ah, let me pray, my enemies
Speak justly, if in this alone,
To this I set Life's energies,
To free my country from their throne.

My comrades, trusting me to death,
Called to me, 'ere they sank in strife.
God! then Thou mad'st Thy test of faith
The long-drawn agony of life.
Because I have endured the pain
Of waiting, while my comrades died,
Let me be swept in war's red rain
And friends and foes be justified.[43]

MacSwiney and MacCurtain were certainly not the only IRA leaders troubled by their inaction during Easter Week. Austin Stack, who served as minister for home affairs in the Republican government, and who had commanded the Irish Volunteers in Tralee during the Rising, suffered from the charge that he had taken no action to prevent Sir Roger Casement's capture by the British forces on Good Friday. Michael Collins's needling of Stack for his non-performance during Easter Week was a constant source of friction between the two, with Stack later emerging as one of Collin's most bitter critics for his support of the Anglo-Irish Treaty. According to Seán Ó Luing, at one meeting Collins, referring to a project undertaken by Stack in home affairs, caustically remarked: "I hope you won't make a mess of this the same as you did of the Casement landing."[44]

Others who had not "come out" in 1916, and who played prominent roles in the 1919-21 Anglo-Irish war, included Dan Breen and Sean Treacy. The two men were later responsible for the Volunteer attack against a party of RIC men at Soloheadbeg, County Tipperary on 21 January 1919, an event credited as the opening shot in the Anglo-Irish war. Speaking of himself and Treacy, Dan Breen stated that "we were both bitterly disappointed that the fighting had not extended to the County. We swore that should the fighting ever be resumed, we would be in the thick of it, no matter where it took place."[45]

MacSwiney's decision to go on hunger strike from the time of his arrest was a unilateral one. No sanction was sought or given by either the IRA's general headquarters or the Republican government. In his biography of Michael Collins, Piaras Béaslaí, a Republican propagandist who had published MacSwiney's essays in *Irish Freedom* some years earlier, contended that IRA general headquarters' position was that "while a hunger strike for treatment as a 'political prisoner' or 'prisoner of war', or for the redress of grievances, was sound policy, a hunger strike for release was inexpedient, as it must in the long run force the enemy to an extremity in which they could not consistently give way."[46]

The British government's decision in May 1920 to release twenty-seven IRA hunger strikers at Wormwood Scrubbs was influenced by a strike launched by Irish trade unions which paralysed a number of British-owned industries. That release, however, along with the success he had himself achieved in an earlier hunger strike, may have fuelled a belief on MacSwiney's part that his decision to refuse food would result in the British government once again backing down, especially in light of his public position as lord mayor of Cork, and successor to a mayor who had been murdered by the RIC.

However, as Béaslaí has noted, "In the case of MacSwiney the issue was knit, and the English Government took up the challenge."[47] Béaslaí was also direct in his criticism of what appeared to him to have been a precipitate action on the lord mayor's part.

I still think it was undesirable to have brought this thing to an issue, whose result was to kill the effectiveness of the hunger strike as a weapon. The world-wide sympathy which the heroic martyrdom of MacSwiney evoked was no doubt a valuable asset to Sinn Féin, but not a very tangible weapon in our warfare with the Black and Tans. The death of this brave and gifted man was undoubtedly a blow to the cause.[48]

MacSwiney's wife had not approved of her husband's first hunger strike. In a letter written to him after it had ended, she wrote: "Beloved, you took the only thing off my mind that was really troubling me, the hunger strike. You see, I never ever believed in it, which made things worse."[49] Muriel may have tried to intervene directly with Michael Collins to have her husband "ordered off" his hunger strike now. MacSwiney's colleague, Tomás Ó Ceallaigh, insisted in the years after the lord mayor's death that Collins had in fact so acted.[50] Other contemporaries have argued that Collins could not have done so, since MacSwiney was not a member of the IRB, but Collins was the leader of the IRA and MacSwiney's military superior. Collins's attitude to the use of the hunger strike as a device for protest certainly suggests that, while he grew in awe of his fellow Corkman's tremendous courage, he viewed the protest as an unnecessary loss of life, particularly in light of MacSwiney's position in the movement and his role as lord mayor of Cork.

In the final analysis, Terence MacSwiney threw his life at the British government wilfully. The British government showed itself willing to match him: there would be no further surrender to Republican hunger strikes.

Notes
1. Moirin Chavasse, *Terence MacSwiney* (Dublin 1961) p. 141.
2. Testimony of Muriel MacSwiney before the US Commission on Conditions in Ireland, published in *The Nation*, p. 752.
3. Ibid.
4. Eithne MacSwiney to Etienette Beuque, 21 January 1928, MacSwiney Collection, UCD Archives, P48c/61.
5. Florence O'Donoghue, *No Other Law* (Dublin 1954) p. 89.
6. Ibid.
7. Ibid. pp 87-88.

8. Ibid.
9. Ibid. p. 92
10. Piaras Béaslaí, *Michael Collins and the Making of a New Ireland* (Dublin 1927) vol. II, p. 73.
11. Margery Forester, *Michael Collins: The Lost Leader* (London 1971) p. 162
12. O'Donoghue, *No Other Law*, p. 89.
13. Ibid.
14. Michael Collins to Art O'Brien, 9 October 1920, SPO/Dáil Éireann Files.
15. Ibid.
16. See T. Ryle Dwyer, *Michael Collins* (Cork 1990) p. 92.
17. Kenneth Griffith and Timothy O'Grady, *Curious Journey* (London 1982) p. 138
18. Testimony of Muriel MacSwiney before the US Commission on Conditions in Ireland, published in *The Nation*, 20 December 1920, p. 753.
19. Ibid.
20. Draft of statement to cabinet from Sir John Anderson, 25 August 1920, CO 904/168, pp. 14-16.
21. *Observer* (London) 28 August 1920.
22. Ibid. 19 September 1920.
23. *Cork Examiner*, 18 August 1920, as cited in MacSwiney Collection, 48b/452.
24. Ibid.
25. Forester, *Michael Collins: The Lost Leader*, p. 162.
26. Remarks of Mary MacSwiney, New Orleans, LA, 25 February 1921, as published by the American Association for Recognition of Irish Republic, New Orleans Chapter.
27. C. J. Street, *The British Administration of Ireland 1920*, (New York 1920) p. 218.
28. *Cork Examiner*, 18 August 1920.
29. MacSwiney's inaugural address to Cork Corporation, Cork Municipal Archives.
30. Testimony of Muriel MacSwiney before the US Commission on Conditions in Ireland, from *The Nation*, p. 752.
31. Ibid.
32. *Cork Examiner*, 18 August 1920.
33. Ibid.
34. Ibid.
35. Ibid.
36. Ibid.
37. Ibid.

38. Ibid.
39. Ibid.
40. Ibid.
41. Ibid.
42. Terence MacSwiney to Cathal Brugha, 30 September 1920, MacSwiney Collection, P48b/416.
43. MacSwiney Collection, Cork Municipal Archives.
44. Taylor, *Michael Collins: The Big Fellow*, p. 108.
45. Dan Breen, *My Fight For Irish Freedom* (Dublin 1981) p. 27.
46. Piaras Béaslaí, *Michael Collins*, vol. II, p. 54.
47. Ibid.
48. Ibid.
49. Muriel MacSwiney to Terence MacSwiney, undated letter from 1918, MacSwiney Collection, P48b/114.
50. Tomás Ó Ceallaigh to Brian O'Higgins, 7 December 1943, MacSwiney Collection, P48c/245.

Chapter VI
Diary of a Hunger Strike

IN THE EARLY hours of 18 August, Lord Mayor Terence
MacSwiney was placed on board a British naval sloop
bound for South Wales. From there the prisoner was sent
by train to London, arriving there at 4 a.m. on Wednesday
morning. The journey proved a strenuous one for a man who
had already been on hunger strike for almost a week.[1]

His chaplain, Fr Dominic O'Connor, OFM, CAP,
described him as "wan, wasted, and haggard-looking".[2] He
entered the gates of Brixton Prison, already in a weakened
physical condition, as Prisoner No. 6794, and as early as 30
August, reports were being despatched to the *Irish World* and
American Industrial Liberator in the United States stating
that MacSwiney was "not expected to survive the night". The
papers cited a physician's verdict that "The Lord Mayor
could live but a few hours."[3]

At Brixton he was placed in a large unoccupied hospital
ward containing seven beds, several large windows and a
fireplace. The bed upon which the lord mayor lay was in the
left-hand corner of the big room. He was not the first Irish
patriot from that period to occupy the ward; Sir Roger
Casement had also been confined there during the weeks
before his trial.

His family and friends were allowed to visit on an
unrestricted basis at first. Muriel, accompanied by Fr
Dominic, visited him on the Friday following his arrival.

Throughout his confinement at Brixton, appetising foods
were brought at regular intervals to his room by the prison
staff. The assumption, held by some who had never endured
a protracted fast, that the desire for food eventually left the
protester, was rebutted by MacSwiney himself. At one stage
he candidly admitted to Fr Dominic that he would "give
£1,000 pounds for a cup of tea".[4]

MacSwiney wanted to stay alive for as long as possible. He did so both out of a hope that the British government might reverse itself, and failing that, out of a desire to ensure that his sacrifice might be prolonged so as to draw world attention to the Irish cause. He preserved his energy by remaining in bed, but the bed-sores he developed after weeks on hunger strike proved a major source of pain. Eventually, he reached the stage where the bedsheet touching his body was agonising. He became unable to bend his knees as the flesh wasted from his joints.[5] Fr Dominic,* his almost constant companion at Brixton, placed MacSwiney's agony in context in an essay written after his death: "Try and conceive the pain you suffer in your shoulder and back, and in your knees, the stiff numbing pain in the calves of your legs, the agony in your heels, instep and ankles if you remain for even a quarter of an hour outstretched on your back."[6]

A first-hand account of the manner in which the body consumes itself in search of nourishment during starvation is provided by Ernie O'Malley, the IRA guerrilla leader who joined in a hunger strike at Kilmainham Gaol in 1923 in a protest against the policies of the Free State government. O'Malley's own hunger strike lasted forty-one days.

> The unimportant tissues, seemingly, are first affected; the unimportant muscles waste, then more vital organs are attacked, memory and sight impaired. My people sent the family doctor in to see me ... "When muscle wastes too much it cannot repair," he said. "Your back and thigh muscles are far gone now."[7]

In Brixton Fr Dominic was granted access to the facilities

---

*Fr Dominic O'Connor had previous experience as a chaplain during an armed conflict. His first call during wartime came as a chaplain to the British forces in Greece during the Great War. Upon his return in 1918 to his native Cork, during the midst of the anti-conscription campaign, he was appointed by Tomás MacCurtain as chaplain to the Cork city brigade of the Volunteers, soon to become the Irish Republican Army. From there, Fr Dominic proceeded to appoint battalion chaplains for the Volunteers in Cork, and came to know Terence MacSwiney well. One of the first individuals to arrive at Tomás MacCurtain's home following his murder, he remained as chaplain for the IRA in Cork, and upon the commencement of Terence MacSwiney's hunger strike he became his "spiritual director". In all these actions, the priest acted with the permission of his superiors in the Capuchin Order - one that had become closely identified with the Volunteers since the Easter Rising. He died as a result of an automobile accident in the United States in 1944.

he needed by the bishop of Southwark, Dr Amigo, who also granted him permission to say mass in MacSwiney's prison ward. Early in his protest, Fr Dominic anointed the lord mayor with the last rites of the Catholic Church. The priest recalled that MacSwiney had requested this "so that all his thoughts might be on God and his preparations for death, and so that thoughts or rumours of release might not spoil his preparation".[8]

MacSwiney can have had few worries about his wife's and daughter's financial well-being. Even though his personal income was limited to his pay from Dáil Éireann as an organiser for the Irish Volunteers, he had married the daughter of one of the wealthiest families in Cork city. In an interview given in New York city during the hunger strike, his brother Peter surmised that Terry was able to risk death by hunger strike secure in the knowledge that his wife and daughter would be provided for. "Muriel MacSwiney is a wealthy woman," he told one reporter. "She is the daughter of one of Cork's leading businessmen and will never know want."[9] In terms of a bank balance in his own name, however, MacSwiney's resources were modest. As he entered his fourth week without food, on 8 September a letter from the manager of the Munster and Leinster Bank in Cork city to Muriel MacSwiney indicated that "the credit of the Right Honorable Terence MacSwiney at this office is £51.12s.4d".[10]

As MacSwiney's hunger strike continued, it provoked numerous editorials and a voluminous correspondence in the pages of the British press. Foreign correspondants also covered the story. An analysis from London early in September, by the correspondant of the French journal *Le Populaire*, offered a concise view of what was at stake: "The situation is tragic. The drama is poignant. Two wills confront each other. One is in prison. The other is in a palace. Which will be the stronger?"[11] A reporter for London's *Daily News* noted the considerable interest which the lord mayor's hunger strike had engendered in the pages of the European press:

> One of the first things that strikes the average Englishman abroad is the fact that the case of the Lord Mayor of Cork seems to be exciting even greater interest in the foreign press than in

our own ... In Paris and Rome, most of the papers treat the case as the most important of the news items, and some of the French papers are running it as the daily feature. This case, together with the treatment of Ireland generally, is undoubtedly reviving on the Continent something of the feeling against England and the English during the Boer War, and it is hard to understand why the Prime Minister who is supposed to live with his ear to the ground, has not come back ready to realise that the present policy of repression in Ireland is doing not a little to injure British and French unity.[12]

During MacSwiney's hunger strike, the *Chicago Tribune's* editorial page argued that "The Irish question seriously involves the U.S. and the case of MacSwiney is the Irish question at its highest point of drama."[13] Similarly, the *Neue Frie Presse* wrote that "If MacSwiney dies, if this modern Winkelried diverts all arrows of racial hatred to his own heart, the Lord Mayor of Cork will, perhaps, be more powerful in his death than the powerful Prime Minister or the King of England.[14]

The Irish Self-Determination League, the pro-Sinn Féin group in Britain, worked to supply the Republican version of events to the media. "I may say," Art O'Brien informed Michael Collins in a memo of 25 August, "that both the *Independent* and the *Freeman*, the Press Associations and the American Press Agencies are kept constantly supplied with news ... Yesterday, for instance, messengers were sent down to these on six occasions with different reports and news items."[15] Terence MacSwiney's hunger strike was already providing a major source of international propaganda for the Republican cause.

In his native Cork, MacSwiney's protest led the Gaelic Athletic Association to abandon all its competitive fixtures whether inside or outside the county, as a gesture of solidarity with him.

If he could not get MacSwiney to end his protest, at first Michael Collins considered other means for getting him out of prison alive. In a 26 August memo to Art O'Brien, under the subject heading of "Lord Mayor of Cork", an escape attempt is apparently what Collins was alluding to:

As already indicated to you, men have gone across last night, and three others went this morning. You will get our people together – that is to say —, yourself, and mobilise every possible bit of assistance that can be secured in London. One man who accompanies the Cork men is already known to you, and to —. He will be their guide.[16]

Collins appears to have believed that, considering MacSwiney's deteriorating condition, if an escape attempt were to be made, it had to occur soon. The names of some of those who were blanked out in Collins's communication with O'Brien are revealed in his response to his chief:

Re your special memo on the 26th instant re the Lord Mayor of Cork. Murray arrived here yesterday, and Fitz last night. I am wondering if you had sent me any previous note on this matter which had gone astray. — gave me a note from you, the contents of which seemed to suggest that you had sent some previous memo. The note of introduction which — brought and the special memo of the 26th instant, are the only news that I had from you. Everything possible is being done here. — last night, and preliminary arrangements were made. I will let you know how things are proceeding later.[17]

But while such an undertaking may have been discussed in some form between Collins and his subordinates in England, an attempt to free MacSwiney never materialised.

Consideration was clearly given in the contact between Collins and O'Brien to maximising the propaganda value of MacSwiney's death, Collins's own feelings on the subject of hunger strikes notwithstanding. Of particular interest to O'Brien in a memo to Collins on 28 August was the prospect of making public opinion more aware of the use of questionable evidence against MacSwiney by the British government at the court-martial.

Assuming that the English Government allow him to die in prison there will be an inquest. I believe that in the case of the prisoner dying in prison the rules governing the inquest are very strict and give a great deal of power to the Government. I understand that it is also possible in certain circumstances that the relatives of the prisoner should be represented by a solicitor, and that this solicitor may claim the right of calling witnesses and cross examining them. Assuming that this position arises, it would probably be advisable that all details of evidence given at the Court Martial in Cork should be available. I think it would be advisable that it should be procured at once, and sent over here.[18]

A week later O'Brien told Collins, apparently in reference to the individual who had been sent over to London, that he was "in touch with – and his friends ... Some of them are a bit restless." O'Brien also described his first visit to MacSwiney:

> I was very much alarmed at his appearance. What impressed me most, however, was the great contrast between his practically lifeless body and the mind so thoroughly alive and alert, as shown by the expression in his eyes and face. I only stayed with him two minutes. He was too weak for conversation. One thing he said however, which was of note is, "In another week this will be finished one way or another." It seems extraordinary that he should have hoped of lasting another week. This is, of course, for your own information.[19]

The lord mayor, of course, would endure for an additional eight weeks, but with the passage of the days, the veiled discussions of escape attempts between Collins and O'Brien ceased. Instead their talk turned to the making of funeral preparations and the sending of an Irish Volunteer honour guard. On 14 September, Collins wrote to O'Brien and told him that "in the event of his death we shall, of course, send a Guard of Honour. The Volunteers forming the Guard would not be armed." Noting "some hitch" which prevented him from writing at greater length, Collins went on to ask O'Brien to "please tell the men for the same reason I was unable to send them a reply today, but it will go tomorrow without fail".[20]

By the second week of MacSwiney's hunger strike, expressions of concern from Irish sources loyal to the crown began to mount. Virtually all of them warned of the negative outcome that would be provoked by the lord mayor's death. In retrospect, it seems that many of the alternatives offered would have allowed the government both to save face and to avert the final outcome.

On 20 August 1920, John Healy Scott, the high sheriff of Cork, wrote to home secretary Shortt, whom he had served as an aide during the latter's service as Irish chief secretary. While describing MacSwiney as a "very obstinate man", he argued that "it would be calamitous if anything happened to him while on hunger strike".[21] Four days later, Scott made the same observation to King George V. He also offered a way out of the impasse by suggesting that the government accept a request from him in his role as high sheriff of Cork to release MacSwiney for hospital treatment. He went so far as to provide a draft announcement for use by the Coalition: "In compliance with a request contained in a petition forwarded by the High Sheriff of Cork on behalf of certain loyal citizens, the Home Secretary has been pleased to issue an order that Mr MacSwiney be given hospital treatment outside of Brixton Prison at present." Scott noted that he had taken his post as high sheriff at the "pressing request of the Lord Lieutenant when it was not possible to get a citizen to take the office, or run the risk of taking it". It was his contention that the British government, by showing leniency toward MacSwiney at the request of the loyalists of Cork, would have the effect of "showing that we have some influence and that our advice may be valued".[22]

A similar suggestion came to the government from the former Irish Party MP A.M. Sullivan in a letter of 26 August, in which he recommended acceptance of a proposed resolution favouring MacSwiney's release from "a really representative meeting of the men who should be governing Ireland". Under his proposal the government would release MacSwiney "subject to re-arrest".[23]

By far the most important correspondence received by the cabinet seeking leniency for MacSwiney was that forwarded on the monarch's behalf by his private secretary, Lord Stamfordham. The issue became a major source of friction between the king and his government, and another manifestation of the king's displeasure with the conduct of the government's Irish policy. Previously, in questioning the efficacy of their policy of coercion and reprisals, the king asked the chief secretary for Ireland "If this policy of reprisals is to be continued, and if so where will it lead ... ?"[24]

The weekly *Nation* argued, somewhat tongue in cheek, given its usually anti-monarchical stance, that MacSwiney's case represented an occasion for the monarch to vindicate his constitutional right and protest the growing autocracy of the cabinet.[25] Appeals to King George V by southern Unionists and Catholic moderates seeking leniency for MacSwiney did, in fact, gain the monarch's attention. The question as to whether the king could intervene through the use of his prerogative erupted as a major issue in the MacSwiney case by the end of August. On 24 August, George V received a joint plea from the Irish Peace Conference, a group of moderate southern Unionists that included Sir Horace Plunkett and Lord Monteagle, amongst others, to "most respectfully implore Your Majesty by the exercise of your Royal prerogative to order forthwith the release of the Lord Mayor of Cork, now lying at the point of death in Brixton Gaol. We base our prayer in circumstances of unparalleled national emergency upon the highest grounds of all public policy, the necessity of a great act of conciliation to open the path to peace which we are seeking to achieve, domestic peace in Ireland and international peace between Ireland and Great Britain. We submit that this great object transcends in importance any question of mere administrative principle."[26]

The bulk of the correspondence exchanged between George V and the cabinet on the MacSwiney matter occurred during Lloyd George's holiday in Lucerne. In his stead, Arthur Balfour was left to handle matters in the cabinet. On 25 August, in a statement issued from Lucerne in response to appeals for the lord mayor's release, Lloyd George stated: "If the Cabinet departed from its decision a complete breakdown of the whole machinery of law and government in Ireland inevitably followed. Whatsoever the consequences, we cannot take the responsibility."[27] But on the same day a telegram from the king to Balfour read: "King is seriously perturbed by newspaper reports of grave condition of affairs in Ireland and asks whether the government is considering any fresh measures or change in their policy to cope with a situation which seems to become worse daily."[28]

Two days later came a handwritten letter from Balfour to the king. Balfour expressed his "regret that your Majesty has not been kept adequately informed about the case of the Lord Mayor of Cork now causing so much excitement".[29] Balfour goes on to describe the situation in Ireland as the cabinet saw it.

> The South and West of Ireland is the scene of a deliberate and skilfully organised scheme of rebellion. This would have no chance of success if the machinery of the government including the Royal Irish Constabulary had been maintained in a thoroughly efficient state. The result has been that the machinery of the law became paralysed. Judges, magistrates and jurymen were unable to carry out their duties and as the King's courts no longer functioned, the Sinn Féin Courts began to take their place. Substitution of Military Courts, which could not be intimidated, for Civil Courts which could, was partial remedy for this state of affairs, and the Revolutionary Party, being thus foiled in their efforts to prevent sentence being passed, tried to prevent them from being effectually carried out by employing the device of the hunger strike. The Cabinet many weeks ago resolved that they would not permit justice to be defeated by the threat of suicide, and the penalty announced by the Prime Minister in reference to the Lord Mayor of Cork is merely application to a particular case of the general principle deliberately adopted by His Majesty's Government. Mr. Balfour ventures to add this further observation re the Lord Mayor. It is stated quite truly that he was convicted of no offence more serious than that of having in his possession a secret police code. Even if this were a crime as trivial as it seems, it does not justify his deliberate attempt to impede by hunger strike the operation of the law ... Whether the Lord Mayor of Cork shares with other members of the Sinn Féin Party the guilt of organised assassination Mr. Balfour does not know.[30]

Stamfordham responded on the king's behalf immediately, pointing out that George V's request had not been met. "The King assumed from your telegram that you are inclined to discount such representations as mere opinions of an unimportant section of the public, ill-informed about political affairs, but there is no disguising the fact that even among the educated public there is an idea that the Sovereign, even in extreme cases, should exercise his authority." Reminding Balfour of the actions taken by his own colleagues vis-à-vis the king a decade earlier in their opposition to Home Rule for Ireland, Stamfordham reported that "His Majesty's mind goes back to 1911 and he remembers the exhortations of many of the leading representatives of the unionist opposition to exert His Royal Powers and to giving guarantees to his government for the creation of peers."[31]

A private correspondence between Stamfordham and J.C. Davidson, a key legal advisor to the cabinet who had apparently taken it upon himself to apprise the king of what he saw as the folly of the government's policy in the MacSwiney case, sheds greater light on the controversy. Davidson was the regular recipient for the cabinet of the daily reports "forwarded from Brixton Prison" on MacSwiney's medical condition. In a 28 August letter to Davidson from Balmoral Castle, Stamfordham noted that he was "amused at the P.M. at Lucerne out of touch with what was being done. ... Was there ever such a method of Government as now!" he exclaimed.[32] The most significant statement in Stamfordham's letter concerned the king's differing views from his government's on the MacSwiney matter:

> The King feels that the probable results arising from MacSwiney's death will be far more serious and far reaching than if he were taken out of prison, moved into a private house, where his wife could be with him but left under strict surveillance so that he could not escape and return to Ireland.[33]

The king's private secretary also noted George V's awareness of the arguments advanced by General Macready and Chief Secretary for Ireland Greenwood that the lord mayor's release would exacerbate the situation in Ireland by encouraging the revolutionaries and worsening the police morale. "But if MacSwiney dies," he argued, "the trouble will probably not be confined to Ireland." He acknowledged that the volume and range of the letters of protest at the government's policy received by the king had had an impact on the monarch's views. "But you cannot," Stamfordham continued, "get away from the fact that a considerable and weighty part of the public are for release." He then mentioned correspondence containing alternative policies by which the government could save face, including those submitted by Horace Plunkett, C.P. Scott, publisher of the *Manchester Guardian*, Lord Dunraven, and other leading British and Irish public figures of moderate bent. Stamfordham sums the situation up neatly:"The King and A.J.B. [Balfour] are at issue because H.M. merely asks that the government should remind the public that the King cannot exercise his prerogative except on ministerial advice. A.J.B. argues that nobody but ignoramuses wish he could and it would be a mistake to raise the question."[34]

On 27 August the *Manchester Guardian* reported that "The King, it would appear, was prepared to exercise his prerogative of clemency, but was unable to secure the assent of the Government, and has not felt himself justified, under the Constitution, in acting without it."[35] The British Press Association also reported on that day that "The view in government quarters is that the evidence vs. the Lord Mayor of Cork is too grave to justify his release merely because he declines food, and that the matter of bearing or increasing the penalty is in his own hands." The report went on to state that "The appeal to which the King took action ... and to which sympathetic acknowledgement had already been forwarded by Lord Stamfordham, the King's Private Secretary ... [who] said it would receive immediate and careful attention."[36]

Balfour finally complied with the king's wishes on 28 August and publicly released this comment to the press:

> You ask me what is the constitutional practice with regard to the exercise by the Sovereign of the prerogative of mercy. The practice is quite clear and is in accordance with accepted constitutional principles. The prerogative is exercised on the advice of Ministers. For that advice, they alone are responsible. If it be mistaken, they alone are to blame. To them, therefore, and only to them does it seem proper to address censure or praise, encouragement or remonstrance.[37]

Nonetheless, the question of royal intervention in some form persisted, apparently with the backing of Stamfordham, whether out of a desire to change the government's approach towards MacSwiney or to at least seek a way to distance the monarch as much as possible from the policy the coalition had chosen to pursue. On 31 August 1920, Stamfordham forwarded a draft reply to Balfour which was to be sent under the queen's name in answer to a plea received from the Society of Friends in Manchester. The draft stated:

> Her Majesty cannot express an opinion on merits of dispute, but in any political controversy human life should not be sacrificed on either side. Therefore as a woman she hopes King's Ministers who have the power and are humane men may see their way to spare Ireland from additional sorrow."[38]

In his covering note to Balfour, Stamfordham added the caveat that "Her Majesty would propose to send this reply to Manchester, but would not if it would embarrass the government."[39] The government's reply, however, was swift and predictably negative. Worthington Evans, answering for Balfour on the following day, emphasised that

> The Queen cannot express an opinion on the specific point raised by the Society of Friends, which raises political and administrative questions of great difficulty. Accordingly, the government suggested that the Queen's reply should centre on a general comment, that "Her most earnest desire is to see peace restored and harmony prevail in all parts of the United Kingdom and among all classes of the population'"[40]

Stamfordham would himself take the opportunity of issuing a response stating the king's position on the MacSwiney matter to be the definitive response for public consumption.

Despite the continued hard line taken by the government, both publicly and in communications with the monarch, within the cabinet itself the seriousness of the threat posed to the government's Irish policy by MacSwiney's hunger strike was evident. The minutes of a cabinet meeting held on the evening of 25 August, with Balfour and Churchill in attendance, indicate how serious the situation had become. Home Secretary Edward Shortt explained that there was a growing demand on all sides for MacSwiney to be released from Brixton Prison, "and practically the whole press took this line".[41]

At the session, Sir Ernley Blackwell stated that "there was

a very distinct line of demarcation in the public mind between a political and criminal prisoner". He went on to state his view as to the futility of the government's attempting "to apply the Cat and Mouse Act in this case as MacSwiney had stated quite definitely that he would only begin to eat again in receipt of a statement in writing that he would be unconditionally released."[42] He implied that MacSwiney's deteriorating condition necessitated a change in the government's response, but with the late arrival of Winston Churchill at the meeting, any inclination on the cabinet's part to reverse its course evaporated. The lack of representation from the Irish executive was cited in the minutes as the reason for their inability to make any such revision. At the same time, minutes for the meeting, written by Davidson, indicated that the prospect of a change had been contemplated: "It was decided that if General Macready expressed strong views against his release then the Cabinet decision should stand."[43] Davidson's record of the meeting would only be circulated to Balfour and Shortt. Macready, in fact, would make his opposition known.

The government's refusal to compromise in MacSwiney's case was exacerbated by the increase in the number of attacks against the crown forces in Ireland. The report to the cabinet's Irish Situation Committee by the British military command, for the week ending 30 August 1920, stated that "The number of serious outrages committed during the week again shows a large increase, the total figures being 192 as compared with 140 for the previous week." The report also noted that "the most noticeable feature of the week's lawlessness was the increase in the number of raids for arms which rose from 59 to 110".[44]

On 26 August, the home office received the opinion of medical specialists who confirmed that MacSwiney's condition was worsening but recommended against force feeding at that time.[47] Two days earlier it had been confirmed that the lord mayor was suffering from tuberculosis. The government was kept well-informed about MacSwiney's condition.

Although recognising the threat posed by MacSwiney's hunger strike, the British government refused to bend. In its view, the lord mayor of Cork was a criminal convict who was inflicting harm upon himself of his own free will, and thus did not deserve any leniency. A cable from the cabinet to George V on 26 August reiterated this position, basing it on the advice of the Irish Administration at Dublin Castle: "Mr. Secretary Shortt deeply regrets that the decision of the Cabinet must stand. The Irish Chief Secretary informed Mr. Sec. Shortt that the release of the Lord Mayor would have disastrous results in Ireland and would probably lead to a mutiny of both military and police in South of Ireland."[46] On the same day, the reply of Lloyd George to a letter from Mary MacSwiney, the Lord Mayor's sister, received wide circulation in the press.

Nevertheless, discussion as to finding a way out of the problem continued to take place within the government. One of the most involved suggestions came to Balfour from Sir John Anderson, the chief British civil servant at Dublin Castle, whose remarks also show that the government's contention that the Irish administration was totally opposed to leniency in MacSwiney's case was inaccurate. While Chief Secretary for Ireland Hamar Greenwood may indeed have continued to hold to a hard line on this and all other aspects of Britain's Irish policy, it is apparent that many in Dublin Castle saw a need for urgent change. Anderson based his recommendation to Balfour on a conversation that Bishop D'Arcy of Cork had with the lord chancellor, in which he reasoned that since the evidence used to convict MacSwiney by court-martial might have been inadequate had he been tried before a civil court, the "offer might be made of retrial before Special Commission judges conditional upon his abandoning hunger strike". Anderson noted that while "It seems very doubtful whether the Lord Mayor would accept such an offer ... I gather Lord Chancellor feels that fact offer was made would at least strengthen hands of Government."

There were other options the government contemplated at a high level. On 6 September Bonar Law, forwarding his ideas through J.C. Davidson in a correspondence to Crown Solicitor Sir Ernley Blackwell, wondered "whether either through the agency of the Prison Doctor or some other official who comes into contact with Lord Mayor MacSwiney's friends it would not be possible to suggest that they should invoke the Dáil Éireann to issue an order to MacSwiney to stop hunger striking". Davidson emphasised that this "naturally should be done without any suggestion of inspiration and possibly would meet with no success". However, his concluding comment that "as the Roman Catholic Irish are not very good at fighting a losing battle, the determination of the Government to let MacSwiney die might perhaps be an inducement to the Sinn Féin organisers to make him live," indicated the persistence of the government's view that, by staying the course with its policy, it would prevail.[47]

A cabinet conference held on 2 September proved decisive, both in terms of Terence MacSwiney's life and the future conduct of British policy in Ireland. Arthur Balfour, who chaired the meeting in the prime minister's absence, acknowledged that "in view of the strong representations which have been made for the release of the Lord Mayor of Cork from Brixton Gaol, he had conferred with the Home Secretary and the Secretary of State for War".[48] The home office replied that:

> In the view of the Home Office, the detention of a prisoner during a protracted hunger strike until his death was subversive of prison discipline and administration. It could also be urged on behalf of the Lord Mayor that he was a political prisoner and that it was impossible in his case to feed him forcibly as had been done with success with other hunger strikers. On the other hand, to release him would, in effect, be equivalent to giving up the Coercion Act recently passed.[49]

On the basis then of ensuring that the intent of the Coercion Act was not compromised, the conference proceeded to recommend "no change in the Cabinet's decision". Balfour reminded his colleagues that "the Cabinet had decided against the release of hunger strikers and that the decision had been announced and defended by the Prime Minister in his published letter to the Lord Mayor's sister".[50] The government was not willing to back down. The question of the lord mayor of Cork's hunger strike would not be taken up again by the cabinet for another month.

But the issue would not go away, and in a letter to Bonar Law from Lucerne, Lloyd George made clear his view that "enough has not been done to put our case before the British public – or the foreign public – which is very important". The need to more effectively explain the government's handling of MacSwiney's case, he argued, should form a central part of such an undertaking. "I trust," he wrote, "concerted effort will be made to make clear to the British public opinion that our refusal to release this man is not attributable to any cruelty or even obstinacy on our part but to high policy which we cannot depart from without sacrificing the supreme interests of the British Empire." Nonetheless, it is evident from the prime minister's letter to Law that at one stage the release of Terence MacSwiney had at least been contemplated, if only to be rejected in the end.

> I have received no communication during the last few days indicating what the view of the Irish Government is of the deten-tion of the Lord Mayor of Cork to the point of death. When I sent my wire I had been definitely informed that if we let him go it would completely disintegrate and dishearten the police force in Ireland and the military. Apart from that it struck me that if we released him we might as well give up again attempting to maintain law and order in Ireland.[51]

A similar view was conveyed by J.T. Davies of the prime minister's senior secretarial staff to Lord Stamfordham two weeks later. In his letter, Davies also told Stamfordham that the prime minister had been receiving "a good number of threatening letters on account of the refusal of the Government to release MacSwiney, and we are taking extra precautions to protect him from any attack".[52] Davis also indicated Lloyd George's suspicions about MacSwiney's ability to endure without food.

> The Lord Mayor of Cork still lives. I am enclosing a copy of today's medical report with regard to him, and also a copy of the medical report of ten days ago, from which you will see that besides a certain amount of physical deterioration there is very little change in his condition. The Prime Minister and other members of the Government are unable to understand how it is that he is kept alive, but they have no definite information that he takes any nourishment privately, although very remarkable stories are flooding around as to the different methods by which

he is fed – one being that his wife feeds him on the quiet. The Government still adhere to their determination that if he wishes to commit suicide he must be allowed to do so.[53]

"Policy or humanity," the *Cork Examiner's* lead article for 7 September stated, "might indeed have influenced real statesmen to differentiate between strict legalism and a more generous line of conduct, and if the balance turned in favour of the latter, few or none would chide the Ministers for having taken a merciful course." Citing a previous edition of the London *Observer* as having stated that the "majority of the Public Opinion and the Press in Great Britain is unquestionably for the Lord Mayor's release", the *Examiner* went on to argue that "the unctuous Ministers with whom Lloyd George has surrounded himself need have felt no compunction in conforming to the popular wish".[54]

The belief persisted that MacSwiney would in fact die sooner rather than later. Ireland itself entered a prayerful mode in showing its support for him. On the morning of Wednesday, 1 September, some 4,000 Dublin workers joined a procession to a Carmelite church, where at a mass offered for the lord mayor, the faithful heard the celebrant, Fr D.B. Devlin, liken the British government's unwillingness to end MacSwiney's hunger strike by releasing him to the fiddling of Nero while Rome burned. He also lent spiritual legitimacy to the dying man's protest. "Terence MacSwiney's dying," Fr Devlin said, "will appeal more eloquently to the world for Ireland than a thousand tongues. ... I ask you all to pray fervently to Almighty God for a really great man now in his death agony." The response of the congregation to Fr Devlin's call was described in *The Irish Times* of the following day: "The roll of the response of the 'Hail Mary' and deep chanting by the whole congregation of the 'Hail Holy Queen' concluded a scene not soon to be forgotten by those present."[55] Following the mass, the workers reformed their procession and headed for work at such Dublin mainstays as Jacobs' Biscuit Factory, Smith's Silversmiths, McCren's Shirt Factory, and Co-operative Bookbinders.

This incident and others shows the position of the Catholic Church in MacSwiney's hunger strike to have been far more sympathetic than during similar protests undertaken by Republican prisoners during the Irish civil war – little more than two years after the lord mayor's death. While neither the Catholic hierarchy in Ireland nor Rome took a definitive position in the case of Terence MacSwiney, the ambivalence it exhibited undoubtedly provided priests like Fr Devlin and Fr O'Connor with the latitude to embrace his cause openly. The attitude of the Church on the broader issue of the morality of his hunger strike is a subject for wider discussion elsewhere in this account.

The month of September also witnessed a formal protest by the British labour movement along with the Labour Party by way of telegrams against the government's handling of the MacSwiney case. On 3 September, the Labour Party forwarded to Lloyd George in Lucerne an appeal "to the Prime Minister and the Government to reverse their decision to allow him [MacSwiney] to starve to death in prison rather than release him". In words that echoed the Labour Party's "Report on Conditions in Ireland", the letter argued that the Coalition's policy "has already seriously jeopardised the hope of any early settlement of the Irish problem on the basis of conciliation and appeasement and has stained the name of Britain with dishonour in the eyes of the civilised world".[56]

The opposition of the British Trade Union Congress was equally strong. In a 6 September telegram to Bonar Law, the TUC conveyed the warning that "we in the name of the whole organised labour movement will hold the government responsible for the death of the Lord Mayor of Cork and remind them that such blind stupidity will render a reconciliation between Ireland and Britain almost impossible".[57]

The response issued for the government by Bonar Law, however, revealed no desire to change: "The Government's position has been made clear in the public statement issued August 25th to which there is little to add."[58] The Coalition was determined to blame MacSwiney for his own plight:

> From the moment of his arrest he sought to defeat the ends of justice, and to reduce the forces of the Crown to impotence by refusing food, no doubt in the belief that that course would lead to his speedy release. It is the clear duty of the Government not

only to take every step possible to suppress disorder in Ireland, but also to protect those brave men who are carrying out their duties as servants of the Crown, in daily peril of their lives. To release prisoners, who, like the Lord Mayor, have been guilty of complicity in a movement which uses as one of its main instruments assassination and outrage would be nothing short of betrayal ... Since the arrest of the Lord Mayor fifteen officers have been brutally and treacherously done to death ... Surely the sympathy which has been given in such full measure to the Lord Mayor, whose condition has been brought about by his own deliberate act, is due rather to the bereaved widows and families of the murdered Irish policemen.[59]

A somewhat telling remark, when viewed against the backdrop of the internal disagreement between the king and his ministers over the handling of the MacSwiney episode, was this comment in Law's letter: "The Government fully realises how large a part sentiment plays in all human affairs, and if it were possible they would have gladly taken the attitude of the English King who said of an opponent, 'He is determined to make himself a martyr and I am equally determined to prevent it.'"[60]

Sinn Féin seized on Bonar Law's statement and argued that it was full of glaring contradictions. The lord mayor's fellow TD and lifelong friend from Cork, Liam de Roiste, was selected by the Cork Municipal Corporation to issue an official response to Law's statement. "We are to take it," he began, "that Mr Law's reply to the English Labour Party is the considered answer of the English Government to all appeals that have been made for the release of the Lord Mayor of Cork from prison and all demands for the cessation of the English Government's terrorist regime in Ireland."[61] De Roiste's comments pointed to some of the more glaring inconsistencies in the government's attitude toward MacSwiney, as well as attacking what were in fact baseless comments regarding the nature of his conviction.

Mr. Law states he [the Lord Mayor] was arrested while actively conducting the affairs of a rebel organisation under the cover of a Mayoral Court. No charge of conducting the affairs of a rebel organisation was made at the court martial. If there was basis of

[*sic*] such a charge why was it not brought forward? Mr. Law
speaks of a "Mayoral Court." The courts established in Ireland
under the authority of Dáil Éireann for the maintenance of law
and order are courts set up by and with the consent of the Irish
people ... The courts deal only with legal business. They are not
a cover for anything. Therefore, we must assume that, in the view
of the English Government, to set up Courts that the Irish people
have confidence in, to maintain order and discipline, to dispense
justice, is a capital crime.[62]

De Roiste focused particular attention on Law's use of the term
"avowed rebel" in relation to MacSwiney, and challenged
Law's statement that under universal practice MacSwiney
would normally have been shot. "Since when," de Roiste
asked, "has it become 'the universal practice of civilised
nations' to immediately shoot on capture an unarmed man –
even an 'avowed rebel'" Noting Law's open support for
Carson and the Ulster Volunteers in their challenge to the
British government over the Home Rule Act a decade earlier,
de Roiste stated: "At one period of his existence, Mr. Law
declared himself an 'avowed rebel' ... There were others also,
now high in power in England, who also declared themselves
rebels, and gloried in the title."[63]

MacSwiney's friend and colleague argued that despite
Law's and his fellow Unionists' claim that the British government was the lawful authority in Ireland, "they declared they
would overthrow that Government by force of arms, over-
ride the decrees of what they acknowledged as a lawfully
elected Parliament, defy an Act assented to and signed by the
King to whom they say they are loyal ... Will Mr. Bonar Law
hold that the practice he now lays down, 'the universal
practice of civilised nations', according to him, should have
been applied to himself and his friends when they were
'avowed rebels'".[64] Likewise, Law's contention that
MacSwiney had been tried by a "legally constituted tribunal"
was rejected outright by de Roiste. "The English Government," he stated, "has not the consent of the Irish people to
rule Ireland ... Its tribunals therefore are not legally constituted ones." As for Law's claim that it was the duty of the
government to suppress disorder, de Roiste offered a line of

reasoning that was consistent with democratic principles outlined more than a century earlier by Jefferson and Madison during the American Revolution.

> That it is the duty of a government to suppress disorder and protect its servants is admitted. But the Government must be a lawful government, a just government, ruling with the consent of the people governed, and supported by the people governed. A government ruling and acting in defiance of a people's will does not and cannot suppress disorder. It is itself the creator and fomentor of disorder.[65]

Actions taken by the British military against Irish civilians, together with pogroms against Catholics in the north, provided de Roiste with further ammunition: "Since Mr. Law's statement was written, the evening press of London of this day reports the shooting dead of two boys on the roadside at Ballyvourney, Co. Cork, by soldiers firing from a military lorry ... What has Mr. Law to say about the expulsion of men from employment in Belfast, the burning of houses there and at Lisburn by persons waving the Union Jack?" When Bonar Law and his associates answered these questions, de Roiste concluded "they may then talk of 'law, order, justice, good government'".[66]

On 6 September Law's remarks also met with a public rebuke from Annie MacSwiney, sister of the lord mayor. She characterised his comments as "an insult to freedom, honour, truth, and every democratic principle ... Do you call the Poles rebels because they are determined to be free; why then do you call the Irish rebels and persecute them because they desire likewise?"[67]

A personal undertaking to the conference of the Trades Union Congress at Portsmouth on 9 September by Mary MacSwiney, who wanted the TUC to declare a general strike in support of her brother, received a swift rebuff. The written protest issued to the British government would prove to be the extent of the British labour movement's involvement at an organisational level. In fact, Mary MacSwiney's effort to address the conference's delegates herself was blocked directly by TUC President J.H. Thomas, who took a particularly patronising approach towards her. Rejecting her request to speak, Thomas informed the delegates that, "If any of you think for a moment of the torture that woman has been through for the past three weeks then it would be madness to allow anything of the kind ... The torture she is going through ... naturally imposes a strain that becomes difficult to bear." He then proposed that "instead of allowing her to come before Congress and talk to you, I suggests you agree to sending another telegram to the Prime Minister showing that we are wholeheartedly in sympathy with her and anxious to do all we can".[68] The following exchange then occurred between Thomas and some of the delegates:

> A delegate asked if there had been any reply to the first one. Mr. Thomas: "No, but you have seen the official reply. Do you agree to leave it to the Parliamentary Committee to take the necessary steps?" A delegate asked should the Parliamentary Committee interview Mr. Lloyd George at once, and convey to him the opinion of the Congress in regard to the Lord Mayor. Mr. Thomas: "I do not think that is a good thing for our movement to merely invite rebuffs, unless you are going to meet them some way. I think we have got too much into the tendency of assuming that the mere threat of doing something will accomplish something. Personally, I do not believe it does anything of the kind. We have already been personally to the Government, and the Parliamentary Committee could have done no more." It was agreed to adopt the course suggested by Mr. Thomas.[69]

The British labour movement would contemplate a general strike only if its direct interests were involved. Thomas would later serve in British Labour and Coalition governments as colonial secretary, dominion secretary and lord privy seal.

Art O'Brien continued to send regular reports to Michael Collins from London apprising him of MacSwiney's condition. The two men expressed amazement at the lord mayor's endurance. "I was astonished to find very little change in his facial appearance from the last time I was there," O'Brien told Collins in a communication of 9 September. "The expression in his face and eyes was full of life and keenness, and his mind – as shown by his conversation – was as alert as ever."[70] O'Brien, however, went on to note:

He did not on this occasion make any effort to greet me with his hand. The effort was evidently beyond him. He told me he was quite prepared for the end, he felt that life was going from him. If it was God's will that he should die he was resigned, but he had a feeling that God would let him live, and by doing so the victory over the enemies of his country would be greater. We should be prepared for this, and he spoke to me about a possible nursing home, and other matters, and finished saying, "but there is no immediate hurry to go into details. I can see you later about these." The contrast between the inert body and the alert mind is most impressive.[71]

There was an even more pressing matter which led MacSwiney to ask O'Brien to visit him on that Saturday in September. It forms the basis for what is surely one of the most important revelations to emerge in the course of the lord mayor's long and arduous ordeal: MacSwiney made it clear to his visitor that he believed future hunger strikes would be an exercise in futility. MacSwiney was particularly perturbed over comments attributed to Eamon de Valera in the United States, to the effect that the president of the Irish Republic would assume MacSwiney's place as a hunger striker in the event of his death.

This has greatly distressed Terry and he asked me to write and give you his opinion as follows: the English government have determined to forcibly feed all hunger strikers, and Governors of all prisons have been instructed to this effect. Many of our men have been forcibly fed in English prisons, and have given up the hunger strike. In his own case they made the mistake of letting him go too far and could not forcibly feed him without grave danger. People in Ireland were greatly misled by the Thomas Ashe incident – the doctor responsible in that case was clumsy and bungled the operation – it was quite easy for experienced doctors to feed through the nose, etc., without danger, and the process could be kept up indefinitely. By the mistake they made in his case in Cork, they enabled him to put up this fight against them. But if Dev came over they would arrest him, impose a heavy sentence, and would start forcibly feeding him at once, and would continue the forcible feeding for the rest of his sentence. He thought their present experience should be the end of the hunger strike as a weapon. In future those imprisoned by the enemy should be considered as casualties, and they should suffer their term of imprisonment without resistance, unless for some important purpose.[72]

In the end, soon after MacSwiney's death, Collins and Griffith ordered the nine remaining striking prisoners in Cork Gaol off their hunger strikes. The men complied. It was a tragedy that Collins and Griffith had not given the order while the lord mayor was still alive, and when it was still possible to spare the prisoners further agony.

In the event, as the condition of the lord mayor deteriorated, so did those of eleven Republicans on hunger strike in Cork Gaol. They were accused of a range of offences against the crown, ranging from possession of arms to the killing of members of the RIC and the British army. Neither Michael Fitzgerald nor Joseph Murphy, who would both die on hunger strike, had been convicted of the offence for which he was imprisoned. Fitzgerald had been imprisoned since September 1919 for the killing of a British private. Joseph Murphy was arrested in July 1920 and charged with possession of a incendiary device. The two began their hunger strikes in August of that year. Fitzgerald, who would die one week before Mac-Swiney, was commandant of the First Battalion of the Cork No. 2 Brigade. He was held on remand without trial, under the official explanation that he was too weak to appear before a military tribunal, without formal charge or trial throughout his eighty-one day hunger strike. Joseph Murphy died within hours of MacSwiney, at the age of twenty-two.

Appeals were made to the British government on behalf of the prisoners in Cork Gaol, largely on the basis that the men should be shown leniency since they had not been convicted of a crime. In one instance, P.H. Barry, the former high sheriff for County Cork, wired the prime minister on the prisoners' behalf, noting that "Even Mr. Bonar Law's letter in answer to the Labour Party's appeal does not attempt to justify the detention of untried or unconvicted men."[73] The response from Lloyd George's office countered that leniency was not justified since the eleven men "had reduced themselves to a physical condition that renders them unfit for trial, and the Government are advised that it is legally impossible to try them for the grave offences with which they are charged in their absence or until they are certified to be fit to undergo trial". The Coalition held that "It is impossible for the Government to allow men charged with such grave offences to escape trial by their own act ... If this were permitted, there would be an end to the possibility of the enforcement of law and the administration of justice."[74]

Terence MacSwiney served as the inspiration for the eleven Republican hunger strikers in Cork, whom he referred to as "my boys" to visitors at Brixton.[75] Despite his admission to Art O'Brien earlier in the month, in a public statement released on 21 September, the fortieth day of his own hunger strike, MacSwiney spoke for both his comrades in Cork Gaol and himself in attempting to explain why he felt they had been able to endure thus far.

> I attribute this to the spiritual strength which I receive from Daily Communion bringing me bodily strength assisted by a world of prayers, of which the intensity is so apparent. My comrades, who are fasting two days longer than I, are clearly sustained in like manner. I believe God has directly intervened to stay the tragedy for a while for a Divine purpose of his own: I believe he has intervened not solely for our own sakes. We have laid our offering at his feet to be accepted or not, according to his Divine Will.[76]

MacSwiney then sought to explain his belief that divine intervention had prolonged his own hunger strike as well as those of the others "for our enemy's sake ... It is incredible ... that the people of England will allow this callous and cold blooded murder to be pushed to the end ... If it is pushed through it will leave a stain on the name of England, to which there is no parallel (even in her history) ... I think God is giving them a last chance to pause and consider." Making it evident that he was quite reconciled to assuming the mantle of martyrdom for himself and his comrades, MacSwiney stated that "We feel singularly privileged in being made the instruments of God for evoking such a world-wide expression of admiration and support for the cause of Irish independence, and the recognition of the Irish Republic, and if we are to die, we are called to even the greater privilege and happiness of entering the devoted company of those who died for Ireland."[77]

From these words, and from his letter of 30 September to Cathal Brugha, Terence MacSwiney evidently drew consolation from the belief that he and others would be able to join with the martyred dead of Easter Week and before.[78] He and the men of Cork would be coming out after all. On the fifty-seventh day of his hunger strike, the lord mayor asked the hunger strikers in Cork "to join with me in the following prayer for our people suffering such persecution in the current crisis". The "prayer", which he composed himself, was reminiscent of Patrick Pearse's message in the *The Sovereign People*.

> Oh, my God, I offer my pain for Ireland. She is on the rack. My God, thou knowest how many times thine enemies have put her there to break her spirit, but by Thy mercy, they have always failed. I offer my sufferings here for our martyred people, beseeching Thee, O God, to grant them nerve and strength and grace to withstand the present terror in Ireland, not only for two months but two years if need be, that by Thy all powerful aid, the persecution may end in our time, and Ireland arise, at last triumphant. The spirit of prayer will defeat the cunning of Satan. Thy power, O God, is stronger than the malice of the devil. I offer everything Thou askest for Ireland's resurrection. It is Thy Will.[79]

The lord mayor went on to ask God to "Accept our willing sacrifice for our people." The notion of achieving Ireland's redemption through human sacrifice, echoed not only Pearse but the fundamental basis of Roman Catholicism itself. "Comrades," he exclaimed, "if we twelve go in glorious succession to the grave, the name of Ireland will flash in a tongue of flame through the world and be a sign of hope to every people yearning to be free ... Let the thought inspire us, and let our dying prayer be an exhortation to each other and to our people, that everyone be prepared to sacrifice everything and God will at last redeem our country."[80]

The attitude towards the medical officials attempting to treat the Republican hunger strikers in Cork, as relayed to them by the IRA, was of a somewhat less spiritual tone than the remarks attributed to the lord mayor. They were instead the recipients of death threats. On 6 September 1920, the deputy governor in charge of Cork Gaol reported that the chief medical officer there had received a threatening letter from someone representing himself as "the Officer in Charge of the Cork No. I Brigade IRA".[81] According to a phone message forwarded by the deputy governor to Dublin Castle, the threatening letter stated:

> As your professional attendance upon the eleven hunger strikers in Cork Gaol gives a tinge of legitimacy to the slow murder being perpetrated upon them, you are hereby ordered to leave the Gaol at once and the country within 24 hours of this date – 3 o'clock p.m. September 6th. Failure to comply with the order will incur drastic action.[82]

At about the same time, the IRA officers of the Cork No. 1 Brigade also threatened other physicians who had been sent to Cork, according to the Irish administration "for the purpose of giving necessary additional medical attendance required owing to the condition of health of the eleven prisoners who are on hunger strike".[83] In the latter threat, the IRA informed the physicians that "we hold you responsible for the lives of the men at present on hunger strike in Cork Gaol. Should any of them die," the warning noted, "either in Gaol or after release you will be guilty of a crime punishable by death under the laws of the Republic." The statement concluded that if the doctors wanted to "disclaim responsibility for the present treatment of these men, you can make this fact public by sending a notice of your resignation to the Press tonight".[84] Following the threat, the British government sought to act in the physicians' defence by stating in the press that the responsibility for the hunger strikers imprisonment, "rests entirely and solely with the Government". The official statement contended that the two physicians threatened by the IRA – Dr McCormack and Dr Kinsella – "as soon as they had examined the prisoners thus placed under their medical care ... strongly recommended to the Government that on medical grounds the prisoners should be released".[85]

Contacts between MacSwiney and the Cork inmates were made possible through channels established by Donald O'Callaghan, the deputy lord mayor of Cork, and Fr Dominic. In a 22 September letter to Fr Dominic, O'Callaghan stated that "It was with a view to getting Fitzgerald to change his mind on the matter of medical attention that I wrote to London asking particulars with regard to Terry's treatment, as obviously the longer the men can be kept alive the better ... However, he fears the doctor would avail of the opportunity to play tricks and there the matter ends." O'Callaghan also noted that "The men already receive Holy Communion daily." He added also the cryptic comment that he "was not sure yet with regard to the other message you sent – I must have a talk about it".[86]

Communication between Michael Collins and Art O'Brien concerning MacSwiney's condition continued to be frequent and detailed. It was not to the cabinet of the Irish Republic or to its president that O'Brien, an IRB man himself, wrote, but to the IRA's principal strategist and head of the IRB. Collins's role as the primary source to which O'Brien and the Irish Self-Determination League turned for direction during the lord mayor's protest is illustrated in this memo from London to the "Big Fellow" on 11 September, relating to the need for further instructions in the event MacSwiney died.

> Terry is now very bad indeed, and we have to face the position that at any moment the end may come. From present indications, it seems certain that they intend to let him die in prison. It is very necessary in these circumstances that I should obtain from you your advice as to what tactics we are to adopt in several ways.[87]

O'Brien went on to restate the various legal options that existed for them should an inquest be held following the lord mayor's death; but a key cause for concern revolved around whether or not the British government would in the end consent to handing the body over to MacSwiney's family. O'Brien told Collins that a contact named "Mac" had informed him that "he has made a search for any act or statute, which would give the Government power in such a case to hold the body and he cannot find anything that would give them such power. ... On the other hand, he tells me that at the time of the Chartist rising, the bodies of two Chartists, who died in prison, were held and buried in the prison, on the ground that their release and the subsequent funeral would cause public disturbances."[88] In the mean time, while O'Brien and his comrades awaited their instructions from Collins, MacSwiney's Volunteer uniform was readied, having already been brought over to London. A large tricolour that would eventually be used to drape his casket had likewise been secured.

In a communication to O'Brien later that month, prompted apparently by an attempt on the part of someone in the lord mayor's party in London to terminate the medical care given him, Collins made clear the position of IRA general headquarters on the subject of the medical treatment then being accorded MacSwiney. "I may say that it was very wrong of anybody to suggest the discontinuance of medical treatment. ... The view is that medical treatment should be availed of. ... We would rely on the etiquette of the profession insofar as the administering of nutriment is concerned."[89]

Collins communicated to Art O'Brien the view that MacSwiney's "prolongation of life seems to be absolutely wonderful – in fact little short of miraculous".[90] Three days later, he added his praise for the eleven hunger strikers at Cork Gaol: "The miraculous thing is that not one of the whole crowd had any organic defect. This is more remarkable in Terry's case than in the others as he has had such a trying time for the past four years and a half." He also told O'Brien that there was no need to see MacSwiney on a regular basis, "So long as we are kept informed ... . As the days pass, we will marvel more and more at the fight being made by him and by our men in Cork." MacSwiney's family had made it clear earlier that visits should be kept to a minimum in order to conserve his strength.[91]

Whatever about the lord mayor's frame of mind, there appears to have been division between his wife Muriel and his sister Mary about the continuation of the hunger strike. As previously noted, it is clear Muriel was strongly opposed to her husband's earlier hunger strike. Muriel accompanied Fr Dominic to Brixton from Ireland on 20 August. She remained there throughout most of the hunger strike, but made occasional trips back to Ireland. One of them involved a visit to Alderman Tom Kelly, the lord mayor of Dublin, with a personal plea that he issue a statement asking her husband to end his protest.[92] Kelly appears to have drafted such a statement and submitted it to the *Irish Independent,* but after a visit by Mary MacSwiney, he withdrew the letter.[93]

Throughout the short duration of her marriage to Terry, relations between the two women appear to have been strained. While in prison in December 1917, MacSwiney indicated he was aware of this when he wrote to Muriel that she would be "glad" of Annie's company. "I know you don't want Min [Mary] or many visitors," he acknowledged.[94] In refusing a request from one biographer that she be allowed to interview Muriel MacSwiney some years later for details on her husband's protest, Mary explained: "Poor Muriel could not be expected to be a stoic like the MacSwineys all were."[95]

Collins's admiration for MacSwiney's courage and staying power did not outweigh his opposition to hunger strikes. According to one account, that of their mutual friend and fellow Corkman Sean Murphy, sometime in October Collins took the step of ordering MacSwiney off his protest. Describing the episode some three decades later, Murphy recalled that he had stopped off in London (en route to Paris) to visit the offices of the Irish Self-Determination League. There he was shown a copy of Collins's order to MacSwiney:

> When I got to Art O'Brien's office, there were present Art O'Brien, Sean McGrath, Mary MacSwiney, Fred Cronin of Cork ... and to the best of my recollection Peter MacSwiney and a Dublin Volunteer dispatch carrier. Michael Collins' letter was in his own handwriting, and was handed to me, and my comment on it was the same as all in the room with the exception of Miss MacSwiney. We were unanimous that he should carry out Michael Collins' order. Miss MacSwiney would have "no surrender" and she was very emphatic that she would beat the British Government. She stated she would interview Commander Kentworthy that night in the House of Commons and get him to accompany her to a Labour Congress that was then sitting, to the best of my memory in Brighton, the following day, and get them to declare a general strike ... [96]

It was Murphy's contention that Collins' "order" was issued in response to an appeal made to the IRA leader, and that

Collins stated to MacSwiney that while he had "put up a glorious fight for the cause and have done as much as is humanly possible", it was time to end the protest. Murphy maintained that Collins stated that he had "information that the British Cabinet mean to finish this hunger strike weapon of ours, and do not intend releasing you ... I now order you to give up the strike as you will be ten times a greater asset to the movement alive than dead."[97]

Whether or not Collins actually issued such an order to MacSwiney – Murphy's account was vehemently denied by Florence O'Donoghue – and, if so, if it was communicated to him, the fact remains that he did not end his hunger strike. Indeed, given the ferocity of his commitment to waging his protest at this stage, it is unlikely that anything could have lead him to alter his course, short of his release from Brixton. If he had ended his protest voluntarily at this late stage, it is also unclear whether he would have lived, or if he had, what his prospects for recovery to anything resembling full health would have been.

Dr Mannix, the Catholic archbishop of Australia, visited MacSwiney for a second time in late September. The County Cork born Mannix had himself been banned from entering Ireland by the British government under the Defence of the Realm Act. On 29 September, Art O'Brien wrote to Michael Collins:

> You will have seen Archbishop Mannix's remarks to the Press: "It is a miracle." I have seen the Archbishop since, and these words actually convey his opinion. He tells me that he saw no change in Terry since his last visit, which as you know, was about three weeks ago.[98]

O'Brien's letter also dealt with a more sombre topic. He informed Collins that he was able to provide Dublin sculptor Albert Power with photographs of the lord mayor which could be used in the creation of a bust.[99]

The attitude of the IRA in the field towards MacSwiney's heroism and agony is candidly recalled by Ernie O'Malley in his account of the Anglo-Irish war. "The result was inevitable," he wrote. "We hoped he would not be released when his body was almost used up."[100]

A steady flow of information between the medical team and prison officials at Brixton Prison, and the prime minister and home office, focused each day on Prisoner No. 6794's physical deterioration. The reports began on 23 August with the report of W.D. Higson, the medical officer in charge at Brixton Prison, to the home office, which stated that "The prisoner is becoming progressively weaker."[101] The physician noted that MacSwiney stated that he was "getting dried up". An internal correspondence from the home office to Bonar Law cautioned that "the Medical Commissioner of Prisons is of the opinion that it would be injudicious to add anything to the water which the prisoner drinks, without his knowledge. ... Mr. Bonar Law should also be informed that the prisoner is constantly supplied with appetising soups, jelly and custard. He would not be in the least likely to take water which he knew had been doctored."[102]

Dr Higson's report of the next day stated that in his opinion "the above named prisoner is now dangerously ill owing to his refusal to take food. ... Unless he can be induced by some means to take nourishment ... the consequence will prove fatal."[103] A conversation which the physician had with Dr Mannix following his visit with MacSwiney left him, according to an accompanying note, with the view that the situation "would end in a tragedy and be no good either for this country or Ireland". The account describes MacSwiney asking Higson, before drinking water, "Is it nothing but water?" MacSwiney's determination was clear to the prison staff: "Dr. Higson does not think it likely that he will take any food and that McSwiney [sic] thinks it would be a help to Ireland for him to be martyred. McSweeney [sic] has expressed this to him." After noting MacSwiney's temperature of 97.2 with a pulse rate of 50, Higson's letter concluded: "I need hardly say that I have done everything possible, with the exception of physical force, to induce the prisoner to take food, and have interviewed his wife, sister and spiritual advisors, repeatedly, in the hope of their assisting me to overcome the prisoner's almost fanatical determination not to take food while he is under detention here."[104]

On 28 August Dr Higson reported to the home office that there was "no marked change in this prisoner's general condition. ... He is a little paler and looking more worn." The extreme uneasiness of the nights spent by the lord mayor is revealed by Higson's comment that "he was restless during the night and slept 2 a.m. until 4 a.m". The extent to which MacSwiney would drink substances other than water was also noted by Higson: "He has agreed to take a mixture of citrate and carbonate salts, and already the acetate odour of his breath is not so marked, and the urine less acrid."[105]

While the British government persisted throughout the duration of MacSwiney's hunger strike in labelling his condition as the result of a self-inflicted course in which the prisoner was determined to take his own life, it was also evident that the Catholic Church did not, openly at least, view the lord mayor's protest as suicidal. In a conversation he had with Dr Higson, as communicated to the government on 29 August, it is clear that MacSwiney was well aware of his position and in fact appeared to take some comfort from it:

> When discussing with the prisoner, this morning, the general principles and ethics of his conduct, also including the position of those associated with and morally supporting him, he replied to the effect that the matter had been fully considered by the Church, and it had been decided that his death would be a "sacrificial" one and not "suicidal", otherwise he could not have been given the blessing of the Church, and Sacraments by the Priest.[106]

The presence throughout his ordeal of Fr Dominic could only serve to confirm MacSwiney's resolve and his sense of approbation by the Catholic Church. On 29 August, Muriel MacSwiney and the bishop of Cork, Dr Cohalan, met with hospital medical officials who, in Higson's words, "clearly explained to them the critical state of the prisoner's condition". On that day, Higson also apprised the home office that "A one half dracha dose of Adrenalin Chloride solution has been added to the saline mixture", and that the lord mayor had again slept for only two and a half hours the previous night.[107]

Over the course of the next two days the lord mayor's physical decline became increasingly apparent. On 31 August, Dr Higson reported that "the prisoner is generally weaker: is looking more pale and worn, and body wasting is

perceptible". He noted further that MacSwiney had complained "of a tingling" and a sensation of "pins and needles
in the right arm, probably due to bed pressure as I find no
objective signs of obstruction of the circulation to account for
them". It was during this period that MacSwiney began to
develop a tubercular condition in which the physicians noted
that his lungs "for the first time began to show signs of
oedema at the bases behind". It was understood by the
medical staff at Brixton Prison that the "oedema is merely
part of his enfeebled condition and position in bed and may
be expected to increase from day to day".[108]

Terence MacSwiney entered what was to be the last full
month of his life with a grim determination to endure to the
bitter end. On 2 September G.B. Griffiths, the medical officer
assigned by the home office to monitor MacSwiney at Brixton
Prison, reported that he had a "consultation with Dr. Beddard
yesterday and he appeared rather surprised to find his
[MacSwiney's] strength so well maintained".[109] He noted,
however, that MacSwiney's condition was "distinctly worse
than yesterday". Griffiths also observed that the lord mayor
"appears quite grateful for the methods taken for his comfort
but seems quite determined to take no food".[110] In order to
avoid abstaining from water and medicine on the nights prior
to his receipt of Holy Communion, MacSwiney assured the
prison doctors that he would make his own arrangements.

On 4 September, the most foreboding account of
MacSwiney's condition to date came to the home office from
Dr Griffiths. "Judging from his condition generally," he
wrote, "I should say that he is liable to sudden collapse at any
time and that if the deterioration in health progresses in the
same ratio as comparing today with yesterday, death is
probably in a few days".[111] Neither MacSwiney nor his
captors could have known that at this stage the lord mayor
was less than one quarter of the way through the course of his
hunger strike. Griffiths stated that the prisoner "tells me that
he feels much weaker" and noted "a slight acetone smell in
his breath".[112]

The correspondence between the prison's medical staff and
the government was not confined to monitoring the lord
mayor's condition. It also took on an aspect of collusion

between the government and prison authorities in devising various stratagems for encouraging MacSwiney to end his protest. In one instance, on 6 September, home office official Edward Troupe approached J.C. Davidson in the cabinet with a suggestion that a means might be sought in which Sinn Féin might actually be involved in encouraging MacSwiney to end his fast.[113] Troupe conceded, however, that such an under-taking probably stood little chance of success. "I believe," he wrote, "the Sinn Féin organisers think the Lord Mayor will be worth more to them dead than alive." On the following day, Troupe reported to Davidson that "The prison doctor spoke to MacSwiney's friends yesterday of the seriousness of his condition and of his own anxiety that they should appeal to Dáil Éireann to stop the hunger strike – but the suggestion was coldly received and he does not think anything will come of it."[114]

Troupe, however, did suggest that British Trades Union Congress head J.H. Thomas, who had been involved in organ-ised labour's appeal to the government for leniency on MacSwiney's behalf, "be invited" to see the lord mayor and seek from him a pledge that in exchange for remission of his sentence he would "do everything in his power publicly and privately to stop the killing of policemen in Ireland". The home office official likened the idea to the "Kilmainham Treaty" of 1882 in which Charles Stuart Parnell was released from prison in exchange for a similar undertaking.[115] There is no evidence that the government took up the suggestion.

Attached to Troupe's 7 September communication were notes of Dr G.B. Griffiths, who related his latest encounter with the lord mayor's family and friends. Griffiths under-scored the refusal of those closest to MacSwiney to make any effort to co-operate with the authorities in their effort to persuade him to end his hunger strike. In his report to the home office for 6 September, on the twenty-fifth day of MacSwiney's hunger strike, Griffiths reported that the lord mayor "complained to me yesterday of feeling rather giddy ... I wished to give him brandy, but he refused." Griffiths added the observation that MacSwiney's body "does not seem to waste as one would expect".[116] On 8 September, a rise in the lord mayor's temperature to 98 degrees was reported, "due probably to over-exertion in talking to people in disposing his affairs. I have warned them that he is not to be allowed to talk so much."[117] On the following day, Griffiths reported to the home office that MacSwiney "complained of feeling faint yesterday and was revived with smelling ammonia".[118] The same report contains the first documented discussion between the prison authorities and MacSwiney himself about force feeding:

> In the course of conversation with him and Mrs. MacSwiney yesterday, I told them that circumstances might arise when he became too weak to resist nourishment or he might become unconscious and that under those circumstances I should take any steps I thought proper as I could not as a doctor stand by and do nothing. They agreed that this would be a proper course, but he added, that when he regained consciousness he would still refuse food. He has referred again to the matter this morning and says that he wants it to be distinctly understood that nothing but release will induce him to take food.

The physician's letter of that day also noted that MacSwiney's sister Mary "appears to think that I as a doctor could do something to get his release by representing his condition to the Prime Minister ... I told her that I reported his condition very fully and I believe accurately to superior authority."[119] MacSwiney eventually became irritated with the prison doctors. On 10 September Griffiths reported that "in order to give him an opening to take some food if he wished, I suggested that perhaps he was now too weak to resist". MacSwiney replied that he "would struggle and would not take any food and that he was 'adamant' on the point". On the following day, the dying Corkman's antagonism only seemed to intensify. Griffiths reported:

> He is irritable this morning and on my offering to feed him if he offered no resistance, refused and said it was only waste of time asking him. He is very bitter and says that he is being as surely murdered by the Government as if he were shot by bandits at the roadside, and speaks of his wonder at the "Medical Association" tolerating it ... He does not seem to see any point but his own apparently and the effort to argue with him or to persuade him to take food seems useless.[120]

Some thirty-four years later, Griffiths, in retirement, stated that he could not provide specific information on his treatment of the lord mayor since "It is so long ago and I have no notes of the case." Nonetheless, he recalled, "What I have clearly in mind is his patience and courtesy in what must have been for him a most trying time."[121]

MacSwiney's apparent bitterness at the British authorities' refusal to back down appeared only to fuel his own resolve. Despite a finding by the hospital physicians, as stated in a report for 12 September, that his "heart sounds are slightly weaker", it was noticed that "he has a fair amount of strength – can move his arms and help to roll himself over in bed for examination".[122] Griffiths reported that "In answer to my usual question as to whether he would take food, he replied, 'I will put it in a nutshell for you. I am here as a matter of duty and my example is a good one for those in Cork.'" The fate of the eleven IRA prisoners on hunger strike in Cork Gaol was obviously very close to his mind. The prison doctor added the observation that MacSwiney appeared "weary and depressed ... He talks rationally except on the subject of food." By this point, the lord mayor's skin was reported as having become so "dry and rough from pressure" that he had been placed on an air bed. Nonetheless, in his account of 13 September, Griffiths again noted that MacSwiney "appears rational".[123]

As his physical condition continued to deteriorate, MacSwiney refused special medicines, probably out of a concern that they might be used to induce him to go off his fast. Dr Griffiths remarked that the lord mayor had become "so huffy at being offered any medicine in addition to those he is taking that I was afraid he was going to decline to take anything". Dr Griffiths added that the lord mayor "said yesterday that he was determined to get out of prison 'dead or alive'".[124] A general characterisation of the lord mayor in succeeding reports was that he appeared "extremely sulky".

On 18 September Griffiths had gone into MacSwiney's ward "unexpectedly about 2 P.M. and found him sitting up in bed being washed. He seems able to take a helpful part in the proceeding himself. The nurse informed me last night that he had been talking a good deal to his friends and had been reading the newspapers."[125]

Edward Troupe of the home office directed a separate letter of Dr Griffiths' to the prime minister, which concerned an attempt by MacSwiney's family to have him examined by "a Sinn Féin doctor".[126] The request, formally made by Mary MacSwiney, had apparently been motivated by a "rumour" that the government would soon transfer the lord mayor to a nursing home in which he would be held in "semi-detention". Troupe recommended the following course of action by the government:

> I propose, if the Prime Minister agrees, to authorise Dr. Griffiths l) to tell Miss McSwiney [*sic*] definitely that there is no possibility of release to a Nursing Home or otherwise. 2) Formally to warn the friends about inducing him to take food in the terms he suggests in the report. They are constantly with him and cannot escape responsibility if they encourage him in the course he is taking.[127]

Each report on MacSwiney's medical condition sent from Brixton Prison to the home office from 23 August to 21 September provided specific details of his condition: 20 September 1920 "has had the pan twice but nothing was passed by the bowels".[128] The concern with such matters suggests the persistence of a belief on the part of the British authorities that MacSwiney was somehow surviving through food smuggled into his cell. The doctor noted that the lord mayor "seemed exhausted after these attempts at defecation". Nonetheless, as Griffiths reported, the prisoner's combative- ness was still apparent:

> He has conversed with me in a fairly strong voice and became very argumentative last night as he said that his medicine was sweet and if there was any "sugar" in it. I told him there was not, he is becoming sulky and unpleasant in his manner and begin- ning to resent very strongly being offered food by the nurse or my asking if he will have some.[129]

That same day MacSwiney gave the home secretary a direct response to his effort to convince him of the futility of his protest. In a statement dictated to prison officials MacSwiney reiterated his position:

> The Medical Commissioner of prisons visited me today to put me

under a medical examination. This he did in a very thorough manner. He confirmed the report of the Prison M.D., Dr. Higson, and informed me that my health was in a very dangerous condition. He impressed on me the gravity of my state and then read a document from you, warning me that I would not be released and the consequences of my refusing to take food would rest with myself.

Nevertheless, the consequences will rest with you. My undertaking on the day of my alleged court martial that I would be free alive or dead within a month will be fulfilled. It appears from your communication that my release is to be in death. In that event, the British Government can boast of having killed two Lord Mayors of the same City, within six months – an achievement without a parallel in the history of oppression. Knowing the revolution of opinion that will be thereby caused throughout the civilised world and the consequent accession of support to Ireland in her hour of trial, I am reconciled to a premature grave.[130]

MacSwiney, confident of his place in the annals of Irish martyrdom, lay ready to join Pearse and the others in eternity.

Winston Churchill, speaking in Dundee at the end of September, sought publicly to lay responsibility for the orchestration of his hunger strike on MacSwiney's supporters, while at the time seeking to shift blame from government policy: "It was during the silly season the Lord Mayor of Cork announced his determination to starve himself to death. He did not want to die, and the Government did not want him to die; but Alderman MacSwiney had many friends in Ireland, who wished him to die. After six weeks fasting, the Lord Mayor is still alive."[131]

The determination on the part of some on the British side to circulate rumours of MacSwiney's cheating on his hunger strike is evident in this entry in the diary of General Sir Henry Wilson:

J.T. Davies read me out yesterday's report on MacSwiney, the Lord Mayor of Cork, by the Home Office doctor. He said that he and another doctor had walked suddenly into the cell and had seen MacSwiney munching something and swallowing it. Later on the nurse found some substance in the basin after he had washed his teeth, and this had been sent to the analyst. The other doctor said that if he had been called to a case such as he found in MacSwiney, he would have ordered gentle exercise.[132]

Wilson's charge, dated to the sixty-first day of MacSwiney's hunger strike, is not supported by the facts, however. Had such an occurrence taken place, there can be little doubt, given the British government's desire to undermine public support for the lord mayor both at home and abroad, that such a statement would have been widely published far beyond Britain itself. Such accusations were circulated on a regular basis, but at no time were they substantiated by any evidence.

The suspicion by the prison authorities and government that MacSwiney was surviving through secret feeding was also shown by a remark from Dr Griffiths concerning the visits of Fr Dominic: "I have made further enquiry about the tablet [communion wafer] which the Day nurse states that Fr. Dominic administers every morning. I was anxious to get a specimen of the solution in which the tablet is dissolved but she says that is impossible as the priest puts the tablet into a teaspoonful of water and the patient drinks it out of the spoon."[133] MacSwiney's hunger strike had undoubtedly wrongfooted the British government. The integrity of his protest together with the support it garnered were something the government found great difficulty in grappling with. Aside from stories of prison officials' analysing the contents of the hard basin in which the lord mayor cleaned his teeth, another rumour circulated that Fr Dominic brought food to MacSwiney hidden in his beard.

While British officials endeavoured to question the integrity of MacSwiney's protest, the prisoner himself gathered the strength to send a final note to his comrade in arms and fellow alderman, Sean O'Sullivan, in Cork. Despite his condition, by then on his seventh week without food, MacSwiney's handwriting remained legible. The letter, in parts sentimental, reflecting on the early days of the Volunteers in Cork, was also defiant. "Do you remember," he asked O'Sullivan, "the first drills when we took the floor eight strong? ... I was in that first square. ... I pray, Sean, you may be spared long to carry on the good work – to come safely through the Battle and live in the honour of victory. ... I'm very weary," he concluded, "and must stop – goodbye Sean, God bless you and give you a long life under a free Republic."[134]

The tedium of the drawn-out course of the hunger strike at Cork Gaol and Brixton weighed on those closely involved in monitoring the situation on the Republican side. This was candidly, if somewhat whimsically, expressed in a letter from Cork's Deputy Lord Mayor Donal O'Callaghan to Fr Dominic on 5 October: "Personally I have long since come to believe that this state of affairs is to continue indefinitely and that we will both find ourselves old men, with the Channel running between us, sending one another periodical messages such as 'situation unchanged', or, as you vary it today, 'no-appreciable change'. Some of the men here seem to suffer somewhat more than they used to." Expressing his concern for MacSwiney, O'Callaghan asked: "Does Troidhealbhach [Terence] suffer much? Please remember me to him."[135]

Concerns about the immediate needs of his family members in London preyed on MacSwiney's mind during the final weeks of his life. During a visit from Art O'Brien on 9 October, MacSwiney told him that he had been worrying a lot about his wife and sister. O'Brien informed Collins that he had complied with the lord mayor's wish that they all be accommodated "under one roof".

> He also made it clear as the life seeped out of him to his sister Annie that it was as a soldier he wished to be remembered first and foremost. At one stage towards the end of his ordeal he asked her to write down precisely the time in which they spoke and to read it back to him as proof that he was a soldier dying for the ideal of a Republic.[136]

Though MacSwiney meant to die as a soldier, he marked passages in his copy of *The Imitation of Christ*, which served as a source of spiritual strength to him during his ordeal. Mary read to him after his eyesight had failed. To a great degree, MacSwiney saw his own struggle and the struggle for an Irish Republic in religious terms. In Book II of *Imitation of Christ* he found solace in the view that "If thou canst but hold thy peace and suffer, thou shalt see without doubt the

Lord will help thee."[137] Similarly, Book I of that work inspired
him with: "The greater the violence thou does thyself the
greater the progress thy shall maked." Another passage read:
"The perfect victory is to triumph over oneself."[138]

At the beginning of chapter five of Book III, the lord mayor
made the following handwritten observation: "This is a most
helpful chapter." He underlined this passage:

> Who sooner is not ready to suffer all things and to resign to the
> will of his Beloved is not worthy to be called a lover. He that
> loveth must willingly embraceth all that is hard and bitter for the
> sake of his Beloved, and never suffer himself to be turned away
> from him by contrary occurrences whatever.[139]

MacSwiney's family continued to seek permission to have a
private physician examine him to confirm that no nourishment had been taken. In late September, the home office
relented to demands that Dr Norman Moore be allowed to
examine the prisoner. Art O'Brien informed Michael Collins
that the intent was not so much to make public Dr Moore's
report as to have it "available at a later date if tricks are
played". Moore declined to estimate how long the lord mayor
was likely to live. Instead he stated, according to O'Brien, that
death would come "in his sleep or very suddenly".[140]

In an attempt to counter insinuations appearing in the
press that Terence MacSwiney had actually taken food
surreptitiously with the help of relatives, his wife, brother and
sisters vehemently defended the integrity of his protest. In a
statement released by the Irish Self-Determination League,
they emphasised that they "have not at any time supplied, nor
are they now supplying food or nourishment in any shape or
form to the Lord Mayor and that even had they supplied any
food or nourishment, the Lord Mayor would not have
accepted it as his determination not to take nourishment
except on his unconditional release remains unshaken".[141]

Convinced that the British press in general had been acting
under the direction of the government and had ceased to
present the family's views fairly on the course of events at
Brixton Prison, MacSwiney's relatives announced their intention of withholding comment from all British publications
and news agencies. The statement, in the form of a manifesto

issued by Art O'Brien through the Irish Self-Determination League, was signed by MacSwiney's wife Muriel, his brother Sean, and sisters Mary and Annie. It was their contention that "a deliberate campaign of misrepresentation and falsehood has been engineered by the English Government, and that the English press is allowing itself to be used as an instrument of this campaign". They argued that during the early stages of the lord Mayor's hunger strike, "most of the organs of the English press treated the matter fairly, or as fairly as could be expected in their columns", but as public opposition to the government's treatment of MacSwiney intensified, the government through the "Chief Commissioner of Police issued a note to the members of the Newspaper Proprietors Association asking them, should certain information come to their knowledge, to withhold it from publication".[142] The family would continue, however, along with the Irish Self-Determination League, to issue bulletins and conduct interviews with the foreign press.

On 7 September Art O'Brien had sent Michael Collins the text of a telegram which had been sent to British publications by the London Police Commissioner:

> In view of the possible death of the Lord Mayor of Cork through hunger striking in Brixton Prison, the Chief Commissioner of Police, General Horwood, is taking certain precautionary measures to protect government property. The Commissioner says it is obvious that these should not be generally known and he would be glad, should information of such measures come into the hands of the press, if they would refrain from publishing any reference to them.[143]

In his defence of the British government's conduct, C.J. Street ("I.O."), in his officially financed book *The Administration of Ireland 1920*, argued in response that it was "hardly necessary to remark that the allegations concerning the influencing by the Government of the opinions of the English press are ridiculous, and show a strong ignorance of the freedom of expression enjoyed by the English newspapers".[144]

Events in Ireland and Britain continued to run a violent course. On 27 September, as Terence MacSwiney slipped in and out of consciousness, the motorcade transporting British army divisional commander General Strickland was ambushed in Dublin. The driver was shot; the general escaped unharmed. Ironically, the attack came on the street that had been named by Dublin Corporation in honour of Tomás MacCurtain, a few miles from the site where MacCurtain himself had attempted to assassinate Lord French. In Britain on that day, summer time was extended by the government in anticipation of a strike by the coalminers. In Dublin the General Post Office again figured prominently in the newspaper headlines as two armed men blew open the building's main safe and made off with several thousand pounds.

While the American press was not included in the protest action taken by the MacSwiney family, issues of contention did arise on occasion. On 14 October 1920 Art O'Brien issued a protest to the *New York Herald* concerning a report in that day's edition which alleged that the lord mayor was voluntarily taking food. The *Herald* also reported the opinion of a group of New York physicians who contended that it was an impossibility that anyone could live for sixty days without food, particularly an individual of MacSwiney's slender build. "One marvels," O'Brien wrote sarcastically, "that men of scientific training should venture to give such emphatic opinions, without taking the elementary precaution of making an inquiry." His letter, however, took on a macabre note with the implication that the medical authorities at Brixton Prison were actually viewing MacSwiney's hunger strike from the vantage point of a scientific experiment.

> What a commentary on the results of what is known as modern education that those who are looked to by the multitude to have knowledge of and to cure the human body, should stand aside scoffing, when the most carefully prepared experiment in a subject of great physiological interest [i.e. the maintaining of a human body without nutriment] is being carried out. For such indeed is the proper explanation of what is happening at Brixton. In none of the known cases of fasting or hunger striking has the same minute care been taken to prevent the waste of tissue, as is being taken today by the English Government at Brixton Gaol. [145]

Few arguments advanced by the lord mayor's adherents were as fantastic as O'Brien's in this letter. No evidence exists, even among the most incriminating of documents on the British government's handling of the MacSwiney case, to support his allegations. Indeed, what is evident from the record, is the British government's frustration over MacSwiney's inexplicable endurance.

On 17 October, after sixty-eight days without food, Michael Fitzgerald, the leader of the eleven Cork hunger strikers, died in Cork Gaol. Terence MacSwiney, now one week from his own death, released a statement which reiterated his public view that the Republic's interests were served by such sacrifices: "We do not know who is to be second to step into the path of immortality, but by offering unreserved sacrifice, we are safeguarding the destinies of Ireland."[146] Ten prisoners remained on hunger strike in Cork. Joseph Murphy, who would die within hours of Terence MacSwiney after a remarkable eighty-one days, rallied slightly as a result of medical treatment, but on 19 October, the Associated Press reported that "severe collapses were suffered by two of the strikers, Donovan and Kenny, early this morning". The report noted that "Sean Hennessy, Reilly and Upton also are in a critical state".[147]

The last week of Terence MacSwiney's hunger strike ended, as it had begun, against a backdrop of continuing revolt in much of Ireland; but it was only to be a harbinger of worse bloodshed to come. Yet a report sent to the cabinet from Dublin Castle for the week ending 23 October 1920 sought to convey the view that the government's policy of coercion and reprisals was working to its advantage. The report stated that "the policy of lawlessness is not only becoming increasingly difficult in the face of measures being taken for suppressing it, but is gradually losing favour with the more responsible elements among its advocates".[148] This optimistic analysis was forwarded by the Irish administration to the government on the eve of what was to be unquestionably the bloodiest month of the Anglo-Irish war to date, November 1920. Nonetheless, the report conceded that the casualties for the British military and the RIC alike "have again been heavy, namely seven police and three military, the same total for the previous week. ... Most of these casualties have been sustained through the ambushing of motor lorries in remote districts which offer the best opportunities not only for the preparation of this form of attack, but also for the subsequent escape and concealment of the identity of the perpetrators." Total Republican "outrages" for that week "numbered 57 as compared with 71 the previous week". Twenty-four trials of civilians by courts martial were reported to the government, with fifteen of that number convicted.[149]

On 19 October a bulletin issued by the Irish Self-Determination League recorded that the lord mayor "had passed a restless day". The doctor was summoned and urged him to take lime juice against scurvy; but this led to an altercation that "excited the patient and left him exhausted, but tonight he was more settled and his condition generally unchanged".[150] The next day, however, MacSwiney entered a state of unconsciousness. The League announced that he had suffered "a serious attack of extreme delirium shortly after 10 o'clock this morning, the sixty-ninth day of his hunger strike". So serious was MacSwiney's condition that all of his relatives were allowed to visit him. Later that day, the lord mayor suffered what the League termed "a second and more violent paroxysm of delirium this afternoon which lasted a considerable time". Shortly afterwards, the sculptor Albert Power arrived to be ready to make a death mask of the lord mayor, at the urging of the poet Oliver St John Gogarty.[151]

In the House of Commons on that day home secretary Shortt dismissed rumours that the government was about to show leniency toward MacSwiney and the ten remaining Republican hunger strikers in Cork.[152] In fact, that night an unconscious Terence MacSwiney was fed by prison doctors with beef extract and brandy. Upon regaining consciousness, the lord mayor accused the doctors of "tricking" him and adamantly refused to take any more of the liquids. Earlier that day MacSwiney's family alleged that he had been forced to take lime juice. In parliament, Shortt sought to avoid the question, contending instead that he could not address the merits of the accusations of force feeding since he had not been able to communicate with the prison doctor. Nonetheless, the home secretary stated that the prison doctors would be justified in using force to feed MacSwiney "in order to keep him alive".[153]

The lord mayor's situation was hopeless. At this stage death would serve to provide a release from his agony. The morphine given him on 20 October to assist in quelling the violent paroxysm of delirium that had inflicted him during the previous forty-eight hours had granted him a temporary relief. He was by now all but blind. And in his fits of delirium he made disturbing comments, which were described in a message sent on 20 October from Art O'Brien to Michael Collins: "I need not relate to you the effect on his wife and sisters of witnessing these terrible paroxysms of delirium, in which he says the most violent things, and added to which is terrible screaming and shrieking."[154]

Press accounts published at this time confirmed the fact that MacSwiney was force fed. On 22 October, the *New York Times*, citing a bulletin released by the Irish Self-Determination League, reported that while MacSwiney "was delirious this morning the prison authorities continued to force food into his mouth in spite of his protests ... About 8:30 this morning a nurse held a spoon of meat juice to his lips but he muttered, 'No. Take it away.' ... The performance was repeated twice, when his head fell back from exhaustion and the spoon was entered in his mouth. By this stage, MacSwiney was no longer cognisant of his surroundings. Nor did he recognise his relatives, including his wife." The *New York Times*' account noted that "This was the 71st day since MacSwiney began his hunger strike, though the strike has now been partially broken by the food administered on Wednesday, yesterday, and today."[155]

Reports that MacSwiney was taking food voluntarily were again circulated by British authorities on 23 October, less than forty-eight hours before he died. An account by London correspondent John Steele, appearing in the *Toronto Globe and Mail* and the *Chicago Tribune* of 25 October, stated that "according to the doctors at Brixton Prison, Terence MacSwiney was resting comfortably today, the seventy-third day of his hunger strike. ... He was said to be in a semi-conscious state and to be suffering no pain. ... Nausea had ceased and the food that was still being administered was being assimilated."[156]

Predictably, this interpretation was greatly at odds with the bulletin issued on behalf of MacSwiney by the Irish Self-Determination League. The league attempted to carry MacSwiney's protest against his forced nourishment to the outside world. "They tricked me, and I didn't know," MacSwiney was quoted as saying in one account. The league's bulletin emphasised that "It should be made clear that the meat extract given the Lord Mayor during his delirium on the sixty-ninth day of his fast was the first nourishment which had passed his lips since his arrest on August 12th."[157]

Written under the direction of Art O'Brien, the league's statement took the government to task for having had Mac-Swiney's two sisters forcibly evicted from the ante room at Brixton Prison when they attempted to visit their brother. The official response was that, rather than acting from any desire to inflict pain on MacSwiney's family, the government and prison officials had in fact restricted visits out of a concern for the prisoner himself, and the restrictions imposed on the family had been urged by the attending physicians as a means of saving MacSwiney's energy.[158] As for the lord mayor himself, the league said that MacSwiney "opened his eyes occasionally, staring sometimes at Fr. Dominic, but gave no sign of recognition, even when Fr. Dominic spoke to him. He moans as if in pain." As with previous statements, the league's bulletin was written to arouse maximum sympathy for the lord mayor's cause. "Mrs. MacSwiney," it noted, "was allowed to be with her husband a little more than an hour yesterday. ... This extra strain and the fatigue placed on her has brought on an indisposition, and she was unable to visit the prison this morning."

As the lord mayor's life began to slip away, his brother Sean and Fr Dominic were allowed to stay in the prison overnight on the evening of 24 October. The Associated Press reported that the two men upon being summoned to his room by the prison medical officers early in the morning of 25 October, "found him lying motionless, with his eyes open but unconscious".[159] Fr Dominic proceeded to whisper prayers into MacSwiney's ear. He did not regain consciousness. Soon Sean MacSwiney and Fr Dominic were joined in the cell by four physicians, along with an observer from the home office.[160] The two Corkmen went to a separate room where they began reciting the rosary in Irish. It was during this time that MacSwiney was given an injection of strychnine in an attempt to revive him. Fr Dominic and Sean MacSwiney had not long started their prayers when they were brought back to the lord mayor's bed and informed that nothing more could be done for him. MacSwiney was given the last rites by the priest. Within minutes he was dead.

Sean MacSwiney and Fr Dominic set out for the West End hotel to inform the lord mayor's wife and sisters of his death. Three hours later the three women arrived, with his in-laws and Art O'Brien, at Brixton Prison to view his remains. Together they prayed over the emaciated body as it lay in the cot.

One report characterised Mrs MacSwiney as appearing "stoical and dry-eyed",[161] but she was soon overwhelmed by a combination of grief and sheer exhaustion. That day a statement was released in her name to the 1,300 branches of the Irish Self-Determination League in the United States with this simple message: "Terence died this morning. Muriel."[162] For the next two days she lay prostrate in her hotel room while MacSwiney's sisters organised the obsequies. A statement released later that morning from London by Fr Dominic said: "Fleet Street, London: 8:47 a.m. Monday, 25 October 1920, Lord Mayor completed his sacrifice for Ireland at 5:40 this morning."[163]

The records of the Republican government's ministry of defence for 25 October shows this entry in its official chronology: "Terence MacSwiney, Lord Mayor of Cork, died at 5:40 a.m. on his 74th day of hunger strike at Brixton Prison. Last words: 'I want you to bear witness to the fact that I died as a soldier of the Republic. God save Ireland.'"[164] On the next line came mention of the death of Joseph Murphy, the seventeen-year-old hunger striker in Cork Gaol. The other incidents listed on the report for that day provide an overview of the violence that had occurred throughout the country:

IRA attack RIC patrol near Grange. Four RIC dead, two wounded.

Later British forces burn premises and stores around Cliffoney and wound and arrest civilians. IRA attempt to surprise garrison at Mallow RIC barracks fails.

IRA attack Tempo RIC barracks and village patrol. RIC surrender. Later Phillip Breen, civilian, shot near his home.

Michael Ryan, president of the local Dáil court, taken from his home at Curraghduff, and William Gleeson taken from his home in Moher, and shot to death by RIC.

Charles Lynch (aged 70) shot dead in his home by RIC.[165]

Art O'Brien made sure that the details surrounding the lord mayor's death were known to Michael Collins as soon as possible:

> You no doubt received news of poor Terry's death early this morning. Ever since he went into delirium on Wednesday last, it has been fairly certain that the end could not be far off. Last night, his brother Peter and Fred Cronin, who had been with him, told me that they did not think he would last the night and their estimate has proved correct. His brother Sean and Father Dominic were summoned to him at twenty-five minutes to five this morning. As he was dying, Sean, immediately afterwards, wanted to telephone me, in order that I might bring the other relatives, but they would not allow him to use the Prison telephone, nor would they allow him to leave the prison until a quarter past six.[166]

The news of the lord mayor's death reached Collins as he was in the process of writing to O'Brien. Late in the evening of 25 October, he wrote to his compatriot in London that "If possible, I shall give you an idea of the arrangements being made before this letter goes, but probably somebody will be going across specially tonight in any case, and will reach you before this letter does."[167]

On 26 October 1920, Arthur Griffith telegraphed this message to Muriel MacSwiney, which appeared in the *Irish Bulletin* pages: "He has proved what he said – that victory in this struggle for Irish freedom is not to those who can inflict the most but to those who can endure."

Of his own longstanding ministering to Terence MacSwiney, Fr Dominic remarked that he had "joined him in Brixton, as a friend, as his chaplain. But 'twas as a brother, a fellow child of St. Francis that I bade farewell to him and sent him to meet 'Tomás' and Eoghan Roe and Joan of Arc."[168]

Although in the days and weeks preceding MacSwiney's death sympathisers had knelt and prayed at the gates of Brixton Prison, the news of his death – which was not released till 9 a.m. – produced little reaction in the vicinity of the prison. If anything, dignity and restraint would characterise those who came to mourn Terence MacSwiney's death in Britain. The Associated Press reported that the usual large contingent of police was outside the prison grounds to prevent any demonstration, but outside and along the road leading to the main highway there were no unusual signs of activity. "No civilians were waiting there as they usually did in the early days of the Lord Mayor's hunger strike."[169]

On the day of Terence MacSwiney's death, the British government released a captured letter dated from May of that year, which it appeared to have had in its possession for some time, addressed to the lord mayor in his capacity of commandant of the Cork No. 1 Brigade, seeking to tie him to the manufacture of hand grenades. The release of the letter on the day MacSwiney died, however, only caused more criticism of the government, especially as MacSwiney had at no time been charged with any offence implied by the communication to him. On 26 October, *The Times* of London stated its objection to what it termed "the attempts by the Government to saddle upon the Lord Mayor the crimes of which he never was convicted. ... Particularly odious is the publication on the day of death the letter referring to the manufacture of hand grenades. ... This action will only intensify Irish feeling," *The Times* predicted.[170]

At the inquest on 27 October, a jury of ten men, after deliberating for twelve minutes, returned a verdict which held that MacSwiney had died as a result of heart failure due to a dilated heart and acute delirium following scurvy, which had been brought about by his refusal to take food for seventy-three full days.[171] Muriel MacSwiney appeared at the proceedings as the sole representative of the MacSwiney family. Dressed in black and heavily veiled, she was described in one account as "the dominant figure of the proceedings". A battle of wills ensued when she refused to concur with the coroner's repeated efforts to characterise Terence MacSwiney's occupation as other than "a Volunteer officer of the Irish Republican Army".

"What was he?" the coroner asked. "An Irish Volunteer," she answered several times until that title was finally accepted.[172]

In its statements, coupled with those of its supporters in the United States and elsewhere, the Sinn Féin leadership sought to compare MacSwiney's death to the sacrifices of the American patriots during the Revolutionary War. In a statement released in the United States immediately after the lord mayor's death, Eamon de Valera compared Terence MacSwiney's determination to die rather than suffer the deprivation of his freedom with Patrick Henry's cry: "Give me liberty or give me death." He argued that "The principles that Mayor MacSwiney ... has given up his life to uphold and the principles for which the remaining comrades are giving up their lives are the principles of the American Declaration of Independence and President Wilson's war aims – the inalienable right to liberty, the privilege of men everywhere to choose their own way of life "[173]

Similar comments came from Arthur Griffith, who held that had MacSwiney been an American, "he would have become one of its most honoured and dignified citizens. ... His crime in England's eyes is that he dedicated these gifts to the service of his oppressed country instead of prostituting them in the service of the oppressors."[174]

De Valera's public remarks were uncharacteristically emotive. Speaking at New York City's Polo Grounds, he stated that the lord mayor "and his comrades gave up their lives for their country. The English have killed them. Tomorrow a boy, Kevin Barry, they will hang, and he alike, will only regret that he has but one life to give. Oh God!" The president of the Irish Republic concluded with a verse from William Butler Yeats's play, *Cathleen Ní Houlihan*:

> They shall be remembered forever,
> They shall be alive forever,
> They shall be speaking forever,
> The people shall hear them forever.[175]

In the immediate aftermath of MacSwiney's death, emotions in London, Ireland and the United States ran high. In Belfast sectarian mobs fought each other, resulting in death and injury. At a rally in New York City on 25 October, an observer narrowly escaped death at the hands of an angry mob of 5,000 protesters after he was accused of making derogatory remarks about the late lord mayor. The badly bruised man was rescued and shuffled off to a nearby cab by a pistol waving policeman.[176] In Sligo, two RIC constables were shot when a group of an estimated 100 IRA men ambushed a patrol.

The deaths of Terence MacSwiney at Brixton Prison and of the two Republicans, Michael Fitzgerald and Joseph Murphy, in Cork Gaol brought a rapid end to the Republican hunger strikes. They were a form of protest that had not officially carried the endorsement of leaders in the Republican government, although their propaganda value was by no means lost on Sinn Féin. Following the deaths of the three men, according to Dorothy MacArdle, "The rest of the Cork prisoners at the request of the Acting President of the Republic, Arthur Griffith, then abandoned their hunger strike." Griffith wrote to Terence MacSwiney's successor as lord mayor of Cork, Donal O'Callaghan, and stated his views on the need to end the hunger strikes: "I am of the opinion that our countrymen in Cork Prison have sufficiently proved their devotion and fidelity, and that they should now, as they were prepared to die for Ireland, prepare again to live for her."[177] Prior to Griffith's action, it appears that he was himself actively lobbied by Michael Collins on the need to ensure that those remaining on hunger strike were taken off it.[178]

In the view of British propagandist C.J. Street, in *The Administration of Ireland 1920*, Griffith's action was proof positive of Sinn Féin's orchestration of the hunger strikes of MacSwiney and the others. "The prompt obedience to the terms of the letter show that the official heads of the Sinn Féin movement are solely to blame for the deaths of MacSwiney, Fitzgerald, and Murphy."[179]

At the same time, Eamon de Valera, still in the United States, evinced a pragmatic attitude toward the use of the hunger strike. Joseph McGarrity, the Philadelphia-based head of Clan Na nGael, described a discussion he had with de Valera on the subject in the aftermath of MacSwiney's death:

I told him I should consider it a serious blunder for him if he came
to adopt the hunger strike; that I thought MacSwiney's death had
served all purposes of the method. He said that he must keep an
open mind on that; it might be again necessary to use it. That at
times great sacrifices were necessary of performance as they at
certain times brought results which could not be brought about
by other methods.[180]

Great sacrifices were wrought all through 1920, the most
violent year of the Anglo-Irish War. Two-hundred and thirty
policemen and soldiers were killed and 369 wounded. The
IRA, too, suffered heavy casualties, and there were hundreds
of civilian deaths.

One writer, Patrick O'Farrell, has observed that the lord
mayor's death "was no mere political act, it was firmly and
consciously a religious one, and herein lay both its true signif-
icance as an expression of Ireland's spirit and the reason for
its astounding impact on public opinion."[181]

The presence of Fr Dominic O'Connor at all stages of
MacSwiney's protest highlights the religious dimension of his
actions, with the priest acting on occasion both as his
spokesman and spiritual advisor. The fact that the Carmelite
cleric was allowed by the Irish Catholic hierarchy to act as if
the hunger strike had church sanction is itself significant.

Indeed, MacSwiney's utterances from behind the walls of
Brixton Prison were often as religious in nature as political.
Taken against the backdrop of the Irish revolution in which
an independent Ireland would be sustained by a largely
Catholic ethos, MacSwiney's brand of Catholic mysticism
took on a certain utopianism. In his statements, as Patrick
O'Farrell has noted, MacSwiney sought to characterise "all
that was happening in an orthodox Catholic religious
mould".[182] For O'Farrell, MacSwiney's prayer, released from
Brixton to his fellow hunger strikers at Cork Gaol, confirms
the belief that their protest was the stuff of Christian
martyrdom.

Such sentiments, and MacSwiney's authority to utter them,
went unchallenged by the Irish Catholic hierarchy. "Ireland,"
O'Farrell writes, "religious Ireland, identified with this man
intensely, a man who claimed without challenge, the clerical
prerogative of composing prayers, whose body lay in

Southwark Cathedral while thousands filed past, whose photo appeared on little cards ornamented and garlanded with flowers in the manner of a saint."[183] Even Bishop Cohalan of Cork, amongst the most anti-Republican of the Irish hierarchy, refrained from challenging MacSwiney's remarks; instead he officiated at the lord mayor's funeral mass. Cohalan, however, registered his opposition to hunger strikes two years later during the Irish civil war, by refusing to grant an anti-Treatyite protester the same rites of Christian burial that he had given to the lord mayor.

Despite the impassioned debate on the use of the hunger strike which MacSwiney's protest provoked well beyond the shores of Britain and Ireland, no definitive position was taken by the Vatican. On 17 October, after eight weeks of appeals for a pronouncement by the pope from those both favouring and opposing MacSwiney's action, an official from the Holy See announced that Pope Benedict had referred the matter to the Vatican office under whose purview questions concerning faith and morals came. However, up to the time of the deaths of MacSwiney, and Fitzgerald and Murphy in Cork Gaol, no indication of an official Church position was made public.

Foremost among the few clerical critics of the MacSwiney hunger strike was Fr Bernard Vaughan, an English priest of Irish heritage. In a statement issued early on during Mac-Swiney's protest, Fr Vaughan offered a somewhat guarded personal pronouncement, as distinct from a theological one: "Personally from my reading of theology, moral and dogmatic, I should not feel entitled to administer the rites of the Church to anyone, no matter what his nationality, who was deliberately dying through hunger strike." In his comments, it was evident that the priest sought to avoid a direct clash with those among the clergy, including Cardinal Mannix of Australia, who had refused to condemn MacSwiney's action. "Some moralists," he noted, "deny hunger striking can be justified: others have drawn a distinction between objective truths and subjective ones." Fr Vaughan's comments were denounced by MacSwiney's supporters in Ireland, Britain, and the United States in the most bitter terms. In America, the weekly publication, *The Irish Press*, asserted that "the real purpose of this statement is not the elucidation of the morality of the Mayor's hunger strike, but to cloud the issue raised by the action of the British government in sending him to prison. ... Fr. Vaughan's heartless action is a splendid example of the workings of the Imperialist mind."[184]

The cleric's arguments questioning the morality of Terence MacSwiney's hunger strike were also challenged by Mary MacSwiney, who offered him a theological interpretation of her own. Citing the words of Christ that "greater love than this no man hath, that a man lay down his life for a friend", the lord mayor's sister attacked the validity of Fr Vaughan's view that the sacraments of the Catholic Church should be denied to those who risked their lives through hunger strike. It was her contention that MacSwiney's death "will do more ... to destroy the evil thing which is the British Government in Ireland, than if he led a whole army into battle and lost the lives of his men as well as his own. ... Would that be suicide?" she asked rhetorically. "To die for a great principle is a noble death, and not even this material age has dared to decry it." In her belief, "The method of the death is immaterial but inasmuch as the prolonged agony of a hunger strike calls for greater character, for more strength of conviction and purpose, it is the more heroic."[185] Fr Vaughan's opinions had, in fact, aroused such a level of opposition that he was forced to refrain from uttering them in public. A lecture he was scheduled to give in Glasgow was cancelled following alleged threats.

In effect, MacSwiney was able to conduct his hunger strike as a Roman Catholic with the active encouragement of his personal chaplain Fr Dominic, Dr Mannix of Australia, and a number of other high-ranking Catholic clerics. He was also free to draw religious parallels to his experience and that of the other hunger strikers.

MacSwiney's actions found support in the pages of *Studies*, a Catholic quarterly. A hunger striker motivated like Terence MacSwiney did not, in the view of one author, have death as his objective, "quite the contrary, he desires to live".[186] Other supporters of MacSwiney argued that since his was a protest against injustice, and death was not certain "because there are conditions which, if fulfilled will break the fast", his intent was not suicide.[187]

A far less sympathetic tone came from the archbishop of Canterbury, Dr Randall Davidson, who avoided taking any public posture in relation to efforts to gain MacSwiney's release. On 15 October, the archbishop, in a letter to Mary MacSwiney, described the lord mayor as "an honest man setting himself deliberately to commit suicide". Like the British government itself, the archbishop stated that "our sympathy with the sorrowing homes of the men heartlessly murdered in the plain discharge of their duty carries with it the obligation of preserving order and protecting those whose duty it is to maintain".[188]

Mary MacSwiney's public reply to his statements was predictably caustic: "I should certainly have expected more straight thinking from one in Your Grace's position than is shown in the accusation that my brother is setting himself deliberately to commit suicide." Citing the example of the Egyptian Pharoah, she warned the archbishop that "If you harden your hearts, you must take the consequences as he did. ... No one has been 'heartlessly murdered'," Miss MacSwiney argued, "by the Irish. ... Some spies have been shot not 'for the plain discharge of their duty' as you say, but for the direct contravention of their duty – for taking as Judas did, the money of the foreigner to betray their own people."[189]

In the days after Terence MacSwiney's death, the Vatican sought to convey a prayerful and respectful tone. The *San Francisco Examiner* reported that when "Pope Benedict was informed of the death of the Lord Mayor, he showed deep regret and then knelt, remaining a long time in silent prayer".[190] However, in an account to the foreign office of a private meeting he had with the pontiff shortly after MacSwiney's death, the British representative in Rome stated that Pope Benedict had questioned whether the lord mayor had taken nourishment during his hunger strike.

> The Pope then referred to the case of the Lord Mayor of Cork. Reference had been made to the Vatican with regard to these hunger strikes and the matter was being considered. For his own part he did not see that such proceedings could be advisable. Moreover it seemed to him that in the course of the strike MacSwiney must have taken nourishment; no other supposition

was possible. And at the funeral there was too much parade. There was a certain element of farce to it all. I quite agreed but suggested that, as there frequently was to the comic opera side of the Balkans, there were tragic endings.[191]

The Church's public position on the morality of hunger strikes would continue to be an ambivalent one well beyond MacSwiney's day. The ten Irish Republican prisoners who died in Northern Ireland in 1981 and who drew inspiration from the lord mayor of Cork's example, met with differing reactions from within their own Church. Each, however, enjoyed the rites of Christian burial accorded by the Roman Catholic Church, unlike previous Republican hunger strikers during the early years of the Irish Free State. The English Catholic hierarchy, in response to British government pressure, sought to condemn the 1981 hunger strikes as suicide, while their counterparts in Ireland did not.

Writing in a context not unlike that of Terence MacSwiney's hunger strike, one Catholic theologian observed that in light of the pressure on the Church from all sides to issue a moral judgment favourable to their respective interests, "We are witnessing a mobilisation of Catholic moral theology for an essentially political purpose. Moral teaching," Fr Raymond Helmick wrote, "is sought as a way of condemning and discrediting the hunger strikers, or as an apologetic for them." His comparison between the context of Gandhi's hunger strikes and that of the Irish Republicans of 1981 is also useful in reflecting on MacSwiney's own protest.

> Hunger strikes have generally been judged, despite the opposition we have to suicide, as a means of non-violence, even "the supreme" means of non-violence, rather than as a means of violence. ... Gandhi's hunger strikes occurred in a context of non-violence. Most were carefully designed elements in non-violent protest against British policy in India. ... The Northern Ireland hunger strikes, by contrast, occur in a context of violence. ... Nevertheless, the fact that these hunger strikes happen in a context of continuing violence, that soldiers and police and rioters and innocent civilian bystanders get hurt and killed in the growing conflict over the hunger strikers themselves is itself an endorsement not only of a political cause, but of this very context

of violence in which we perceive their action colours our response, moral and human to it.[192]

In his account of the 1981 Republican hunger strikes at Long Kesh Prison, Padraig O'Malley pointed to the relevance of Terence MacSwiney's sacrifice. MacSwiney's example, he wrote, "became the theology of mystical Republicanism, the philosophy of non-violence of physical force separatism, the embodiment of the warrior without weapons, the fighting man as the apostle of passive resistance".[193]

However, Terence MacSwiney persisted as an unrepenting disciple of physical-force Irish separatism to the end. Repeatedly throughout his ordeal, and up to the final moments of his life, he wanted it understood that he was dying as a soldier for Ireland. When stripped of every last resource, including his freedom, MacSwiney used his body as a weapon against the empire. His hunger strike was an act of protest, but it was not an act of non-violence. By doing violence to himself, MacSwiney sought to do greater harm to Britain.

At the same time, MacSwiney became a prisoner to the purity of his own protest. By mid-September 1920, realising that the British government would not give in, MacSwiney found himself hopelessly locked into continuing with his protest. He could not turn back. For a man who had written so much about valour and patriotism, he knew that to do so would be for him a fate worse than death.

This, and the intensity which MacSwiney brought to his protest from the moment of his arrest, makes it clear that no external force, whether direct orders from IRA general headquarters or family pressures, would have deterred him from this course. Likewise, no one else, his sister Mary included, can be shown as having been an *eminence grise* who forced him to remain on hunger strike.

MacSwiney made his decision to commence a hunger strike at the time of his arrest in August 1920. He was determined to stay the course unless the British government relented. Nonetheless, facing the reality of the British government's refusal to back down, MacSwiney hoped to prevent others from following his example; his comments forwarded to the IRA command via Art O'Brien in London make this clear. This was so, despite the public utterances released in his name

from Brixton offering encouragement to his comrades under-
going similar agony in Cork Gaol. Indeed, perhaps some of
the suffering that has occurred in Ireland in more recent times
might have been averted, had this aspect of Terence
MacSwiney's ordeal been better known and understood.

Notes

1. P.S. O'Hegarty, *Terence MacSwiney*, p. 90.
2. Ibid. pp. 91-92.
3. *Irish World* and *American Industrial Liberator*, 30 August
   1920.
4. O'Hegarty, *Terence MacSwiney*, p. 94.
5. Ibid.
6. Ibid. p. 92.
7. Ernie O'Malley, *The Singing Flame* (Dublin 1979) pp. 258-59.
8. O'Hegarty, *Terence MacSwiney*, p. 93.
9. *New York Times*, 26 October 1920.
10. Munster and Leinster Bank to Muriel MacSwiney, 8 September
    1920, MacSwiney Collection, UCD Archives, P48b/417.
11. As cited by *Irish Independent*, 8 September 1920.
12. *Daily News* (London), as cited by *Irish Independent*, 13
    September 1920.
13. As cited by Pádraig Colum, *Ourselves Alone* (New York
    1959)p. 233.
14. Ibid.
15. Art O'Brien to Michael Collins, 25 August 1920, SPO/Dáil
    Éireann Files.
16. Michael Collins to Art O'Brien, 26 August 1920, SPO/Dáil
    Éireann Files.
17. Art O'Brien to Michael Collins, 27 August 1920, SPO/Dáil
    Éireann Files.
18. Art O'Brien to Michael Collins, 28 August 1920, SPO/Dáil
    Éireann Files.
19. Art O'Brien to Michael Collins, 4 September 1920, SPO/Dáil
    Éireann Files.
20. Michael Collins to Art O'Brien, 14 September 1920, SPO/Dáil
    Éireann Files.
21. John Healy Scott to Edward Shortt, 20 August 1920, Bonar Law
    Collection, HLRO 102/9/3.
22. Ibid.
23. A.M. Sullivan to Lloyd George, 26 August 1920, HLRO
    102/9/93.
24. Harold Nicholson, *George V* (London 1952) p. 348.

25. *The Nation.*
26. Irish Peace Conference to George V, telegram, 24 August 1920, HLRO 102/9/2.
27. *Manchester Guardian*, 26 August 1920.
28. George V to Arthur Balfour, telegram, 25 August 1920, HLRO 102/3/1.
29. Arthur Balfour to George V, HLRO 102/9/24.
30. Ibid.
31. Lord Stamfordham to Arthur Balfour, 27 August 1920, Bonar Law Collection, HLRO 102/2
32. Lord Stamfordham to J.C. Davidson, 28 August 1920, HLRO 99/4/22.
33. Ibid.
34. Ibid.
35. *Manchester Guardian*, 27 August 1920.
36. Ibid.
37. Bonar Law Collection, 28 August 1920, HLRO 102/9/5.
38. Lord Stamfordham to Arthur Balfour, 31 August 1920, HLRO 102/4/6.
39. Ibid.
40. Worthington Evans to Lord Stamfordham, 1 September 1920, Bonar Law Collection, HLRO 102/9.
41. Cabinet Minutes, 25 August 1920, CAB/23/2l.
42. Ibid.
43. Ibid.
44. Ibid.
45. Ibid.
46. Edward Shortt to George V, cable 26 August 1920, Bonar Law Collection, HLRO 102/9/3.
47. J.C. Davidson to Ernley Blackwell, 6 September 1920, Bonar Law Collection, HLRO 102/9/7.
48. Minutes of Cabinet Conference, 2 September 1920, CAB 23/22.
49. Ibid.
50. Ibid.
51. Lloyd George to Bonar Law, 4 September 1920, Bonar Law Collection, HLRO 8/31/l/44.
52. J.T. Davies to Lord Stamfordham, 17 September 1920, HLRO F/29/41/8.
53. Ibid.
54. *Cork Examiner*, 7 September 1920.
55. *Irish Times*, 2 September 1920.
56. Labour Party to Lloyd George, telegram, 3 September 1920, Bonar Law Collection, HLRO 102/9/12.

57. TUC to Bonar Law, 6 September 1920, Bonar Law Collection, HLRO 102/9/115.
58. Bonar Law to Labour Party, telegram, 5 September 1920, Bonar Law Collection, HLRO 102/9/115.
59. Ibid.
60. Ibid.
61. Liam de Roiste, statement, released for publication by Sinn Féin Publicity Bureau in response to remarks of Bonar Law, undated, MacSwiney Collection, P48b/427.
62. Ibid.
63. Ibid.
64. Ibid.
65. Ibid.
66. Ibid.
67. Annie MacSwiney, statement, 6 September 1920, MacSwiney Collection, P48b/427.
68. *Cork Examiner*, 10 September 1920.
69. Ibid.
70. Art O'Brien to Michael Collins, 9 September 1920, SPO/Dáil Éireann Files.
71. Ibid.
72. Ibid.
73. P.H. Barry to Lloyd George, telegram, undated, Bonar Law Collection, HLRO 102/9/21.
74. Lloyd George to P. H. Barry, September 1920, HLRO 102/9/87.
75. Chavasse, *Terence MacSwiney,*.p. 170.
76. Terence MacSwiney, statement, 21 September 1920, MacSwiney Collection, P48b/435.
77. Ibid.
78. Terence MacSwiney to Cathal Brugha, 30 September 1920, MacSwiney Collection, P48b/452(2).
79. Chavasse, *Terence MacSwiney*, pp. 170-1.
80. Ibid.
81. Statement of Deputy Governor of Cork Gaol, 6 September 1920, C.O. 904/168 p. 5, no. 29.
82. Ibid.
83. Statement released by Dublin Castle, John Anderson Files, C.O. 904/168.
84. Ibid.
85. Ibid.
86. Donald O'Callaghan to Fr Dominic O'Connor, 22 September 1920, MacSwiney Collection, P48/b.

87. Art O'Brien to Michael Collins, 11 September 1920, SPO/Dáil Éireann Files.

88. Ibid.

89. Michael Collins to Art O'Brien, 25 September 1920, SPO/Dáil Éireann Files.

90. Ibid.

91. Michael Collins to Art O'Brien, 28 September 1920, SPO/Dáil Éireann Files.

92. MacSwiney Collection, P48c/273.

93. Ibid.

94. Terence MacSwiney to Muriel MacSwiney, 12 December 1917, MacSwiney Collection, P48b/27.

95. Mary MacSwiney to Etienette Beuque, MacSwiney Collection, P48c/273.

96. Sean Murphy to Moirin Chavasse, 16 January 1954, MacSwiney Collection, P48c/75.

97. Ibid.

98. Art O'Brien to Michael Collins, 29 September 1920, SPO/Dáil Éireann Files.

99. Ibid.

100. Ernie O'Malley, *On Another Man's Wound* (Dublin 1979), pp. 258-9.

101. Report of W.D. Higson to Home Office, 23 August 1920, HLRO 102/9/23.

102 Ibid. Home Office to Bonar Law, 23 August 1920.

103. Ibid. Report of W.D. Higson to Home Office, 24 August 1920.

104. Ibid..

105. Ibid. 28 August 1920.

106. Ibid. 29 August 1920.

107. Ibid.

108. Ibid. 31 August 1920.

109. Ibid. G.B. Griffiths to the Governor, Brixton Prison, 2 September 1920.

110. Ibid.

111. Ibid. 4 September 1920.

112. Ibid.

113. Edward Troupe to J.C. Davidson, 6 September 1920, HLRO 102/9/18.

114. Edward Troupe to J.C. Davidson, 7 September 1920, HLRO 102/9/19.

115. Ibid.

116. G.B. Griffiths to Home Office, 6 September 1920, HLRO, 102/9/12.

117 Ibid. 8 September 1920.

118. Ibid. 9 September 1920.

119. Ibid.

120. Ibid. 11 September 1920.

121. Chavasse, *Terence MacSwiney*, appendix.

122. G.B. Griffiths to Home Office, 12 September 1920, HLRO 102/23.

123. Ibid. 13 September 1920.

124. Ibid. 17 September 1920.

125. Ibid. 18 September 1920.

126. Letter of Dr. Griffiths forwarded by Troupe to Cabinet, 18 September 1920, HLRO 102/9/23.

127. Edward Troupe to J.T. Davies, 18 September 1920, HLRO 102/9/23.

128. G.B. Griffiths to Home Office, 20 September 1920, HLRO 102/9/23/

129. Ibid.

130. Terence MacSwiney to Edward Shortt, 20 September 1920, Cork Municipal Archives.

131. *The Times* (London) 25 September 1920.

132. C.E. Callwell, *General Sir Henry Wilson* (New York 1927) vol. II, p. 265.

133. Dr. Griffiths to Home Office, undated, September 1920, Bonar Law Collection, HLRO 102/2.

134. Terence MacSwiney to Sean O'Sullivan, 24 September 1920, Cork Municipal Archives.

135. Donald O'Callaghan to Fr Dominic O'Connor, 5 October 1920, MacSwiney Collection, P48b/418.

136. Art O'Brien to Michael Collins, 9 October 1920, SPO/Dáil Éireann Files.

137. Chavasse, *Terence MacSwiney*, p. 217.

138. Ibid.

139. Ibid.

140. Art O'Brien to Michael Collins, 25 September 1920, SPO/Dáil Éireann Files.

141. Statement by MacSwiney family, 28 September 1920, MacSwiney Collection, P48b/428.

142. Ibid.

143. Art O'Brien to Michael Collins, 7 September 1920, SPO/Dáil Éireann Files.

144. C.J. Street, *The Administration of Ireland 1920*, p. 113.

145. Art O'Brien, *New York Herald*, 14 October 1920, MacSwiney Collection P48b/430.

146. New Orleans *Times Picayune*, 26 October 1920.

147. Associated Press account in *New York Times*, 20 October 1920.

148. Irish Administration Report to British Cabinet, 28 October 1920, C.O. 904/168.

149. Ibid.

150. Bulletin of Irish Self-Determination League, 19 October, SPO/Dáil Éireann Files.

151. Ulick O'Connor, *Oliver St John Gogarty* (London 1964) p. 183.

152. *New York Times*, 21 October 1920; see House of Commons debates for 20 October 1920.

153. Ibid.

154. Art O'Brien to Michael Collins, 20 October 1920, SPO/Dáil Éireann Files.

155. *New York Times*, 22 October 1920.

156. *Toronto Globe and Mail*, 26 October 1920.

157. New Orleans *Times Picayune*, 26 October 1920.

158. Ibid.

159. Associated Press account as reported in New Orleans *Times Picayune*, 26 October 1920.

160. Ibid.

161. Associated Press account as reported by Atlanta *Constitution*, 26 October 1920.

162. *New York Times*, 26 October 1920.

163. Fr Dominic O'Connor, statement, 25 October 1920, MacSwiney Collection, P48a/III.

164. Chronology Part III, Section 2, 25 October 1920, Ministry of Defence, Dublin. As cited by Pádraig Colum, *Ourselves Alone*, p. 234.

165. Ibid.

166. Art O'Brien to Michael Collins, 25 October 1920, SPO/Dáil Éireann Files.

167. Michael Collins to Art O'Brien, 25 October 1920, SPO/Dáil Éireann Files.

168. *Irish Independent*, 26 October 1920.

169. Associated Press account as reported by New Orleans *Times Picayune*, 27 October 1929.

170. *The Times* (London) 26 October 1920.

171. Associated Press account in San Francisco *Examiner*, 28 October 1920.

172. *New York Times*, 26 October 1920.

173. *San Francisco Examiner*, 26 October 1920.

174. *New York Times*, 27 October 1920.

175. *San Francisco Examiner*, 26 October 1920.
176. *New York Times*, 26 October 1920.
177. Dorothy MacArdle, *The Irish Republic*, pp. 391-2.
178. Piaras Béaslaí, *Michael Collins and the Making of a New Ireland* (Dublin 1927) vol. II, p. 73.
179. C.J. Street, *The Administration of Ireland 1920*, p. 113.
180. Sean Cronin, *The McGarrity Papers* (Tralee 1972) p. 91.
181. Pádraic O'Farrell, *Ireland's English Question* (New York 1972) p. 290.
182. Ibid. p. 291.
183. Ibid.
184. *Irish Press* (US), 4 September 1920.
185. Reply of Mary MacSwiney to Fr Bernard Vaughan, MacSwiney Collection, P48b/436.
186. P.J. Gannon, *Studies*, September 1920.
187. See lead article, *America*, 11 September 1920, and Michael Hogan, S.J., *The Ecclesiastical Review on Morality of the Hunger Strike* (1933).
188 Archbishop of Canterbury to Mary MacSwiney, 15 October 1920, MacSwiney Collection.
189. Mary MacSwiney, MacSwiney Collection.
190. *San Francisco Examiner*, 27 October 1920.
191. Despatch to Curzon from Rome, 13 November 1920, C.O. 908/185/132.
192. Raymond Helmick, "Northern Ireland in Moral Focus," *The Tablet*, 30 May 1981.
193. Padraig O'Malley, *Biting at the Grave* (Beacon Press 1990) p. 27.

Chapter VII
The Aftermath

IRA VOLUNTEER Connie Noonan believed that the lord mayor's death, "and the hanging of Kevin Barry on November lst, affected us deeply, but in ways it strengthened our resolve".[1] Historians such as F.S.L. Lyons agree that these deaths "set the stage for the terrible events of November 1920, by any reckoning the worst month in the entire Anglo-Irish war".[2] D.G. Boyce records that MacSwiney's death "caused a surge of shame in England, and Londoners lined the route in respectful silence as the coffin passed through the streets on its way to Holyhead".[3]

The lord mayor's death was covered extensively in the world's press; to that extent, at any rate, MacSwiney had succeeded in drawing international attention to the Irish question. In the United States, even those regions lacking a large Irish-American population expressed admiration for MacSwiney's courage. The *New Orleans Times Picayune* wrote that "Whatever men may think of the conflict in Ireland, however widely they may differ regarding the wisdom of his hunger strike and the effectiveness of his sacrifice, we think that all will honor Terence MacSwiney for his courage and devotion."[4] The *New York Times*, while clearly seeking the middle ground, acknowledged that, however mistaken Terence MacSwiney might have been in his decision to "starve himself to death, and however impossible it was for the English Government to surrender to a hunger striker, the world will at present consider the outstanding results ... It sees an Irishman willing to die if only the cry of his nation can be heard. Call it folly, call it madness, there it is just the same – a gesture of deep tragedy on a stage where all mankind looks on."[5] The *Boston Globe* published one of MacSwiney's final poems, "Teach Us How To Die", on its front page.[6]

Unlike the generally sympathetic tone displayed towards MacSwiney in the editorial pages of the American press, the Canadian reaction was somewhat critical. The *Toronto Globe and Mail*'s editorial posture leaned heavily towards the British government's position. "The only certain result of the death of the Mayor of Cork will be a fresh stirring of the dregs of hatred and bitterness and a widening between the two sections of the Irish people." The lead article went on to criticise those who had turned what it saw as a blind eye towards MacSwiney's active support of violence against the Royal Irish Constabulary:

> It is a deplorable casuistry that would define his condonation of crime or maintain that voluntary starvation is not a form of suicide. Even conceding that his hunger strike was an act of courage, what good purpose has it served? It can only add fuel to flames which must be quenched if Ireland is to be successful and prosperous.[7]

In Europe, the Dutch nationalist organ *De Voorts* thought MacSwiney's death would strengthen Irish nationalism, and nationalism, including Dutch nationalism, in general. The *Neuiwe Courant* concluded that "the English are famed for their chivalry to a courageous or a beaten foe. Here is a unique opportunity to show it."[8] From Brussels came a report to Lord Curzon at the Foreign Office on 16 November 1920 that a "requiem Mass was celebrated ... for the late Lord Mayor". The report also noted that "Mr. Gavin Duffy was present."[9] Duffy at that time served in a variety of roving diplomatic capacities for the Republican government on the continent.

Under the heading "Government Assaulted by Press for Death", the *San Francisco Examiner* reported that "Articles on the death of Terence MacSwiney occupied much space in the morning's newspapers, regardless of their political views." The paper cited *The Times* of London as saying, "that the effects of his death will not be confined to the British Isles." It cited the *Daily News* comment that "the Government imprisoned MacSwiney as a criminal and converted him into a martyr and must bear responsibility for his death".[10]

Similarly, the Canadian press also highlighted British news and editorial accounts on the death of the lord mayor in its coverage. The *Toronto Globe and Mail* cited a *Westminster Gazette* editorial which argued that "The Government may urge a thousand reasons to prove it could do nothing but what it did do ... Nevertheless, it has been beaten by Lord Mayor MacSwiney".[11] At the same time, the *Globe* cited an editorial in the government's defence from the pro-Coalition London *Evening Standard,* which argued that the responsibility for MacSwiney's death lay with the lord mayor himself and not with the government: "His death is as truly a case of self-murder as if he had opened a vein on the first night of his incarceration," the *Evening Standard* opined.[12] On the following day, the *Toronto Globe and Mail* reported that the "London press is still discussing the genuineness of MacSwiney's hunger strike, but almost without exception the newspapers pay high tribute to his unselfish courage."[13]

In Britain, the *Manchester Guardian*'s denunciation of the government's handling of MacSwiney was particularly severe. "The Lord Mayor of Cork is dead, and it is now possible to see why he has been allowed to die," the paper lead off.

> The King, it became plain, did not wish it. Mr. Bottomly did not wish it, and a multitude of people in between were of the same mind. The pressure on the Prime Minister was general. It might even have been thought to be irresistible, for he is not usually adamant in face of a widespread popular opinion. But he resisted and the Lord Mayor is dead. Obviously it is part of a policy, the policy of ruthlessness. Ireland is to be terrorised, opposition is to be crushed. To have shown clemency at this stage weakened the effect of that policy. It might even have suggested the application of another – that of redress. So the Lord Mayor has to die, and there are quite a number of other prisoners in like cases who will all die in due course.[14]

The Times of London reported the reaction of the nationalist press in Ireland. "The nationalist newspapers today were published with heavy black borders, and their contents were concerned almost entirely with accounts of the life and death of the late Lord Mayor of Cork ... Their leading articles denounce the Government with extreme bitterness and

regard Mr. MacSwiney's death as a heavy blow to any reasonable settlement of the Irish question."[15] The flag of the Irish
Republic was lowered to half mast outside the Mansion
House in Dublin, while in Cork city the Shandon bells tolled
over the River Lee.

On Wednesday evening, after the inquest had been
completed, Terence MacSwiney's body was removed to St
George's Roman Catholic Cathedral in Southwark. Five
thousand people waited for the body to arrive, and through
the evening a guard of honour was relieved at three-hour
intervals while the lord mayor lay in state. Beneath his IRA
commandant's uniform, MacSwiney's emaciated figure wore
the rough brown habit of the Third Order of St Francis, the
same religious order to which Tomás MacCurtain before him
had belonged.

The following morning, 28 October, some thirty thousand
people, Irish and non-Irish alike, filed past the bier, draped in
a green, white and orange tricolour. Among those who came
to the cathedral was a young British army officer named
Clement Atlee who, some twenty-five years later, would
succeed Winston Churchill as prime minister. The *Cork
Examiner* noted that "on many occasions members of the
gathering were overcome and had to be helped into the open
air and attended to".[16] Amongst those who journeyed from
Ireland for the funeral were MacSwiney's successor as lord
mayor, Donal O'Callaghan, the Cork Municipal
Corporation, and members of Dáil Éireann who were not on
the run from the crown. Requiem mass was celebrated by Dr
Cotter, Bishop of Portsmouth, assisted by Dr Mannix of
Australia. MacSwiney's coffin of polished mahogany was
placed before the high altar, his Volunteer's hat resting on the
casket. A large throng of lay people and some 400 members
of the clergy jammed the cathedral. Representatives of Dáil
Éireann and the Cork Harbour Board joined officials from
British bodies, including the lord mayor of Southwark, the
mayor of Fulham and the mayor of Battersea. Absent,
however, was Muriel MacSwiney. Overcome with grief, her
courage had given way to the awful reality of her husband's
death. She remained in England, missing her husband's burial
in Cork also.

After the service in the packed cathedral, the journey back to Ireland began with a 10,000-strong procession from the cathedral that included contingents from virtually every Irish society in London. Perhaps an even greater source of concern to the British government, however, was the response of the British public, who lined the streets in respectful silence.

Upon their arrival in Holyhead, the mourning party accompanying the lord mayor's body found that the British government had ordered that, rather than being allowed to go to Dublin, where a demonstration of public grief had been planned by Sinn Féin, and would be followed by a train trip across Ireland, the remains would instead be sent directly to Cork. An ugly scene occurred at Holyhead, the result of this surprise announcement.

The decision to re-route the lord mayor's body had come at the insistence of General Sir Henry Wilson. In an entry in his diary for 28 October 1920, Wilson's decision to go over the head of Hamar Greenwood, the Irish secretary, was made clear.

> I talked to Macready and told him that Hamar Greenwood told me last night that the Government could not prevent the lord mayor's body from being taken through Dublin, so all precautions must be taken. I then went to Winston, and I stormed about it to such an extent that he raced over to see the Prime Minister, with the result that the body will not be sent through Dublin, but will be shipped straight to Cork. This is good.[17]

As a result of General Wilson's intervention, the train to Holyhead was visited at 9:15 p.m. by a police inspector at Crewe station, who made his way to the chief mourners' carriage in search of Muriel MacSwiney. He brought a letter addressed to the widow from Sir Hamar Greenwood. On being informed that she was not on board the train, the inspector presented the letter to the lord mayor's brother, Peter, who had journeyed from New York. Its contents caused consternation in MacSwiney's family.

> I am advised that the landing and funeral of the late Lord Mayor in Dublin may lead to demonstrations of a political nature. I regret, therefore, that the Irish Government cannot allow disembarkation of remains of the late Lord Mayor in any other part

of Ireland except his native City of Cork. In order to save you
further inconvenience, the Government has directed the London
Northwestern Railway Co., to provide a suitable steamer to
carry the remains directly to Cork from Holyhead. This steamer
will also convey you and twenty of your friends if you so desire.[18]

The government's attempt at largesse was rejected outright by
the family. Art O'Brien, acting on their behalf, protested that
the government was seeking to violate what he said had been
a "contract", agreed to by the government in London, that
the lord mayor's remains were free to be transported from
Holyhead to Dún Laoghaire for a public memorial service to
be held in Dublin, and then by rail to Cork. The inspector
responded that he was obliged to carry out his orders.[19]

The train stopped abruptly at Holyhead station rather than
at the pier, and almost instantly railway porters began to
shout, "All change here and go to the boat at North Wall
wharf". The presence of the 300 police who had boarded the
train at Euston station, which the travellers had assumed were
for purposes of assisting in crowd control in Holyhead, now
took on a more menacing meaning. The doors to each car
swung open as the policemen emptied out to join in formation with a large body of Auxiliary Police and military who
stood waiting on the platform. The Black and Tans had
arrived from Dublin on the morning boat. The inspector
shouted to the passengers to disembark.

The mourners eventually left the train, but a number, led
by Mary and Peter MacSwiney and Fr Dominic, headed for
the van in which the lord mayor's coffin lay and took up
positions around it. Attempting to ignore them, a railway
superintendent told his men to continue moving forward a
truck for the purpose of transferring the body to the waiting
steamer, the *Rathmore*. The scene grew uglier as the mourners
tried to prevent the authorities taking the coffin. The railway
inspector left to make a telephone call to his superiors to
determine if the orders stood, but returned moments later
accompanied by a number of railway officials whom he
ordered to transfer the remains to the vessel. When
MacSwiney's family and friends continued to stand their
ground, some twenty policemen approached the van and
began pulling the mourners aside. A core group consisting of

MacSwiney's brothers and sister Mary, along with a number of members of the clergy, held on from inside the van. The *Cork Examiner* reported that "When Miss MacSwiney was thrown to the floor, her brother, Mr. Sean MacSwiney, promptly went to her assistance, but he was also subjected to rough usage. Another policeman rushed at him, seized him by the throat and violently dragged him away."[20] Soon the van was cleared and Terence MacSwiney's remains taken from it. The casket was wrapped in a stretcher of sackcloth and a crane raised it onto the steamer.

Every member of the mourning party refused to board the vessel. The order was given for it to proceed directly to Cork, and the lord mayor's body was accompanied on its journey by members of the British military. As the ship left the dock, Fr Dominic began reciting the rosary in Irish. The angry mourners knelt and prayed with him aloud.

The mourners boarded the mail boat for Dún Laoghaire, intent on going ahead with the memorial service which had been planned for Dublin, even without MacSwiney's body. In the event, the thousands of British soldiers called onto the streets of the capital could only stand and watch as the city's masses turned out to honour the lord mayor. On Friday morning requiem mass was celebrated at the Pro-Cathedral by Archbishop Walsh, assisted by Dr Spence, Archbishop of Adelaide, and Dr Clune of Perth. One of the priests who assisted at the mass was Fr Augustine Hayden, who had only minutes earlier returned from a last visit with eighteen-year-old Kevin Barry, scheduled to be hanged in two days' time at Mountjoy Jail.

Tragedy compounded tragedy as Ireland prepared for further mourning. The British government sought to portray a different version of events. C.J. Street gave this account, largely for American consumption. It ended on a note of irony that bordered on sarcasm.

> The lack of animus on the part of the Government was shown by the fact that MacSwiney's funeral cortege, decked with every conceivable Republican emblem, and escorting a coffin upon which an inscription in Republican terms was allowed to pass publicly through the main streets of London in the middle of the

day. Naturally, however, such an incitement to rebellion could not be permitted in Ireland without grave risk of disorder endangering innocent lives. The funeral party were therefore informed during the journey to Holyhead that a special steamer had been placed at their disposal to convey the body direct to Cork ... The purely political outlook of the Republicans on the whole incident was then once more shown. The guard of honour and MacSwiney's relatives preferred to proceed direct to Dublin in order to take part in the celebrations which had been prepared there in expectation that the coffin would be landed at Kingstown; whilst the body of Terence MacSwiney was allowed to proceed unattended by mourners, and under the care of a party of the R.I.C.[21]

At 1:45 on the afternoon of Friday, 29 October, MacSwiney's remains arrived in Queenstown (now Cobh), County Cork. There the British Auxiliaries were met by a problem of a different complexion. In an action that was probably planned, none of the hundreds of mourners assembled at the dock came forward to claim the body, forcing the authorities to transfer the body themselves from the *Rathmore* to the British admiralty tug, *Mary Tavy*. At 4:15 p.m., the *Mary Tavy*, with its blue ensign flying at half mast, arrived at Customs House Quay. After an absence of two-and-a-half months, Terence MacSwiney had finally returned home.

The mourning party from Dublin arrived in Cork that evening, and the body was removed from the tug and placed upon the quay. At 9:30 p.m., MacSwiney's remains were carried into City Hall on the shoulders of an honour guard of Irish Volunteers, accompanied by acting president of the Irish Republic Arthur Griffith, Liam de Roiste and several other members of the Dáil, along with a large retinue of clergy.

On the day of the arrival of the lord mayor's remains in Cork, an open letter from Bishop Cohalan appeared in the *Cork Examiner*:

I ask the favour of a little space to welcome home to the city he laboured for so zealously the hallowed remains of Lord Mayor Terence MacSwiney. For the moment, it might appear that he has died in defeat. This might be conceded if there were questions merely of the individual, but it is not true when the resolve of the nation is considered. Was Lord Edward Fitzgerald's death in vain? Was Robert Emmet's death in vain? Did Pearse and the other martyrs for the cause of Irish freedom die in vain? We are the weaker nation in the combat ... Special questions such as the questions of the land, of local government, of housing, or education, for a time engage our whole attention. But periodically the memory of the martyr's death will remind a young generation of the fundamental question of the freedom of Ireland ... Terence MacSwiney takes his place among the martyrs in the sacred cause of the freedom of Ireland ... We bow in respect before his heroic sacrifice. We pray the Lord may have mercy on his soul.[22]

Dr Cohalan's patriotic tone is unconvincing, given his antipathy to republicanism up to this. Three years later he wrote another letter to the *Cork Examiner*, explaining his decision to deny the rites of Christian burial to Republican hunger striker Dennis Barry in the aftermath of the Irish civil war. Despite stating that he knew Barry "to be a very good man", Cohalan said that the use of the hunger strike had become exceedingly irreverent, "and even blasphemous". In denying Barry the last rites, the bishop held that he was "but enforcing the law of the Church".[23]

The people of Cork came in their thousands to offer their respects at the lord mayor's lying in state and to his funeral, though there were some who said no more young men should die on hunger strike. A letter to the *Cork Examiner* asked: "I wonder is it hopeless to appeal to those whom the hunger strikers in Cork Gaol recognise as their authority to consider whether an order should not be made that these men now take food?" In the same issue, an individual calling himself only "A Parish Priest" stated: "Without going into the ethics of the question, as we have now three martyrs who have nobly given their lives for their cause and principles as it seems clear that the British Government will 'suffer their deaths gladly', I wish to ask the Irish Republican Government is it necessary to make a further holocaust of the brave boys in Cork Gaol?" The cleric suggested that there were other ways in which the men could serve their country.

Are they not too good to die so? Is not their cause sufficiently vindicated in everybody's eyes. Why not even at this eleventh hour, command them to retire. There is still a chance that they live to help their country in her struggle for freedom. By doing so their names will live in history as well as the men who have died.[24]

The *Manchester Guardian*, reporting on MacSwiney's lying in state at Cork's City Hall, observed that "the people of Cork have filed past the open coffin in unending procession all day".

> The interior of the Hall is plain and bare of ornament. Below the large organ that fills one end there are stacks of wreaths and flowers, and crepe hangs from the railing around the gallery. More wreaths surround the coffin which rests in the centre of the Hall. The austere figure within it is clothed in the uniform of a Brigadier of the Republican Army. It is the only uniform there, but Volunteers in mufti stand rigidly on either side of the coffin and form a cordon along the street outside.[25]

In an act of malice the night before, however, the black mourning draping that had been placed above the entrance to City Hall was torn down, and was found floating in the River Lee. Outside City Hall, the public stood in a line, running half-a-mile through the city's streets. The *Guardian* wrote that many of the mourners "fell silent when their turn comes to enter the Hall ... Among them," the paper noted, "are many children, some very young; one feels thankful that they are not tall enough to look into the coffin as their parents lead them past it."[26] Those who came to view the lord mayor's bier entered in single file, proceeded around the coffin and exited by another door. P.S. O'Hegarty's account of paying respects to his dead friend is particularly poignant.

> To me who had been intimate with Terry it was a queer experience ... The first glimpse of his dead head, from afar off, was unmistakably Terry ... then as you went nearer it seemed to be unlike him. The face was also the face of a bronze statue, but that was not the unfamiliar thing about it. The lines were different, for it was a face in which all the tissue had gone but the fundamental things. It was a face in fact in which the real Terry, the fundamental Terry first appeared. And what was left now was essentially a warrior face. Nobody had been accustomed to regard Terry as primarily a fighter, in that sense.[27]

After a requiem mass celebrated by the Bishop of Cork, assisted by four Irish bishops and two Australian archbishops, the lord mayor was buried on Sunday, 31 October. In County Longford on that day, the hand of fate moved against the local district inspector of the RIC. The IRA's general headquarters had earlier conditionally approved of orders to execute him in the event of the death of either Terence MacSwiney or Kevin Barry. The district inspector accordingly was shot on 31 October, the day of the lord mayor's burial. On the following day Kevin Barry was hanged. The Anglo-Irish waltz with death continued.

Soon after her brother's burial, Mary MacSwiney received a letter of condolence from one of her former teachers at Cambridge University, from which she had received a teaching degree some twenty-five years before.

> It was only quite recently that I learnt that you are the same Miss MacSwiney that was one of my students at Cambridge and I want therefore to send you a few words of warmest and deepest sympathy in your grief and trouble. I feel that it would not be so strange if you should dislike the idea of any communication just now with anyone English ... I want you to believe that we hate and abhor what is being done in Ireland – that when we think of the death of your heroic brother and the suffering of the other Irishmen and women we are filled with bitter shame and sorrow, that we are not only hoping and praying for an end to these horrors, but the moment we can stop them we will ... The English people cannot long tolerate, when once they really know, the things that are being done in their name.[28]

In the autumn of 1920, fighting in Ireland intensified. As IRA attacks on convoys of British Auxiliary troops and RIC increased dramaticallly, the government introduced martial law in Cork and the south-western counties. The British policy of reprisals against military and civilian targets alike, reached a new height in December, when "Black and Tan" troops burned the centre of Cork city. By the spring, however, lines of communication were opened between the British government and Sinn Féin, and the terms of a truce were hammered out. Hostilities ceased on 11 July 1921.

The Government of Ireland Act of the previous year had

provided for a separate jurisdiction in Northern Ireland, and
in negotiations which continued through the autumn of 1921,
the British government offered Southern Ireland the status of
a dominion of the British empire. The eventual terms of the
Anglo-Irish Treaty, signed by Arthur Griffith and Michael
Collins in London, provided for a partitioned island wherein
both parts would pledge allegiance to the king. Terence
MacSwiney's memory served as a rallying point for those
committed to the preservation of the Republican ideal in its
more uncompromising form.

In the private session of Dáil Éireann which debated the
Anglo-Irish Treaty on the evening of 17 December 1921, Mary
MacSwiney, who had taken her brother's place in the Dáil,
invoked his memory in pleading for her colleague's rejection
of the treaty's terms. Throughout the course of the often
acrimonious public and private sessions of the Dáil on the
treaty, she was amongst the most strident in her opposition
to the agreement and the most venomous in attacking those
who spoke in its favour. Although not the only instance in
which she sought to interject Terence MacSwiney's name into
the proceedings, her 17 December speech was perhaps one of
the most emotional delivered in the Dáil during the debate. It
merits quotation in full:

> Search your souls tonight and in the face of every martyr that
> ever died for Ireland take an oath now that you will do what is
> right no matter what influences have been brought to bear on
> you. I do not speak of my right anymore than I do of the others
> to allude to those who have gone but I do ask those here tonight
> who are putting expediency before principle to kindly leave the
> names of the dead out of their speeches. I consider myself in a
> different position from most of those who have suffered, for
> every other person who lost one near and dear to her lost him
> suddenly. I did not. For 74 days I sat and thought and let me tell
> you in 74 days you have much time for thinking. I weighed the
> cost. I weighed every thought. I am not a fool ... I do not think I
> am a fool and sitting there by that deathbed the like of which has
> never been known in the world before I looked at this question
> from every possible angle, from the orthodox, from the national
> point of view, and I asked myself, when talking with my dying
> brother I asked him, was it worth the cost, and we decided it was,

and one of the last things he ever said to me was, "Thank God there will be no more compromises now."[29]

The memory of the dead figured in Michael Collins's concluding remarks in the Dáil on 19 December, in support of the treaty and in vindication of his role in bringing it about.

> Deputies have spoken about whether dead men would have approved [the treaty] and they have spoken of whether children yet unborn will approve of it, but few of them have spoken as to whether the living will approve it. In my own small way, I tried to have before my mind what the whole lot of them would think of it ... There is no man here who has more regard for the dead men than I have.[30]

The Dáil ratified the treaty by a majority of seven votes, but two weeks later Mary MacSwiney again did her utmost to ensure that no compromise would be reached between those who stood in favour, and those who stood against the agreement. On 7 January 1922, having been defeated by Arthur Griffith for the presidency of the Dáil, Eamon de Valera stood in a hushed chamber, apparently fumbling for an answer to a plea from Michael Collins to "come in behind us and help us get the best out of the treaty", Mary MacSwiney jumped to her feet and shouted: "No! We won't go in with you, nor help you in any way. You are worse than Castlereagh ..."[31] DeValera allowed her remarks to stand, giving no formal response of his own to Collins's call for co-operation.*

But the spectre of Terence MacSwiney and his dead comrades continued to haunt Collins. In Cork city in June 1922, on the eve of the "Pact Election", he was barred by armed anti-Treatyites from entering the Republican plot at the cemetery where MacSwiney was buried. Collins was so enraged that he had to be dragged away by his companions.[32]

MacSwiney of course did not live to see the civil war which sundered the national movement, but, having done so much to realise Irish independence, his memory remained very much

---

*Some eighteen years later, de Valera as head of the first Fianna Fáil government, and operating within the margins of the Irish Free State apparatus that Collins had asked him to join, became the target of attacks from Mary MacSwiney, who said that he had also betrayed the ideal of the Irish Republic. Like Collins, he had become another "Castlereagh".

alive all through this period. In a 27 February 1921 entry in her diary, Lady Augusta Gregory, commenting on the Abbey Theatre's production of *The Revolutionist*, remarked on the "splendid audiences". The change in the public attitude in the months following the lord mayor's death was also evident to her.

> I feel so happy that we have been able to keep the Abbey going, if only for this week, with the production of a national play of fine quality by one who has literally given his life to save the lives of others. For by his death and endurance he has made it unnecessary for other prisoners to protest through hunger strike; he has done it once for all. It is strange to see the changes in political thought now, the audiences cheering the revolutionist who stands up against the priest's denunciation, denounces his meddling in return. They applauded also fine sentences. "Life is a divine adventure. She will go farthest who has most faith."[33]

Pádraig Colum wrote that "it would be impossible to overestimate the effects of Terence MacSwiney's ordeal and its conclusion on the Irish and British public". He gives a useful analysis of how MacSwiney's hunger strike helped to change the attitudes of the British and Irish publics.

> Ordinary English people did not believe that the Irish really wanted to separate themselves from the United Kingdom and the British Empire – they didn't know what the Irish wanted, but it couldn't possibly be that. But here was a man gaoled in a suburb of London who was letting his life waste away ... They did not think his ordeal and death, as the French and Italians did, as heroic, for they could not sympathise with the passion that was behind it, but they saw in it something sporting (the word is used in the fine sense) and an admiration for the spirit of the "Shinners" came to them, an admiration that was to lead to the formation of another image of the Irish nationalist than the one they were used to. In Ireland, amongst those who had gone over to Sinn Féin, the ordeal of Terence MacSwiney meant a dedication at a higher pitch. But there was a large section in Nationalist Ireland that had not gone over, for whom Sinn Féin as well as the Gaelic League denoted fanaticism. Now the emotions of these people were deeply stirred: they sympathised with men whom they had thought trouble-makers and with a cause they had thought dangerous. Now

thousands of men and women mourned for Terence MacSwiney, and in mourning for him made his cause their own.[34]

MacSwiney's hunger strike helped to personalise the Anglo-Irish conflict in graphic and awful terms. It allowed the Irish independence movement to exploit his suffering and death as an example of British cruelty in Ireland, both against the individual and against the kind of small nation whose rights the British claimed to have championed in the Great War.

Charles Townsend has argued that MacSwiney's death "proved a decisive blow to the hunger strike policy, a fact which might in the long run have outweighed the emotional impact of martyrdom".[35] It can be argued, however, that MacSwiney's death quite possibly made further Republican hunger strikes unnecessary, and hastened Arthur Griffith's decision to call the remaining hunger strikers in Cork Gaol off their protest. And the impact of MacSwiney's death in galvanizing opposition to British policy in Ireland cannot be ignored. No single event up to that time had served to greater effect to draw international attention to the Irish independence struggle. Indeed, in Britain itself, the government was severely jolted when ordinary people with little or no Irish connections came out on the street to mark MacSwiney's passing. And, in the months after MacSwiney's death, George V, who had hoped for a compromise during the hunger-strike impasse, began for his part to play a more active role in encouraging his ministers to seek a negotiated settlement in Ireland.

An important platform for exploiting MacSwiney's hunger strike to the maximum was provided by the American Commission on Conditions in Ireland. Set up by Dr William Maloney, it consisted of more than sixty members of Congress, governors and other elected officials. The commission, in the course of fourteen days of public hearings, from 19 November 1920 to 21 January 1921 in Washington DC, took testimony from thirty-seven witnesses, eighteen of whom came from Ireland. Among them were Muriel and Mary MacSwiney, the wife and sister of Terence MacSwiney. MacSwiney's death had received worldwide attention and nowhere was this more the case than in the United States, where efforts were made by local, pro-Irish separatist organ-isations to hold up MacSwiney as a martyr to British oppres-sion. The appearance of the two MacSwiney women, dressed in black, coupled with the lengthy, emotional yet poignant testament of MacSwiney's sister Mary, of several hours duration covering a session and a half, were not helpful to Britain's image in the eyes of the world.[36]

In May 1921, Muriel and Mary MacSwiney were joined in the United States by MacSwiney's successor as lord mayor of Cork, Donal O'Callaghan. At the request of the British government, the US State Department attempted to deport O'Callaghan for entering the country as a stowaway, but the opposition of the burgeoning American labour movement succeeded in allowing him to remain in the US, using the excuse that he had in fact travelled from Ireland as a seaman on an American steamship. O'Callaghan made use of his stay in the US to attack the British government for the murder of Tomás MacCurtain, and for the unyielding vindictiveness it had displayed towards Terence MacSwiney throughout his protest.

In the years after MacSwiney's death, the antipathy which had developed between Mary MacSwiney and Muriel was made abundantly clear. Refusing permission for the publica-tion of extracts from her brother's letters to his wife, Mary told one would-be author in 1937 that Muriel was "not normal and her views on all that concern Ireland are warped and distorted".[37] The writer was refused access to the letters, and received no help in locating Muriel.

Three years after her brother's death, Mary MacSwiney had a bitter clash with Cork's Bishop Cohalan, when he refused to allow Republican hunger striker Denis Barry full burial rites. Dismissing her criticism of his action, the bishop claimed that Mary MacSwiney "was not a republican at all in 1916", and "prevented the call for a rising to reach the Volunteers of Cork". He levelled a further charge, that she had prevented her brother from ending his hunger strike.

> Later, she gambled on the life of Terry. It occurred in this way, just as in the late hunger strike; she encouraged Terry to continue the strike. She never believed it would go to a fatal end. She

thought he would be released, and that she would share in a sunburst of cheap glory. She solicited intervention here, there and everywhere; she was hoping that Terry would live until the re-assembling of the British Parliament, to get help even from that quarter. She gambled too long. It was not a "win out". And then the theory was started that, in justice to the memory of Terry, it should be a Republic or an Ireland reduced to ruin.[38]

While Bishop Cohalan's comments about Mary Mac-Swiney's alleged efforts to prevent a rising in Cork may be seen as disingenuous, in the context of his own role in urging the Irish Volunteers to lay down their arms, his remarks concerning her conduct during Terence MacSwiney's hunger strike must be considered. Mary MacSwiney wrote letters to Cohalan's Irish superior as well as to the papal nuncio in Ireland, and threatened legal action against the bishop, but no action was taken. In a letter drafted to the papal nuncio, Monsignor Paschel Robinson, several years after the bishop's attack on her, she sought to raise the issue again. "In all these years I have had no reply to my appeals to his Holiness. I feel deeply both the calumnies of the Bishop and the long delay in obtaining the satisfaction to which the laws of the Church entitled me."[39] She received no satisfaction, however. For a woman who showed no hesitation in criticising the hierarchy of her church, as she did when she criticised Bishop Cohalan among other Catholic bishops for issuing an edict of excommunication for IRA membership, her relative timidity in this instance might be viewed as surprising. She also appears to have sought no public forum from which to refute Cohalan's charges.

And what of MacSwiney's widow, Muriel, and their little daughter Máire? The life that lay ahead for Muriel and Máire MacSwiney was filled with considerable sadness. Indeed for Máire, the support given her by her father's sister, Mary, served as an important source of stability in her early life. Her relationship with her mother was one of great uncertainty. Muriel MacSwiney's sudden mood swings create a picture of a deeply troubled woman. In her own words, Máire MacSwiney states that "The main problem with my mother was that she had some psychiatric illness."[40]

At the same time, Máire MacSwiney expressed an appreciation of her mother's many fine qualities. "In every other way, she was a wonderful person," she wrote, "loving, caring, brilliantly intelligent, of great integrity and full of concern for those not well off." In the aftermath of her husband's death, however, Muriel MacSwiney found it increasingly difficult to cope. Máire recalled that when "her illness hit a bad patch she just retired to bed, opting out of life entirely ..."[41]

Such behaviour may also have occurred when Terence MacSwiney was alive. During her mother's periods of depression, little Máire often found herself in the care of her grandmother in Cork. There she was in the care of butlers and a special nurse. Muriel's difficulties may have lain at the heart of Terence MacSwiney's decision, taken on his death-bed, to assign their daughter to joint custody with his sister, Mary. As to the depth of her mother's problems, which may have been manic depressive in nature, Máire MacSwiney Brugha speculates that her aunt, Mary MacSwiney, "probably saw a clearer picture of my mother than any of the others".[42]

Following Terence MacSwiney's death, Muriel and three-year-old Máire continued to reside in Cork. Muriel communicated with the child only in Irish. It was a difficult period for both mother and daughter. One incident, dating to July 1922, stands out particularly in Máire's recollection of their time spent together. In their flat in Dublin, when the little girl was four:

> This evening I refused to eat my supper, to be precise my egg, and my mother said if I didn't eat it she would go away and leave me. I decided to chance my bluff and right enough she was gone next morning leaving me with the maid and I didn't see her again for twelve months ... As far as the world at large was concerned, the Civil War had broken out (that's how I know the date) and my mother had taken herself off to the Hammond Hotel where de Valera and Brugha were trying to deal with the situation. There were some other women there. I don't know whether my mother was needed or merely added to the difficulties the men were having.[43]

The widow of the executed 1916 hero "The O'Rahilly" took the child into her care, and she was cared for as a daughter in their household of five boys, but at the end of autumn 1923 Muriel reclaimed the child. They went to Germany, and spent the next decade away from Ireland. Central to Muriel's actions was a desire to keep Máire away from the influence of Mary MacSwiney and her husband's other sisters. She was especially determined that her daughter not be raised a Catholic. According to Máire, "One of the main *bête noir* in her life by now was the Catholic Church. She blamed them for all the ills of the poor and every hypocrisy, etc."[44]

Christmas 1923 marked an especially lonely time for the five-year-old child. Her mother had left her near Heidelberg in an avant-garde German boarding school, among strangers, with whom she could not communicate. A promise by Muriel to take the child out of the school for Christmas was not kept. Thereafter, the only periods she would ever reside with her mother came during summer holidays from the myriad of schools she attended.

Máire MacSwiney Brugha believed that her mother lived in Paris while she was in Germany. In Paris, Muriel may have become actively involved in left-wing politics. "Apart from her rejection of religion," Máire writes, "her second obsession was the Communist Party. They became her religion, and as far as I can make out whoever she was in touch with of that persuasion in Paris at that time managed to part her from a lot of money."[45] In Paris, Muriel MacSwiney became involved in a relationship with a French intellectual, and had a daughter by him who was born on 5 May 1926 in Germany. The child was named Alix.

While she remained a boarding student in Heidelberg, Máire received sporadic visits from her mother, who would call her to meet at a railway station. "I don't know where my mother lived during this time; she wouldn't tell anyone," Máire recalled. "I had to learn to adapt to changing circumstances ... I had no vision of any future or any sense of security or continuity."[46] When, in the summer of 1930, Mary MacSwiney wanted mutual Irish friends who were visiting Germany to pay a call on Máire, Muriel whisked the child away, along with baby Alix, to a doctor's home in the Bavarian Alps. The following Easter, Muriel wanted to bring Máire and Alix back to Heidelberg, but Máire refused to go.

Soon after, Mary MacSwiney decided to visit Máire in Germany.
It was a visit which Muriel tried hard to prevent. Máire's
account of what followed reads like a novel from the period.

> My mother got her wind up and sent this gentleman to collect me
> ... They all arrived together! By this time I was resigning myself
> to the inevitable, so was my aunt Maire [Mary] ... she ordered
> the taxi to take her and her friend Mrs Stockley to the station the
> following morning to return to Ireland. When I was saying
> goodbye to Mrs. Kaltenback [with whom she was living at this
> time] ... she suggested that I should go to my aunt in the hotel
> and ask her to take me with her. I ran all the way and found my
> aunt and her companion at breakfast. She didn't understand a
> word I was saying since she understood no German and I had no
> English ... Mrs Stockley who was part German and part French
> couldn't cope with the urgency of the occasion by translating. By
> the time the taxi arrived my aunt understood. I knew the Austrian
> frontier was only a half hour away by a back road and I was able
> to direct them to it, I staying on the floor of the taxi so as not to
> be seen ... We caught a train and made our way back to Ireland
> via Geneva and Paris while the German police were looking for
> us throughout Germany. My mother believed, as was reported in
> the German and English press, that my aunt had kidnapped me
> when in fact I had to do all the kidnapping![47]

Muriel MacSwiney took an action in the Irish courts seeking
custody of the child. However, when questioned by the judge
directly as to her wish, Máire, who was by then fourteen, made
it clear that she wanted to reside with her aunt, and so in 1932
she was made a ward of court and allowed to remain with
Mary MacSwiney. "Losing the case made my mother very
unhappy," Máire MacSwiney Brugha wrote. "She blamed the
Catholic Church for the outcome; they were not involved in
any way in the case, but the fact that I was not being brought
up as a Catholic (which would have been my father's wish)
and the insecurity of my existence weighed with the judge."
Hence the rather extraordinary decision by a judge in an Irish
court to deny the custody of a child to its only living parent.[48]
    Máire was to hear from her mother on only one more
occasion. In 1934 she sent an acquaintance to Ireland with a
letter asking Máire to return to Switzerland, where Muriel

was then living. The letter contained the warning that if Máire did not come, she would never speak to her again. "I had no difficulty in deciding to stay in Ireland," Máire recalled, "having at last found continuity and stability in my life, but I don't think I believed she would carry out that threat forever. But she did."[49]

In the years that followed, efforts made by people to arrange a meeting between mother and daughter were rejected outright by Muriel. On the day of Máire's wedding to Ruari Brugha, the son of her father's close friend and comrade in arms, Cathal Brugha, the bridegroom went in person to the Dublin hotel where Muriel was then staying, to try to arrange a meeting with her, but to no avail.

After 1934, Máire continued to hear of her mother's movements from time to time. Muriel left Switzerland for France, and when World War II came she went with her other daughter, Alix, to England, taking up residence in a number of small hotels. She continued to make occasional visits to Dublin.

When the war ended, Muriel returned with Alix to Paris, where she spent much of the rest of her life. Amongst people she knew, she was often referred to as *L'Irlandaise*. After her daughter Alix trained as a nurse and married a young English veteran, she left Paris and went to live in England. She is now retired in London.

In Máire's estimate, Muriel MacSwiney was "an ill person, who, having cut herself off from her family and friends was left to cope alone." In all, Máire MacSwiney Brugha's view of the life that circumstances left her to live remains free of any bitterness towards her mother. Her memory of her childhood in Germany is filled with the loving families she lived with. "I didn't come to any harm," she wrote, "and at least I was home in my early teens and well before the outbreak of the war in Europe. My father must have been watching over me." Nonetheless, thoughts of how he would have felt at the shape his daughter's life took after his death remain with her. "I sometimes think it must have troubled him greatly on his death-bed that he was leaving me to he knew not what. He fully understood by then that my mother was not capable of looking after me. That is probably why he made my Aunt Mary my joint guardian."[51]

While it would be inaccurate to say that the fragile state of Muriel's health was a consequence of MacSwiney's political activities, Muriel was certainly not helped by the death of her husband, nor the manner of his dying. Muriel MacSwiney died in a London nursing home in October 1982 at the age of ninety. She had lived to see another episode in Irish history when young men starved themselves to death in protest against British rule.

What course Terence MacSwiney would have pursued had he lived cannot be known. Friends with whom he had entered manhood, and who were a part of his earliest literary and cultural endeavours in Cork – Liam de Roiste, Sean and P.S. O'Hegarty – went on to support the Anglo-Irish Treaty. On the other hand, MacSwiney's brothers and sisters were unanimous in their opposition to it, and were led, predictably, by Mary MacSwiney. Life for Sean MacSwiney, Terence's brother, was also filled with its share of difficulties. In the aftermath of the Anglo-Irish Treaty; Sean MacSwiney proved himself a virulent anti-Treatyite, and as a result spent long periods in Irish Free State prisons for his political activities. Later, in 1938, as the result of a crackdown ordered by Eamon de Valera, Sean MacSwiney was again imprisoned, handcuffed to Tomás MacCurtain Jr, the son of the slain lord mayor, for his Republican activities. It is not at all improbable that Terence MacSwiney would have joined them in prison had he lived.

MacSwiney's pursuit of the Republican ideal was uncompromising; it is unlikely that he would have settled for a measure of independence. MacSwiney's Ireland would have been a country governed by a Catholic ethos. Tolerance is not a word which springs easily to mind in describing his outlook; he was conservative, even priggish at times, an advocate of legislation to outlaw certain kinds of music halls. On the other hand, the values he expressed in *Principles of Freedom*, and his anger at "the bribes of those in power to maintain their ascendancy, the barter of every principle by time-servers; the corruption of public life and the apathy of private life,"[52] would find a certain resonance today amongst those concerned about the ideals of public service in democratic society.

MacSwiney's name continues to live on, in Ireland and in other countries seeking national independence. In 1990, an Irish journalist covering the release of dissident Gamsa Kurdia in the Georgian capital of Tiblisi, was informed that Gamsa Kurdia's father had once told Lenin: "One day we will have our own MacSwiney's and Casements."[53]

In Chicago, a stained-glass window, ornate in design and spectacular in scale, was erected in Terence MacSwiney's honour at St Patrick's Church. Today, the "Terence MacSwiney Window", with its inscriptions, "For The Glory of God" and "For the Love of Mankind", perpetuates the definition of the Lord Mayor's sacrifice in religious terms.

In the end, Terence MacSwiney, author, poet, playwright, politician, teacher, IRA commandant and hunger striker, gained the respect of even those who were his adversaries. He had entered Brixton as a handsome young man of forty, and left it on his own terms after almost eleven weeks. Yet from MacSwiney's bed in a prison hospital he served as an unparalleled source of inspiration to the Irish revolution. In death, he entered Ireland's pantheon of heroes, leaving the pain of Easter week behind him. He had indeed endured the most.

Notes
1. Uinseann MacEoin, interview with Connie Noonan, *Survivors*, (Dublin 1987) p. 428.
2. F.S.L. Lyons, *Ireland Since the Famine* (Dublin 1971) p. 428.
3. D.G. Boyce, *Englishmen and Irish Troubles* (Cambridge USA 1972) p. 407.
4. *New Orleans Times Picayune*, 26 October 1920.
5. *New York Times*, 26 October 1920.
6. *Boston Globe*, 25 October 1920.
7. *Toronto Globe and Mail*, 27 October 1920.
8. Report from British Embassy in the Hague to Lord Curzon, 2 November 1920, CO 904/185.
9. Report from British Legation in Brussels to Lord Curzon, 16 November 1920, CO 904/185.
10. *San Francisco Examiner*, 26 October 1920.
11. *Toronto Globe and Mail*, 26 October 1920.
12. *Evening Standard* (London) 26 October 1920.
13. *Toronto Globe*, 27 October 1920.
14. *Manchester Guardian*, 26 October 1920.

15. *The Times* (London) 27 October 1920.
16. *Cork Examiner*, 28 October 1920.
17. C.E. Callwell, *General Sir Henry Wilson* (New York 1927) Vol. II, p. 267.
18. *Cork Examiner*, 29 October 1920.
19. Ibid.
20. Ibid. 30 October 1920.
21. C.J. Street, *The Administration of Ireland 1920*.
22. *Cork Examiner*, 29 October 1920.
23. Bishop Cohalan to the *Cork Examiner*, April 1923, as cited also by the MacSwiney Collection in typescript copy, P48b/197.
24. *Cork Examiner*, 29 October 1920.
25. *Manchester Guardian*, 1 November 1920.
26. Ibid.
27. P.S. O'Hegarty, *Terence MacSwiney*, p. 97.
28. M. Plumet to Mary MacSwiney, 7 November 1920, MacSwiney Collection, P48a/112.
29. Dáil Debates, Private Session, 17 December 1921, p. 246.
30. Dáil Debates, Public Session, 19 December 1921.
31. Dáil Debates, 7 January 1922.
32. Marjorie Forester, *Michael Collins: The Lost Leader* (London 1971) p. 313.
33. Lennox Robinson (ed) *Lady Gregory's Journal* (London 1976) p. 63.
34. Padraig Colum, *Ourselves Alone* (New York 1959) p. 234.
35. Charles Townsend, *The British Military Campaign in Ireland* (London 1982) pp. 350-51.
36. Patricia Lavelle, *James O'Mara* (Dublin 1949) pp. 217-18.
37. Mary MacSwiney to Etienette Beuque, 16 June 1937, MacSwiney Collection P48c/450.
38. Bishop Cohalan to *Cork Examiner*, April 1923; MacSwiney Collection, P48b/197.
39. Mary MacSwiney to Papal Nuncio, 25 April 1932, MacSwiney Collection, P48a/197.
40. Maire MacSwiney Brugha to author, 13 March 1992.
41. Ibid.
42. Ibid.
43. Ibid.
44. Ibid.
45. Ibid.
46. Ibid.
47. Ibid.
48. Ibid.

49. Ibid.
50. Ibid.
51. Ibid.
52. MacSwiney, *Principles of Freedom*, p. 33.
53. Conor O'Clery, *Melting Snow* (Belfast 1991).

Bibliography

Newspapers
Boston Globe, 1920
Cork Constitution, 1918-21
Cork Examiner, 1910-23
Daily News (London) 1920
Evening Standard (London) 1920
Fianna Fáil, 1917
Freeman's Journal, 1919-21
Irish Independent, 1918-21
Irish Times, 1916-1921
Manchester Guardian, August-October 1920
New York Times, August-October 1920
Observer (London) August-October 1920
San Francisco Examiner, 1920
The Nation, 1920-1941
Toronto Globe and *Mail*, 1920

Articles
Garvin, Tom, "Great Hatred Little Room: Social Background and
    Political Sentiment Among Revolutionary Activists in Ireland,"
    The Revolution in Ireland, 1879-1923 (D.G. Boyce ed. London
    1988)
Hogan, Michael S.J. "The Morality of the Hunger Strike,"
    Ecclesiastical Review (1933)
Helmick, Raymond S.J. "Northern Ireland in Moral Focus," *The
    Tablet*, May 1981

Government Documents, Diaries, Letters
Dáil Debates, Public & Private Sessions, Dáil Éireann Files 1919-
    1921, State Papers Office, Dublin
Lloyd George Collection, House of Lords Records Office, London
Bonar Law Collection, House of Lords Records Office, London
MacSwiney Collection, University College, Dublin
MacSwiney Collection, Cork Municipal Museum

Books

Béaslaí, Piaras, *Michael Collins and the Making of a New Ireland* (Dublin 1927)

Bennett, Richard, *The Black & Tans* (London 1959)

Beresford, David, *Ten Men Dead* (London 1987)

Boyce, D.G. (ed.), *The Revolution in Ireland* (London 1988)

Breen, Dan, *My Fight For Irish Freedom* (Dublin 1981)

Callwell, General C.E. *Sir Henry Wilson, Vol. II* (New York 1927

Chavasse, Moirin, *Terence MacSwiney* (Dublin 1962)

Clarke, Kathleen, *Revolutionary Woman* (Dublin 1991)

Colum, Pádraig, *Ourselves Alone* (New York 1959)

Cronin, Seán, *The McGarrity Papers* (Tralee 1972)

Crozier, Frank, *Ireland Forever* (London 1932)

Dangelfield, George, *The Damnable Question* (Boston 1976)

Davis, Richard, *Arthur Griffith and Non-Violent Sinn Féin* (Dublin 1924)

Deasy, Liam, *Towards Ireland Free* (New York 1959)

Dwyer, T.R. *Michael Collins* (Dublin 1990)

Edwards, Sean, *The Gun, The Law and the Irish People* (Tralee 1971)

Forester, Margery, *Michael Collins: The Lost Leader* (London 1971)

Howell, L.G. *Six Days* (Boston 1976)

Lavelle, Patricia, *James O'Mara* (London 1946)

Lynch, Diarmuid, *The IRB and the 1916 Rising* (Cork 1951)

Lyons, F.S.L. *Ireland Since the Famine* (Dublin 1971)

MacEoin, Uinseann, *Survivors* (Dublin 1988)

MacSwiney, Terence, *Principles of Freedom* (Dublin 1921)

Middelmas, Keith (ed.), *Tom Jones Whitehall Diary Vol. III* (London 1972)

Nicolson, Harold, *George V* (London 1952)

O'Farrell, Patrick, *Ireland's English Question* (New York 1972)

O'Malley, Ernie, *On Another Man's Wounds* (Dublin 1979)

O'Malley, Pádraig, *Biting At the Grave* (Boston 1990)

O'Mahony, Sean, *University of Revolution* (Dublin 1987)

O'Connor, Frank, *The Big Fellow* (Dublin 1965)

O'Donoghue, Florence, *Tomás MacCurtain* (Tralee 1971)

O'Hegarty, P.S. *Terence MacSwiney* (Dublin 1922)

Ryan, Desmond, *Sean Treacy and the Third Tipperary Brigade* (Tralee 1995)

Robinson, Lennox (ed.), *Lady Gregory's Journal* (London 1976)

Taylor, Rex, *Michael Collins* (London 1958)

Street, C.J. *The British Administration in Ireland 1920* (New York 1920)

Townsend, Charles, *Political Violence in Ireland* (Dublin 1983)

Townsend, Charles, *The British Military Campaign in Ireland* (London 1982)

Index

Anderson, Sir John 142, 170
Anglo-Irish Treaty 35, 234-5, 244
Anglo-Irish Truce 234
Anglo-Irish War 9, 10, 37, 110, 118, 145, 152, 169, 177, 201, 206, 210, 223, 233-4
Ashe, Thomas 101-2, 116, 179

Balfour, Arthur 164-5, 167, 168, 169, 171
Black and Tans, 153, 228
Blackwell, Sir Ernley 168-9
Breen, Dan 17, 94, 152
British Labour Party 174, 175, 178
British Trade Union Congress 174-5, 191
Brugha, Cathal 69, 119, 150, 157, 241, 243
Casement, Sir Roger 48, 53, 64, 75-6, 245
Catholic Church 43, 57, 173-4, 181, 189, 210-11, 239, 243
Ceannt, Eamonn 59
Ceannt, Tomás 59
Churchill, Sir Winston 168, 169, 195, 227
Clan na nGael 210
Clarke, Kathleen 66, 71-2
Clarke, Thomas 62, 63, 66, 71
Cohalan, Bishop 66, 67, 68, 69, 72, 90, 114, 117, 126-8, 230, 233, 238-9
Collins, Michael 13, 17, 66, 70, 116, 120, 150-2, 153, 180, 184, 185, 186, 187, 203, 206, 234, 235; as Minister

for Finance 109, 111-14, 126-30, 133-4; and IRB 102, 110; Director of Intelligence IRA 118, 119, 141, 160-2, 178, 184-8, 199
Connolly, James 58-9, 63
Cork Celtic Literary Society 22-3
Corkery, Daniel 21, 28, 29, 81
Cumann na mBan 21, 33, 79

Dáil Éireann 94, 104, 109, 123-6, 131-2, 133, 146, 170, 191, 205, 226, 234, 235
Deasy, Liam 58, 120, 128
de Roiste, Liam 22, 48, 49, 115, 128-9, 175, 175-7, 230, 244
de Valera, Eamon 17, 37, 103, 104, 112, 126, 179, 208, 210, 235, 241, 244

Easter Rising 21, 47, 56, 61-7, 75, 79, 80, 82, 87, 90, 96, 97, 102, 151
Emmet, Robert 28, 43

Fitzgerald, Michael 180, 209

Gaelic League 20, 28, 56, 61
George V 10, 163-9, 237
George, Lloyd 117, 144, 164, 171-2, 173, 178, 180
Germany 53, 56, 61, 103
Greenwood, Hamar 170, 227
Griffith, Arthur 37, 38, 66, 76, 80, 111, 126, 180, 206, 208, 230, 234
Gun-running: Howth 50; Kerry 61-2, 64, 65

Hales, Sean 70
Hales, Tom 62, 70
Healy, Timothy 59, 78
Hobson, Bulmer 23, 63
Home Rule 28, 40, 46, 50, 56,
    76, 166, 176
Hunger strikes: Barry, Dennis
    231; Cork 180-4, 185, 193,
    197, 201, 209-10, 231-2,
    237; Gandhi 214; Long Kesh
    1981, 43, 214-5; Mountjoy
    11; Wormwood Scrubbs 11,
    152; *see also* Thomas Ashe

IRA 9, 143, 182, 183, 209, 239
IRB 47, 52, 61, 63, 65, 70, 90,
    102, 110, 140, 184
Irish Party 49, 59, 61, 78, 163
Irish Self-Determination League
    9, 111, 160, 184, 186, 198-9,
    202, 203, 204, 205
Irish Volunteers 48, 51, 56, 58,
    82, 86, 92, 102, 152, 162,
    230; Cork No.1 Brigade 114,
    140, 141, 147, 158, 183,
    207; Cork Volunteers 49, 82;
    West Cork Brigade 58

Law, Bonar 170, 171, 174, 175,
    177, 180, 188
Lynch, Diarmuid 47, 61, 62, 64,
    69
Lynch, Liam 17, 140

MacCurtain, Tomás 9, 48, 49,
    50, 58, 61, 62, 64, 65, 66,
    67, 69, 70, 78, 82, 200; mur-
    der of 114, 118-9, 140, 148-
    9, 151, 207, 238; inquest
    116-7
MacDiarmada, Sean 47-8, 62,
    63, 64, 65, 66
MacNeill, Eoin 48, 49, 51, 63,
    65, 66, 98
Macready, General 165, 169, 227
MacSwiney Brugha, Máire 83,
    98-100, 139, 239-44

MacSwiney, Mary 21, 25, 33,
    62, 67, 71-2, 76-9, 81, 83,
    84, 85, 86, 98, 144, 147,
    177, 185, 186, 188, 192,
    194, 197, 198, 199, 203,
    213, 233, 234-5, 238, 241,
    242, 244
MacSwiney, Muriel (née
    Murphy) 83, 86-100, 121,
    139, 142, 146, 147, 149,
    153, 157, 184-6, 188, 189,
    192, 197, 199, 203, 204,
    205, 206, 207, 226, 227,
    229, 238, 239
MacSwiney, Terence: arrest 174-
    5; court martial 145-50, 161-
    2, 170, 195; on art 85, 90;
    and Dáil 103-4, 109, 114,
    121-6, 128, 131-4; and Dail
    Loan 10, 109, 111-14, 126-
    30; and Easter Rising 38, 47,
    61-70, 79, 81, 87, 97, 150-1;
    education 18, 19, 26, 84;
    father 16-17, 19; hunger
    strikes 90, 94, 149-53, Chap.
    VI; and imperialism 52-54,
    57; and IRB 47, 61; and Irish
    language 18, 58, 82, 84, 86,
    94, 100, 133, 134, 146, 149;
    literary works 27-41, 78, 79,
    81, 87, 100, 151, 236; as lord
    mayor 115-6, 121-3, 131; on
    marriage 54-6, 90, 91-2, 100-
    101; and martyrdom 58, 146,
    150-51, 195, 146, 150-1,
    195, 231; mother 16, 21, 25,
    91; and nationalism, 20, 44,
    46-7, 51, 52-3; and physical
    force 20, 43-4, 46, 53-4, 61,
    70, 81, 97, 119-20, 128, 131,
    134, 224; prison: Belfast 94,
    95, 99, 100, 102; Brixton 78,
    Chap. VI ; Bromyard 86, 90-
    1; Cork 60, 75, 94; Dublin
    75; Dundalk 94-5; Frongoch
    70-1, 76, 77, 78, 79, 80;
    Lincoln 103; Reading 75, 76,

79, 80-2, 84-5; Wakefield 70, 79, 80, 89; Wormwood Scrubbs 75; and religious beliefs 17, 20, 21, 31, 43, 45-6, 47, 61, 66, 78, 95, 99, 101, 123, 181,189, 197, 210-11, 226, 243; and Republicanism 35-8, 57; and Republican courts 115-6, 130-1, 132, 143; and role of women 34-5, 44, 93; and Unionism 44-5, 131; and Volunteers 48-53, 56-7, 60-2, 82, 83, 86, 90, 92-4, 112, 115, 120, 185, 197, 207, 208; and work: in Dwyer and Co. 18-20, 22, 25-6, 26-7; as lecturer in business methods 26; as commercial instructor 27, 58

Mannix, Archbishop 187, 188, 211, 212

Mulcahy, Richard 90, 91, 92, 101, 119, 226

Murphy, Joseph 180, 201, 205, 209

Neeson, Sean 40, 49, 83

Nolan, Sean 112, 113, 128

O'Brien, Art 141, 160, 178-9, 181, 184-8, 186, 187, 197, 198, 199, 200, 203, 204, 205, 206, 216, 228

O'Connell, Ginger 63, 64, 70, 81, 82

O'Connor, Fr Dominic 147, 157, 158-9, 174, 183, 185, 189, 195, 204, 205, 206, 207, 228, 229

O'Donoghue, Florence 48, 49, 50, 52, 56, 62, 64, 69, 140, 141

O'Donovan Rossa, Jeremiah 57-8

O'Hegarty, P.S. 45, 46, 48, 52, 128, 232, 244

O'Hegarty, Sean 48, 49, 64, 244

O'Kelly, Sean T. 61, 80

Pearse, Patrick 13, 17, 46, 57, 62, 63-4, 65, 66, 69, 101, 150, 181, 195

Redmond, John 48, 49, 50, 51, 59

Republican Courts 10, 115-6, 127, 130-1, 132, 140, 165, 176

RIC 9, 62, 68, 79, 94, 94, 117, 118, 119, 142, 145, 148, 165, 170, 172, 202, 206, 209, 230, 233

Shortt, Edward 163, 168, 169, 170, 202

Sinn Féin 76, 103, 112, 119, 123, 131, 144, 153, 165, 171, 194, 208, 209, 227, 236-7

Stack, Austin 64, 151-2

Stamfordham, Lord 163-9, 172

Stafford, General 65, 67

Trade Union Congress 177-8

Traynor, Oscar 94

Treacy, Sean 17, 94, 95, 152

Troupe, Edward 78, 191, 194

Ulster Volunteers 48, 59, 176

Unionism 162-4, 176

United States 10-11, 12, 76, 131, 157, 160, 200, 205, 208, 209, 237-8

Wilson, Sir Henry 195-6, 227